THE WAY OF PEACE

THE WAY OF PEACE

Cecil Kerr

Hodder & Stoughton

LONDON SYDNEY AUCKLAND TORONTO

British Library Cataloguing in Publication Data
Kerr, Cecil
  A way of peace
  1. Society. Role of Christian church
  I. Title
  261.1

ISBN 0–340–53820–1

First published in Great Britain 1990

Published by Hodder and Stoughton,
a division of Hodder and Stoughton Ltd,
Mill Road, Dunton Green, Sevenoaks, Kent TN13 2YA
Editorial Office: 47 Bedford Square, London WC1B 3DP

Photoset by Chippendale Type Ltd, Otley, West Yorkshire

Printed in Great Britain by Clays Ltd, St. Ives plc

CONTENTS

Acknowledgments

The publishers are grateful to the following people for permission to use their photographs.

The four photographs on the cover are by John Callister.

The Christian Renewal Centre, 1990: Alistair Hughes
View over Carlingford Lough: Alistair Hughes
The Centre 1974: Ian Gilchrist
Easter praise: Berti McKee
The bombing at Warrenpoint: private owner
March for Jesus, Dublin: private owner
Filming 'Highway': *Mourne Observer*
Receiving a people of the year award: private owner
Banner of Reconciliation: John O'Connor
Cecil and Myrtle Kerr: Beryl Stone

PREFACE

My primary purpose in this book is to give glory to the God of peace 'who in the midst of conflict and division turns our minds to thoughts of peace'.

I want especially to thank my wife Myrtle who has courageously journeyed with me on the walk of faith. Together we thank God for Ruth, David and Timothy who share us with a wider family.

This story reflects the faith, hope and love of a great multitude of God's people – the brave and gifted men and women, more than sixty since 1974, who readily responded to the call to serve God in Rostrevor; the many short-term helpers from Ireland and overseas who contribute so much to our life and witness; the generous brothers and sisters all over the world who are obedient to God's prompting 'to give the right amount at the right time' – the people who form a worldwide network of prayer for us and for our land.

We are partners with many others who work for peace in Ireland. Ian Ellis has compiled a directory of Peace and Reconciliation projects in Ireland, noting more than eighty groups. In a foreword David Bleakley, the General Secretary of the Irish Council of Churches, notes:

> The good news is that Irish Christians do join hands across the sectarian divide and often at considerable personal sacrifice. Sometimes the work they do is dramatic in its impact, but more often the peace-makers go about their work quietly trying to keep together and repair the fabric of their threatened society.

I am grateful to the members of the community at Rostrevor who made it possible for us to take time off for writing. To Lavinia Bowerman who lovingly and efficiently prepared and typed the manuscript we offer heartfelt thanks. Our good friends William and Paula Curran kindly provided a haven of peace for us in their lovely home in the south of Ireland. I also want to thank Edward England, my literary agent, for all his encouragement and advice. To David Wavre, and to Dick Douglas and Carolyn Armitage of Hodder and Stoughton, I want also to express my gratitude for their help.

My prayer is that all of us may continue to 'live by faith, walk in hope and be renewed in love until the world reflects God's glory'.

CECIL KERR
ROSTREVOR,
EASTER 1990

EVENTS IN IRISH HISTORY

432   Patrick returns to Ireland at God's call to bring the Gospel to the island. Born in Britain he had been taken to Ireland as a slave when he was sixteen.

6th–8th centuries   Missionary outreach to Europe from the Christian communities (monasteries) in Ireland. Among the leaders are Comgall, Columba, Columbanus.

793–950   Vikings from Scandinavia regularly raid Ireland.

1171   Henry II of England encouraged by Pope Adrian IV comes with an army to Ireland. A papal edict of 1155 grants lordship of Ireland to the English king.

1588   Defeat of the Spanish Armada.

1607   Departure of the Earls of Ulster who opposed English rule.

1608   James I of England begins a programme of 'plantation'. English and Scottish settlers given large areas of land, mainly in the north. These 'planters' are mostly Anglicans from England and Presbyterians from Scotland.

1641   Irish Catholic uprising. Two thousand Protestant settlers killed and tens of thousands, stripped of clothing and goods, flee to places of refuge.

1649   Execution of Charles I. English Civil War. Oliver Cromwell with an army of 20,000 arrives in Ireland. Their purpose is the reconquest of Ireland and avenging the massacre of 1641. In the sieges of Drogheda and Wexford thousands of Irish Catholics and some Protestant royalists killed. Protestant ascendancy restored.

1658	Death of Cromwell.
1661	Restoration of Episcopal State Church in Ireland.
1670	Synod of Catholic Bishops meets in Dublin.
1685	Death of Charles II and accession of James II.
1688	Prince William of Orange (Holland), Protestant son-in-law of James II, 'invited' to take the English throne. James flees to France.
1689	William III and Mary II enthroned joint monarchs of England. James II arrives in Ireland. The siege of Derry is relieved by William's army.
1690	William arrives in Ireland, defeating James and his army at the Battle of the Boyne (July).
1691	Treaty of Limerick.
1704	The English Parliament introduces penal laws which severely restrict the rights of Catholics, Presbyterians and Non-conformists.
1728	Franchise removed from Catholics.
1778	Relief Act allows Catholic leasehold and inheritance rights.
1791	Formation of Society of United Irishmen.
1793	Catholics admitted to parliamentary franchise.
1795	The Orange Order founded. Catholic Seminary opened in Maynooth.
1798	National insurrection led by the United Irishmen with support from France. Wolfe Tone's involvement personifies a tradition of Irish revolutionary violence.
1829	Catholic emancipation enabling participation in Parliament.
1845–6	The Great Famine. A million people die and another million emigrate to the USA, Britain, Australia and Canada.
1858	Irish Republican Brotherhood emerges.

1859	Fenian Brotherhood in USA formed.
1869	Disestablishment of the Church of Ireland.
1873	Home Rule League formed.
1912	Ulster Covenant signed on Ulster day (28 September) opposing the introduction of Home Rule for Ireland.
1913	Formation of Ulster Volunteer Force, Irish Citizens Army and Irish National Volunteers.
1914	UVF illegally ship rifles and ammunition from Germany (April). Irish Volunteers following their example carry out a similar but smaller operation.
1916	The Easter Rising at Dublin General Post Office (24 April). The leaders surrender to the British forces on 29 April. Fifteen of the leaders executed.
1919	Irish Volunteers reconstituted as Irish Republican Army.
1920	Government of Ireland Act – independent Parliaments for north and south. Partition of the island.
1921	First Parliament of Northern Ireland opened by George V. Irish Free State established.
1922/23	Armed conflict among Nationalists who accepted partition and those who opposed it.
1937	Eire (Republic of Ireland) Constitution agreed, with a claim to jurisdiction over the whole island of Ireland.
1939	IRA bombing campaign in Britain. Start of Second World War. Republic of Ireland remains neutral.
1947	Education Act provides for free secondary education for all children in Northern Ireland.
1949	United Kingdom government's Ireland Act gives assurance that partition will be supported. 'In no event will Northern Ireland or any part thereof cease to be a part of . . . the

United Kingdom without the consent of the Parliament of Northern Ireland.' Irish Republic inaugurated (April).

1954 – 62   Border terrorist campaign by the IRA.

1964   First meeting of the Prime Minister of Irish Republic, Mr Sean Lemass, and the Northern Ireland Prime Minister, Captain Terence O'Neill.

1967   Northern Ireland Civil Rights Association formed.

1968   Civil Rights march in Derry leading to confrontation with Royal Ulster Constabulary.

1969   Sectarian violence erupts in Belfast. Army drafted to Northern Ireland to help keep the peace.

1970   Provisional Sinn Fein formed. IRA increases terrorist activities and other splinter groups subsequently emerge. Ulster Volunteer Force, Ulster Defence Association and other Protestant terrorist groups become active.

1971   Internment introduced.

1972   'Direct Rule' imposed by British government.

1973   Northern Ireland Assembly created with power sharing executive.

1974   Northern Ireland Assembly disbanded and direct rule reimposed. Bomb explosions with many deaths in Northern Ireland, Dublin, Guildford and Birmingham.

1975   Northern Ireland Convention convened.

1976   Northern Ireland Convention collapses. British Ambassador in Dublin murdered by IRA.

1979   Earl Mountbatten and friends killed in Sligo, and at Warrenpoint eighteen soldiers die in IRA attacks on August Bank Holiday Monday.

1981   Death of Republican hunger strikers.

1985   Anglo–Irish Agreement signed at Hillsborough between the British government and the government of the Irish Republic. The Northern

Ireland Unionist majority not party to the agreement continues to oppose it.

Over 2,800 people have died in the violence in Northern Ireland between 1968 and 1990.

1

THE POWER OF THE CROSS

The only thing I can boast about is the cross of our Lord Jesus Christ. (St Paul)

> *A man that looks on glass,*
> *On it may stay his eye;*
> *Or if he pleaseth through it pass,*
> *And then the heavens espy.*
>> *George Herbert*

'Where the mountains of Mourne sweep down to the sea.' That is where you will find the beautiful little village of Rostrevor; half way between the border town of Newry and the fishing port of Kilkeel. Sheltered by the mountains and on the shore of Carlingford Lough it was a popular seaside resort in the nineteenth century. Over a hundred years ago the Earl of Kilmorey chose a lovely spot to build a modest mansion facing south. The tidal waters of the Irish Sea come almost to the coast road that divides the house from the Lough. The varied Irish weather ensures a changing view almost every moment. Exquisite sunbeams pierce the clouds and move like searchlights across the Cooley mountains on the other side. Behind the house the foothills of the Mournes rise, providing a majestic tapestry of colour in the trees that clothe their slopes. As you walk along the shore you will hear the chatter of the oyster-catchers, the call of the curlews and the sound of many other sea birds that make their home there.

Come along the shore to that old Victorian mansion. It is Easter day in the afternoon. The sound of the sea birds gives way to another song. On the lawn of that large house which is now the Christian Renewal Centre several hundred people are celebrating the resurrection of Christ. Voices and music from many instruments carry the joyful message across the water:

> Thine be the glory, risen conquering Son,
> Endless is the victory thou o'er death hast won.

As you mingle with those who have gathered on the lawn you will be surprised to find people there from so many different backgrounds, Protestant and Roman Catholic, young and old. Some have come from Belfast, others have crossed the border from the Republic of Ireland; some will be visitors from Britain and overseas. From very different backgrounds they have come together to express what makes them one in Christ, the Saviour of the world. An afternoon of praise, worship, sharing of Scripture and fellowship comes to an end as the people fan out and join hands in a large circle to sing:

> Bind us together, Lord,
> Bind us together
> With cords that cannot be broken.
> Bind us together, Lord,
> Bind us together,
> Bind us together with love.

> There is only one God,
> There is only one King,
> There is only one Body,
> That is why I sing:

> Made for the glory of God,
> Purchased by His precious Son.
> Born with the right to be clean,
> For Jesus the victory has won.

You are the family of God,
You are the promise divine,
You are God's chosen desire,
You are the glorious new wine.[1]

Come inside the Centre which has been home for the
Christian community since 1974. Someone will show you
round the older part of the building and then bring you
through the lovely new extension which was completed in
1986. You will be taken to the Upper Room where members
of the community meet to pray together every day. A large
window gives a magnificent view south across Carlingford
Lough. You will notice the way the window is designed. A
large cross forms the centre frame of that window and its
symbolism is crucial for our work.

Shortly after we moved into the old house in 1974 we were
praying in one of the front rooms. Suddenly we realised
that every window in the front of the house had a cross
in the centre of the frame. When we came to build the
extension we wanted to preserve what had been in the mind
of the original architect over a hundred years ago. Malcolm
Chisholm, who designed the new extension, understood its
significance and incorporated a large cross in the window
of the Upper Room.

That cross is a constant reminder to us and to all who
come to the Centre that real healing can only come to our
land and indeed to the world through Jesus.

Long before we came to Rostrevor we were sure that the
foundation for our work of prayer, renewal and reconciliation would be the words of St Paul in Ephesians 2:

For Christ himself is our way of peace. He has made peace
between us Jews and you Gentiles by making us all one
family, breaking down the wall of contempt that used to
separate us. By his death he ended the angry resentment
between us, caused by the Jewish laws which favoured the
Jews and excluded the Gentiles, for he died to annul that
whole system of Jewish laws. Then he took the two groups

that had been opposed to each other and made them parts
of himself; thus he fused us together to become one new
person, and at last there was peace. As parts of the same
body, our anger against each other has disappeared, for
both of us have been reconciled to God. And so the
feud ended at last at the cross. And he has brought
this Good News of peace to you Gentiles who were
very far away from him, and to us Jews who were near.
Now all of us, whether Jews or Gentiles, may come to
God the Father with the Holy Spirit's help because of
what Christ has done for us. (Eph.2:14–18 Living Bible)

Even though we live in one of the most beautiful parts of
Ireland it is an area that has witnessed some of the worst
violence of these past years of conflict. Two policemen
were murdered outside the Post Office in the village a
few hundred yards from the Centre, and in 1979 eighteen
British soldiers were ambushed and killed by the IRA two
miles away at Warrenpoint on the same day that Lord
Mountbatten and three others with him were killed off the
west coast of Ireland. The border town of Newry nearby has
witnessed many terrible massacres. A Christian bookshop
which we ran there for seven years was bombed, fortunately
with no loss of life or major injury.

We realise the reality of the spiritual battle in Ireland.
Demonic forces of hatred and evil are at work in our land.
They have cost the lives of nearly three thousand people,
many of them innocent victims of hate-filled terrorists.
Thousands of others have been maimed and injured. Daily
we are reminded that it is only through what Christ has done
on the cross that men and women can be made friends again
with God and with one another.

From the prayer room then, as we look out, we see our
beautiful but broken land through the cross. Sometimes a
British naval vessel is anchored midway across Carlingford
Lough on the invisible line that marks the border between
north and south. We are reminded that when Jesus died
on the cross of Calvary the first two people to receive
his reconciliation were sworn enemies, the terrorist on the

cross beside Jesus, and the Roman centurion beneath it. The terrorist, driven by nationalist zeal, had taken the way of violence and murder in an attempt to drive out the despised Roman overlords from Palestine. In his dying moments he recognised who Jesus was, saying to his colleagues: ' "We are punished justly, for we are getting what our deeds deserve. But this man has done nothing wrong." Then he said, "Jesus, remember me when you come into your Kingdom". Jesus answered him, "I tell you the truth, today you will be with me in paradise" ' (Luke 23:41–43). The centurion was the army commander who carried out the execution of Jesus and the two terrorists. When he had witnessed the forgiving love of Jesus and listened to the gracious words he spoke, the centurion praised God and said, 'Surely this was a righteous man' (Luke 23:47).

When I read that story in the Gospel my mind goes to two Irishmen who were once sworn enemies and became firm friends and brothers in Christ. You might have met them as you mingled with those who come to the Centre. Al, from the far south of Ireland, was a committed Republican and among the foremost leaders in the IRA, one of the most ruthless terrorist organisations in Ireland. At the height of his terrorist activity Al was literally arrested by the love of Christ. He travelled 200 miles to the Centre to share the story of his conversion. He came during a Bible week which included 12 July, the day when Orangemen march with bands and banners to celebrate the victory of the Protestant William of Orange over the Catholic James II at the Battle of the Boyne in 1690.

Al related how his wife had invited him to a prayer meeting in their town. A nominal Roman Catholic who had not attended church for years, he felt completely out of place surrounded by people praising God. Then a dramatic thing happened. He explained that it was as if a shaft of light came into the room and flashed towards him with great intensity. When he returned home he was driven to his knees in deep remorse and repentance. In trembling faith he turned to Christ and cried for mercy. He knew his sins had been forgiven. He became a new person. The years that followed have proved the genuineness of his conversion to Christ in the way he has worked to change the hearts of people from violence to the way of peace.

Ben was an officer in the British army. He served with distinction in the Second World War and held important positions in the security forces in Northern Ireland. With his wife Gladys, Ben was a frequent visitor to the Centre where he found great joy in sharing his renewed faith in Christ.

In the course of time Al and Ben met each other. To his amazement Ben learned that in his days in the IRA one of Al's assignments had been to stalk him, gathering information on his movements and activities. Al and Ben became firm friends and through their membership of the Full Gospel Businessmen's Fellowship they frequently shared the same platform. Their witness of God's power to turn enemies into friends had great impact, particularly in the heartlands of sectarianism.

Over the years that we have been at the Christian Renewal Centre we thank God for many who have come to the cross of Christ and there laid down their arms of hatred and prejudice. To a watching world, seeing only the bad news from Ireland, we are glad to record another side of the story. As so often happens it is precisely in those places where evil seems to have scored a resounding victory that God's power is revealed to change situations that appeared hopeless and intractable.

The cross in the window is more than a symbol to us. In the darkest days of fear and conflict it reminds us that Christ is the key to the problems of Ireland and can change the hardest hearts.

With many others puzzled by what is happening in Ireland you may often be tempted to despair that a solution will ever be found to our centuries-old problems. In this book we would like you to join us on a journey of hope as we see a little of what God is doing by the power of his Holy Spirit.

2

THE WIND OF THE SPIRIT

You will receive power when the Holy Spirit comes on you. (Acts 1:5)

> *O thou who camest from above*
> *The pure celestial fire to impart*
> *Kindle a flame of sacred love*
> *On the mean altar of my heart.*
> Charles Wesley

Anyone living in Northern Ireland is very conscious of labels. Everywhere you go people want to know 'What are you?' Usually it means one thing. Are you Protestant or Catholic? Even if the question is not asked directly there are all sorts of subtle ways of determining which side you are on. It may be your name, the school you attended, the political party you support or most obviously the church you attend. History has bequeathed this legacy of religious division, which is a potent force in our little island. We live together yet five thousand miles apart.

A personal pilgrimage

My forebears came over from the border counties of Scotland in the late-seventeenth or early-eighteenth century. They came as settlers in the Plantation of Ulster which began in the early part of the seventeenth century. I was

21

born and brought up near Enniskillen in County Fermanagh. Growing up in a part of Ulster that was almost equally divided between Roman Catholic and Protestant I was made aware early in life of the deep differences between the two communities. We were separated by religion, culture and politics. That left enormous gulfs between us even though we lived near to each other. During my school years I can remember only one lasting acquaintance with a Roman Catholic student of my own age. Interestingly we shared some common sports, boating and game shooting!

Like most people in those years in Northern Ireland I was brought up in a nominally Christian environment. Regular attendance at church, Sunday school and religious education in school formed a backdrop of Christian input. Those early experiences laid a foundation for a definite commitment of my life to Christ at the age of fifteen. This in turn led to a clear call for me to dedicate my life to some form of full-time Christian work. Eventually the road seemed to open to prepare for ministry in the Church of Ireland. From Portora Royal School I went to Trinity College, Dublin to read for a degree in Hebrew and Oriental Languages before training for ordination.

Moving to Dublin was an interesting experience, opening many new worlds that I had not encountered in rural Fermanagh. From living in a community divided almost equally between Roman Catholics and Protestants I found myself in a city that was nominally 94 per cent Roman Catholic. Being a student in Trinity College in the 1950s, however, shielded me from the full impact of that. Roman Catholics were still generally banned by their bishops from attending such a 'Protestant' college.

In Trinity I met and fell in love with Myrtle who was later to become my wife. Meeting her was a considerable challenge to my narrow northern upbringing. She had come to university to study English and Irish. I had never before met a Protestant who spoke Irish. Myrtle was brought up in a Church of Ireland family near Mullingar in the Irish Midlands. In a largely Roman Catholic area she had experienced much closer and more neighbourly contacts than I had. My inherited Unionism was something of a shock to her and her understanding of Irish nationalism was an even greater shock to me. Despite that, we shared a deep commitment to Christ which Myrtle had also come to in her teens. Through our involvement in the Christian Union in Trinity College our horizons were widened and friendships made with people from many parts of the world. Friendships with Roman Catholics were still rare, however.

Myrtle and I graduated on the same day. I was ordained into the Church of Ireland to serve in St Patrick's parish in Coleraine on the north coast. Very conveniently Myrtle was appointed to a teaching post in Coleraine High School. We were married in my second year there and set up our first home. Our daughter Ruth was born there and we treasure very happy memories of the many friends we made, working alongside the Rector Canon Stephen Kerr and his wife Peggy. From Coleraine we moved to Belfast where I took up an appointment as Head of Religious Education in Annadale Grammar School.

Queen's University

Moving to be Church of Ireland Chaplain in the Queen's University of Belfast in 1965 brought a great challenge to my life and a real testing of Christian convictions.

Queen's University was one of the few places at that time where young people from Northern Ireland could meet on 'open ground'. Students from separate schools discovered they were freer to explore each other's culture. The five thousand students were almost equally divided between Roman Catholics and Protestants with quite a few coming from Britain and overseas. For the first time I found myself working closely in university affairs with Roman Catholic colleagues, such as Father Patrick Walsh, Dr Ambrose Macauley and Father Tony Farquahar. Together with the

Revd David Turtle, my Methodist colleague, and the Revd Ray Davey, the Presbyterian chaplain, we shared many common concerns in our ministry to students and staff.

Ray Davey's vision of reconciliation was a constant challenge and inspiration to us. While working with the YMCA during the Second World War he was taken prisoner in North Africa. His experiences of sharing with Christians of other denominations in a prisoner of war camp taught him many important lessons about unity in Christ across the traditional barriers. In such a crucible of suffering ancient prejudices were melted. In many ways Ray foresaw the gathering storm in Ulster and in positive ways he and others who shared his vision prepared for it. Under his leadership the community of reconciliation which is now Corrymeela was born. I was privileged to be closely involved with him in some of the early projects in setting up that house of peace on the north Antrim coast. We used to take work parties of students to Corrymeela. Facing the challenge of working together to restore an old building forged lasting friendships across many inherited barriers. Ray and I presided over fervent discussions with the students late into the night. During such times, possibilities opened to us of finding new ways of living together in our divided land.

Like most universities in the western world, Queen's did not escape the questioning of the 'new theology' and the disturbing impact of 'the new morality'. Added to this the campus violence that erupted in many universities took on a much more sinister face in Northern Ireland. When the Civil Rights campaign began in 1968 a volatile situation was easily exploited by radical forces. Intellectual debates about 'Limited Violence to meet the Violence of the System' soon turned into street fighting, bloodshed and murder which has become such a scandal to the watching world.

With many others involved in Christian ministry in Ireland I had to ask myself some searching questions. How could a country which professed so much Christianity erupt into such naked hatred and sectarian conflict? We were living near the centre of Belfast. IRA bombs were devastating the city. Many people were killed including women and children who became random victims in the blitz that caused millions of pounds worth of damage to property. So-called Protestant para-military groups emerged in response to the murderous campaign waged by the IRA. Some of the worst murders recorded in legal history were being acted out. The frightening truth was that they were being done by young men and women, the vast majority of whom had been baptised into some branch of the Church and been exposed to some form of religious education in either Catholic or state schools. We seemed to have enough religion to make us hate each other but not enough to help us love. A primitive blood lust was unleashed that seemed hard to stop.

Personally I felt powerless as I pondered these questions:

- Is there any way that Christianity can meet the awful situation we are in?
- Is there a power that will radically change the face of this land so that we are not eternally committed to an endless repetition of such savage revenge and bitterness?
- Is there any way that we can be released from the prison houses of our history?
- How can the ancient feuds that have bedevilled this island be resolved?

Eventful meeting

A meeting with three Americans one spring evening in 1971 was an important link in a chain of events that was to provide an answer to some of those questions. It was to change the course of life for Myrtle, for me and for our family.

Summer term in Queen's is when the pressure is on for exams. Students allow few things to distract them from the difficult task of catching up on the work of the past year: none the less many of them appreciate a call during the period leading up to exams. In my study I had prepared a list of students to visit in the Halls of Residence near the main university building. Before I went there something prompted me to call on Ed Maginnis who was working for first part finals in Medicine. I obeyed the prompting and have not been the same since, because, on my way back, another student called me over and introduced me to the three Americans from the Church of the Redeemer in Houston, Texas. They were Geoff Schiffmayer, the curate of the parish; Bob Eckhart, a medical doctor; and Bob West, a businessman. After a brief conversation I invited them round to the Student Centre for a further chat and to give them the opportunity of meeting some of our students.

During a number of visits they told us about the miracles that had been happening in the Church of the Redeemer. At first the story seemed remote from the situation in Belfast. Their accounts of the miracles wrought through the Holy Spirit seemed to conservative ears rather unlikely, if not bizarre, but I gradually came to see that what they were saying rang true. Their love, humility and deep devotion to the Lord bore testimony to the authenticity of what they had related.

Situated in downtown Houston the Church of the Redeemer was suffering the fate of many other inner city areas. As the people moved out to the pleasant suburbs, the inner city became a temporary refuge for immigrants. The tree-lined houses of its former supporters became the tenements of Latin Americans and others with little interest in the corner church. Graham Pulkingham, appointed its Rector, assessed the needs of the neighbourhood and energetically set up a programme to make the church relevant to the people. He opened premises for the youth of the area, but they set to work vandalising them. Graham's best plans for advancing the Kingdom of God in that place seemed to come to nothing. In near despair he paid a visit to David Wilkerson in New York, influenced by Wilkerson's book, *The Cross and the Switchblade*, which describe the work of God's Spirit changing the lives of young people in some of the toughest street gangs in the city.

Bob Eckhart quietly told us that his friend Pulkingham, after prayer with David Wilkerson, experienced a fuller awareness of the power of the Holy Spirit. He returned to Houston and quickly found that God was using his ministry in the most unexpected ways, and miracles of healing were being performed that he could never have thought possible.

Over some months Eckhart and others, joining Graham Pulkingham for early morning prayer, became more and more aware of what God was asking them to do in restructuring the life of their church and opening their minds to a new vision. The result led to the total transformation of the Church of the Redeemer. A church that had been dying on its feet became vibrantly alive, serving the needs of the people within its boundaries. Later its influence was to spread to many parts of the world.

And why were these three representatives with us in Belfast? Their answer set me back at first and I received it with some incredulity. They said, 'The Holy Spirit sent us'. They explained that at a prayer meeting one evening in their church a word of prophecy had been given, to the effect that some of the leaders from the Church of the Redeemer were to go to Belfast. They hardly knew where Belfast was. They did not know anyone there and had no idea what they were expected to do. As they prayed about the prophecy they felt more strongly that three messengers were to go to Belfast. So they bought their tickets and here they were. Through their witness I was to learn much more about the amazing work God is doing by his Holy Spirit in the lives of individuals, churches and communities.

Before my new friends returned to America I promised to look them up in Houston while I was researching Pastoral Counselling Centres with a possible view to setting up such centres in Ireland. In the event it was a brief visit but one I shall never forget, particularly the morning service. Bob Eckhart met me and took me along to the church where I was warmly greeted at the door by a very big man who gave me a welcoming hug. The Eucharist was similar to the order we used in the Church of the Resurrection at Queen's University, but there were features of the service which disappointed me – for instance I felt the sermon was not very profound. But the whole atmosphere of the church gripped me, especially the feeling of reality in the worship of the 600 or 700 people who were gathered there. Those folk were singing and praying with a sense of the presence of God in a way I had scarcely experienced before. After the formal intercessions there were prayers for some individuals, and then someone prayed in tongues. It was the first time I had heard this phenomenon, but what followed really impressed me: the whole congregation was caught up in the praise of God and singing in tongues. It lasted for two or three minutes and then quietly died down again and the service proceeded.

As I thought about this strange experience and tried to understand it, it seemed to me that the only explanation was that the worshippers' hearts were so filled with praise that their traditional hymns and songs were not adequate to express what they felt, and God gave these languages in which to praise him. Afterwards I said that what I heard in that 'singing in the Spirit' must be like the countless multitudes in heaven who worship and praise the Lord for ever. I have shared in the experience of singing in tongues or singing in the Spirit on many occasions since then and I am more and more convinced that my first impressions were correct. When I am celebrating Holy Communion and I come to that point in the service when we are asked to join the angels and archangels around the throne who day and night sing 'Holy to the Lord', I feel that this would be a most appropriate point at which to allow the Holy Spirit to lead us into singing in the Spirit.

I left that morning service in the Church of the Redeemer deeply moved because I felt I had participated in worship which was not only relevant but real. However there were questions in my mind, the most important being, was this perhaps just a rather emotional American expression of worship? I wondered about the everyday life of the congregation. I did not have long to wait for an answer as I joined Eckhart and his wife and family.

In response to the call of God Bob Eckhart had given up a lucrative medical practice in Galveston, a rich suburb of Houston. He and his wife and family took up residence near the Church of the Redeemer, and convenient to the clinic he and others ran as an outreach service to the local immigrants who could not afford medical attention. The Eckharts were an extended family, one of forty or more in the parish. These families welcomed some of the broken victims of the society of that city; people in need of the loving acceptance and deep healing which could only come through a caring community. I went with Bob Eckhart to the clinic where he and his staff not only dispensed medicines but also ministered the love of the Lord Jesus to those who came. As I walked around the sparsely furnished school that now served as the clinic, and sat with Bob in his tiny surgery, I realised that it was only through the power of the Holy Spirit that they could go on ministering to people in such need. The strange thing was that I felt again the atmosphere of the reality of the presence of God, which I had sensed in the morning service, as I sat and talked with this humble man of God.

An unconquerable fellowship

As I made my way back to Ireland I reflected on the short glimpse I had had of the work God was doing by his Spirit in Houston. The conviction was borne in on me that that was how the Church should be living in the twentieth century – not that it would be desirable or even possible to translate the work of the Redeemer church into the situation of Belfast – to be so open to the power of the Spirit that it could be an effective witness to the living God. My mind came back constantly to the words of J. B. Phillips in his preface to the Acts of the Apostles,[1] in which he contrasted the impotence of the Church of the twentieth century with the Church of the first century.

> Here we are seeing the Church in its first youth, valiant and unspoiled – a body of ordinary men and women joined in an unconquerable fellowship never before seen on this earth. Yet we cannot help feeling disturbed as well as moved, for this surely is the Church as it was meant to be. It is vigorous and flexible, for these are the days before it ever became fat and short of breath through prosperity, or muscle-bound by over-organisation. These men did not make 'acts of faith', they believed; they did not 'say their prayers', they really prayed. They did not hold conferences on psychosomatic medicine, they simply healed the sick. But if they were uncomplicated and naïve by modern standards we have ruefully to admit that they were open on the God-ward side in a way that is almost unknown today. No one can read this book without being convinced that there is Someone here at work besides mere human beings. Perhaps because of their very simplicity, perhaps because of their readiness to believe, to obey, to give, to suffer, and if need be to die, the Spirit of God found what surely he must always be seeking – a fellowship of men and women so united in love and faith that he can work in them and through them with the minimum of let or hindrance. Consequently it is a matter of sober historical fact that never before has any small body of ordinary people so moved the world that their enemies could say, with tears of rage in their eyes, that these men 'have turned the world upside down'!

In Belfast, immersed in the activities of another academic year, the whole question of the empowering of the Holy Spirit came more and more on my agenda. I attended a conference in the autumn arranged by Tom Smail and David Baillie, where I met two Anglican clergy, Michael Harper from London and Ray Muller from New Zealand, who spoke about the experience. There were many questions in my mind about the theological basis of the Charismatic Movement and I read books such as Michael Harper's *Power for the Body of Christ* and Denis

Bennett's *Nine o'clock in the Morning* in order to sift my thinking on the issue.

The following months were times of deep spiritual hunger in my life. My work as Chaplain in the university appeared to be successful and many students were involved in the activities of the Church of the Resurrection. We had many social service programmes and work camps, and there was a lively worshipping congregation on Sundays. I was actively involved in the pastoral care of nearly a thousand students and spent time and energy in personal counselling. Nevertheless I knew that my ministry was reaching a point of crisis. At times I was saying to myself, either I go on and really give everything I've got to the service of Christ or I give it all up and do something else. Those who knew me would hardly have been conscious of this conflict but I was deeply aware of it most of the time. As I read book after book I seemed so often to be like the people who were 'ever learning but never able to come to a knowledge of the truth'. It is so easy to go on accumulating knowledge of all kinds and to evade the personal truth of Christ and his challenge to total commitment.

I had had a spiritual crisis like this once before during my student days in Dublin when doubts about the very foundations of the Christian faith had assailed me and I seemed on the point of giving it all up. It was the influence of a very dear friend of mine during those days which convinced me of the truth of those things I was tempted to doubt. He was David Torrens, Professor of Physiology in Trinity College, a wonderful man of God. He scarcely ever spoke in public about his faith but it was the spring of all his actions. He was so filled with the love of Christ that one could not help recognising the Lord when one was in his presence. Through the mists of my intellectual doubts his sure confidence in God's Word, and his integrity and willingness to listen to me provided a sure line to a firmer faith.

In this new crisis it was again a network of people in touch with the power of God's Spirit who were used to bring me out of my state of spiritual schizophrenia. From sheer scepticism and suspicion about being baptised in the Holy Spirit I came to a point of praying 'Lord make me willing to be willing'. I have come to believe that that is an important if dangerous prayer!

I had heard from Michael Harper that Graham Pulkingham would be in Britain in the early summer and I immediately extended an invitation to him to visit us in Queen's and to preach in the Church of the Resurrection. He came in late April accompanied by Bill Fara, a young man with a musical talent much used by God. Graham spoke to us on two occasions in the Church of the Resurrection and I remember the challenge he made to us about our status as the children of God. What he said contrasted with so much of the preaching I had been used to for so much of my life. He stressed that God by his grace had called us to be 'the sons and daughters of God' and explained how we might enter our inheritance.

I remember distinctly my conversation with Graham in our home as we drank tea after the evening service. I had a feeling that this may be my opportunity to come to a point of deeper commitment to the Lord. I thought Graham would pray with me with the laying on of hands. I spoke to him about my growing longing and my need for a work of the Holy Spirit in my life. He did not force me or bring any pressure to bear; he simply said, 'The Lord is good and gracious,' and implied that God would deal with me in his own time.

I have always been grateful for that conversation, which humanly speaking was quite a disappointment, indeed an anticlimax. But I have learned since a lesson which we as Christians find such a hard one to learn. We can never do the work of the Holy Spirit. We so easily forget those words of our Lord to Nicodemus, 'The wind blows wherever it pleases. You hear its sound, but you cannot tell where it comes from or where it is going. So it is with everyone born of the Spirit' (John 3:8). God has made each one of us uniquely and deals with us as he knows we need. What he wants is not that we should only enjoy an experience but that we should come to know him ever more deeply and personally.

Renewal in the Holy Spirit

Graham and Bill left us, but the Holy Spirit had begun to work, not only in my own heart but in a number of other people's as well. In that summer term, even though it was exam time, about a dozen of us who were hungry for a deeper awareness of the power of God met together twice a week in the side chapel of the Church of the Resurrection. After breakfasting together we spent an hour or more in prayer and Bible study centred on the early chapters of the Acts of the Apostles. In our togetherness God was speaking to each one of us and that group became a rich fellowship; a foretaste for many of us of what God by his Spirit was going to do in the lives of many more. As the term came to an end some of the men in the group decided it would be a good idea if we could all go away together for a weekend of quiet, where we would continue to pray and study.

About twelve students joined Myrtle and me in Murlough House, a quiet retreat house on the County Down coast. Two of the students, John Kelly and Peter Yarr, had suggested we should invite Roy Millar, a young Belfast surgeon, and his wife Rosemary to share their experience of being baptised in the Holy Spirit and to lead us in Bible study.

For over a year I had carefully studied the Scriptures. I was aware of what the Lord taught the disciples about the gift and empowering of the Holy Spirit. I knew the promise of Christ was true and to be trusted: 'you will be baptised with the Holy Spirit' (Acts 1:5); and 'you will receive power when the Holy Spirit comes on you; and you will be my witnesses' (Acts 1:8). Two fears had haunted me and held me back. One was the fear of what others would think of me. That was answered by the word from Proverbs: 'Fear of man will prove to be a snare' (Prov. 29:25). The second fear was of becoming fanatical. That fear had been progressively dealt with as I met more and more sane, balanced Christians from many backgrounds who had been baptised in the Holy Spirit. I had recognised a new depth of awareness in their lives, a strong gentleness and less interest in being negatively critical of other Christians. In short there seemed to be in their lives more of the grace of our Lord Jesus Christ and the love of God in their fellowship with the Holy Spirit.

During that weekend we praised, prayed and shared Scripture together. One of the Scriptures which came clearly to me as a personal invitation was the word of Jesus: 'If anyone loves me, he will obey my teaching. My Father will love him, and we will come to him and make our home with him' (John 14:23). During one of our times of prayer and praise some of the others felt led to pray for me with the laying on of hands. Nothing happened to me that I was aware of then but I appreciated their prayers for me. Some time later as I was praying in my own room I was aware of the presence of God, like a loving Father offering me all the inheritance he had promised, and asking me to receive it as a gift. This I did without any strange feeling or strong emotion but with a deep sense of inner peace. I learned then what was to become much clearer later as I counselled others. The Lord has his own gracious way with each one of us. To some he gives like he did to Thomas, a vivid visual confirmation of his presence and his powers; to others a growing awareness of his love as they respond to him like a flower opening to the morning sunshine.

I have often tried to explain to others what happened to me that evening in an upper room in Murlough House. They say, 'Surely you had the Holy Spirit before during your life as a Christian and a minister?' The best way I can answer is, 'Yes, I had the Holy Spirit living in me as he does in every believer. But now the Holy Spirit had me in a way that was not so before. And there's a world of difference.' I can say that I increasingly experienced a new awareness of his presence, an overwhelming of his love and a new confidence in his power at work within me as I ministered to others in Christ's name. I found a deeper desire for personal and communal prayer. The services of the church, especially the Eucharist, became more meaningful. I had a new love for Scripture, and found that God spoke in simple and direct ways to me in meditation on his word. Praise and worship became a greater joy. Singing God's praise in old and new hymns and songs was now a delight for me.

It took time for me to experience a release to pray in tongues. I sang in tongues before I could pray in tongues. And that for me was remarkable and the occasion of a miracle of healing. As a young boy in primary school I was asked by my teacher to leave a singing class because I had been singing flat. That apparently simple incident caused a deep hurt. In the years of my ministry it was always a disappointment and frequently an agony to stand at the front of the church leading a service and feel unable to join in the singing of hymns, psalms and canticles. I remember sharing with the students in the prayer group the hurt I had experienced. I told them I was looking forward to heaven when I would receive a new voice to sing God's praise. One of them said, 'You don't have to wait until you go to heaven. Let's pray that God will heal you and release that song of praise for you here on earth.' Some time later that prayer was answered and a long-standing wound was healed when God released in me the gift of singing in tongues or singing in the Spirit.

Much of my time as Chaplain was taken up in counselling students through many and varied crises, a ministry which increased with the onset of the violence, and the trauma and suffering that came in its wake. In the power of the Holy Spirit I found a great resource for ministering. I discovered that through healing prayer, often with the laying on of hands, God could reach deep down into a person's life and touch in a moment what might before have taken hours of counselling.

Shared blessing

In other ways my life as a minister and as a person was deeply enriched. The Lord graciously assured me that a remaining concern was under his control. Though Myrtle was fully supportive of my work in the ministry and carried on effective work with individual students, especially those from overseas, she had missed out on many of the meetings in which I had been involved. When I was baptised in the Holy Spirit I knew that God was saying, 'Cecil, this is not for yourself alone, Myrtle is going to share fully in the blessing that I have for you both.'

I'll let her tell her own story of how this came about.

'As I look back on the late 1960s it was for me a fairly bleak time spiritually and emotionally. Cecil's work with the students seemed to be all-consuming and there were times when I resented the long hours into the night that he felt it was right to spend, either counselling them or listening to their seemingly endless civil rights debates in the Students' Union. Along with the other chaplains he sought to moderate and mediate where he could, and who knows how much worse things might have been but for the moderating influence of the clergy at that time. However, despite everyone's efforts, civil strife broke out in 1969 and before long there was the sound of gunfire at night in the city and the ghastly thud of bombings by day.

'On one occasion I was doing my morning shopping on the Lisburn Road when Lavery's pub on the opposite side of the road exploded into the sky. The sense of powerlessness I felt as people gathered around saying, "There's a man in there," is still very real as I recall the incident.

'Almost dumb from the shock, I asked, "Has anyone called an ambulance?"

' "Yes, someone has," they said.

'Terrorists had planted a bomb in the pub, and Mr Lavery, it emerged, had been carrying it out when it blew up. Like many more, he died in the explosion; and there was hardly time to absorb the shock before the next atrocity.

'In 1970 my mother died having heart surgery. She had been very close to my sister and myself and had been a wonderful mother, so the bereavement, although I don't think I recognised it as bereavement at the time, was deep and painful. We had lost Cecil's mother, very dear to us both, not long before.

'Looking back on 1969–70 those circumstances, civil unrest around us and personal loss, contributed to make them difficult years.

'In 1967 our son David had been born, a great joy and answer to prayer, because we had lost, after our daughter Ruth's birth, two babies, one at three months into pregnancy, and the other, a little girl we called Anne, after a difficult premature birth. Then in late 1969 Timothy was born and we rejoiced in these three little lives in our care.

'Maybe I had post-natal depression, or else had not come to terms with the loss of the two babies and then our mothers, but in spite of having Cecil and three beautiful children, my memories of that time are of "alone-ness" and struggling against depression.

'Then Cecil met the three men from Houston and a whole new approach to life and its struggles was around the corner for us both. These men, somewhat like those Peter spoke of in the New Testament, "could not but speak of what they had seen and heard". God had been working in their home church, the Church of the Redeemer in Texas, in ways we had never experienced. People were being healed, and lives and lifestyles radically changed. I was taken up with the children and did not actually meet these men, but a process had started in Cecil that was to culminate in his asking God to baptise him in the Holy Spirit.

'Meanwhile I was fearful lest all that Cecil was becoming involved in would take him away even more and I was concerned too, as he was, to establish whether all this talk of renewal was scriptural. Around this time a friend of mine, Sheila Kenny, whose husband's work as travelling secretary for the Church Missionary Society took him away quite a lot, used to phone me, and we would have heart-to-heart chats.

' "Have you been baptised with the Holy Spirit?" she asked one evening. She had, and recommended I read *Nine o'clock in the Morning* by Denis Bennett. I did, and I began to open up to God in a new way.

'Eventually I attended a day conference in Ballyholme, sponsored by David Baillie, at which Tom Smail was the speaker. One of our students, Patricia Moore, who was later to join us at the Centre, undertook to look after our two-year-old Tim while the meeting was going on. There was, I expect, praise, worship and exposition of Scripture but the way God spoke to me that day was through Tom Smail.

'Tom said to the assembled group of clergy and others, "In Ireland you have been subjected to a lot of demand preaching; you must do this and you must do that, but nobody tells you how to do these things. I want to tell you there's power for living, power for loving, power for witnessing to Christ, and if you want to receive this power simply ask God to baptise you with his Holy Spirit."

'He quoted the words of Jesus when he said, "If an earthly Father desires to give good gifts to his children, how much more will your heavenly Father give the Holy Spirit to them that ask him." Then Tom invited us to ask God to baptise us in his Holy Spirit as he led us in a simple prayer. I responded, "Yes, please, Lord," and true to his word, God began to answer my prayer. A new peace came, and the beginning of a deep healing from fear and anxiety, a deeper awareness of God's love.

'This must have been perceptible, for when I rejoined my two-year-old after the meeting, he looked at me and said, "You're a different Mummy!" Out of the mouths of babes . . . !

'The same afternoon a brief comment of Truda Smail, Tom's wife, had a deep effect on my life. As we combed our hair in the Ladies, I said to her, "I really don't know much about all this renewal, because I never get to meetings because of being with the children most of the time." She simply said, "That's all right. That's your place just now."

'This was significant for me in two ways. If I had waited until I knew all the theology and read all the books on renewal, I would have missed much blessing, and in the second place, since Cecil's work took him away quite a lot it was very important that I be with the children at that stage and give them the security they needed.

'That experience of God and the power of his Holy Spirit in Ballyholme was not a dramatic or traumatic thing but the beginning of a gentle revolution in my life. I had known the Lord Jesus as my Saviour for many years since my teens, and in fact there never was a time when I did not have an awareness of God as I grew up. Confirmation had been an important milestone in my life in the Church of Ireland, when we sang St Patrick's Breastplate, "I bind unto myself today, the strong Name of the Trinity," and I affirmed for myself what had been undertaken for me when I was baptised as an infant.

'Now however, with being baptised with the Holy Spirit, came the beginning of a new freedom which is the inheritance of every Christian, but which I had lacked; freedom to respond to the love of God in praise, and to share my faith with others. A new joy filled my being, and a new sense of the love of God as my Father, which was to grow, and is still growing deeper as time goes on.

'I was being healed from the inside out, and this healing in me brought a new freedom in my relationship with Cecil too. Now we were able to share our faith more deeply and I gradually became less dependent on him and more dependent on God.

' "God has poured out his love into our hearts by the Holy Spirit, whom he has given" (Rom. 5:5) began to become a reality for me in an undeniable way which I wanted to share with others.'

3

A VISION IS BORN

The eyes of the Lord range throughout the earth to strengthen those whose hearts are fully committed to him. (2 Chron. 16:9)

> *God is at work in us*
> *His purpose to perform,*
> *Building a Kingdom*
> *Of power not of words*
> *Where things impossible*
> *By faith shall be made possible;*
> *Let's give the glory*
> *To Him now.*
> *Graham Kendrick[1]*

'Joy unspeakable and full of glory' is how St Peter described the Christian's experience of the overwhelming love of God. Certainly there is no mistaking that in the account of the first Pentecost in Jerusalem recorded in the early chapters of the Acts of the Apostles. It is not a joy to be hugged to oneself; it is a joy for sharing. And in 1972 we badly needed that joy in the midst of the terrible sorrow that hung like dark clouds over our lovely land. Amazingly in the darkness God was there. We discovered his joy bursting forth in the most unlikely places, even in the areas of greatest conflict in Belfast. It was a spontaneous work of God; his gentle, often invisible but powerful way of answering the demonic powers that fuelled the violence.

St Luke tells us in Acts 2 how the early members of the infant church found a new fellowship. 'Every day they continued to meet together in the temple courts. They broke bread in their homes and ate together with glad and sincere hearts, praising God and enjoying the favour of all the people. And the Lord added to their number daily those who were being saved' (Acts 2:46–47). In our 'new' Pentecost we experienced something similar. Those of us who had found a new release of God's love in our lives began to meet together each week in the Church of Ireland Students' Centre at the university. We passed an invitation round to anyone who wished to join us. We called the time 'Following the Spirit', explaining that it would provide an opportunity to learn more from Scripture, to praise God for what he was doing in our lives and to pray for one another and for the city and our land. After the visit from our American friends those who had been with us in those months of exploration were all from Protestant backgrounds. We had no idea who would turn up for this open meeting.

The day before we were due to meet I had a telephone call from a young medical student. She said, 'I am a Catholic and I am longing to find a group where I can meet other Christians to pray and read God's word. Can you advise me where I can go?' Christine was among those who attended the first meeting. Later we discovered it was a simple sign of what God had begun to do all over the world in what was being called the Charismatic Renewal.

For us it was something completely new. As the weeks and months passed from 1972 to 1973 we saw a remarkable miracle unfolding before our eyes. Roman Catholics and Protestants were meeting joyfully, with obvious love for Jesus and for one another. As I looked round the lounge in the Students' Centre I saw Church of Ireland sitting next to Brethren, Baptist beside Roman Catholic, Presbyterian and Methodist sharing with those from a Pentecostal background. It had to be a work of God. Soon we discovered that our little group was not unique.

Similar groups were springing up all over Ireland, north and south.

I visited a group in University College, Dublin which began soon after Tom Smail, a Presbyterian minister, and Joe McGeady, a Roman Catholic priest, had shared at a meeting of students how they had experienced renewal in the Holy Spirit in their lives. When I entered the meeting room in Dublin and saw that group which included not only many Roman Catholic nuns and priests but Quakers, Brethren, Church of Ireland and other Protestants my heart was strangely warmed. It seemed to be light years away from what I had known in Dublin as a student.

When I shared with Myrtle what I had witnessed we both knew that when God had graciously baptised us in his Holy Spirit he had also baptised us into a ministry of reconciliation. The joy is hard to describe as we met brothers and sisters in Christ whom we had never known before, those from whom we had been estranged and towards whom we had been suspicious. Now we were sharing the rich jewel of a mutual faith in Jesus Christ as Lord and Saviour and being deeply enriched by our fellowship together in him.

Old walls are breaking down

The group which met was far from a 'holy huddle'. We found ourselves being propelled into broken areas of Belfast where we had the joy of sharing with others who were hungry to know more of God's power and peace in their lives. One of those who guided us into West Belfast, scene of much unrest and suffering, was Frank Forte. Frank was a Roman Catholic who owned a café near the centre of Belfast opposite the Europa Hotel, which had the unenviable reputation of being the most bombed hotel in the world. Frank's café had also been wrecked in the bombing but not before his dramatic meeting with Christ. One of his regular customers was a local Pentecostal minister. He and Frank often talked together. Frank had been reading about the beginnings of the Charismatic Renewal in the Roman Catholic Church in the United States and wanted to know more about what was happening. His Pentecostal friend explained what it meant to be baptised in the Holy Spirit and Frank became very interested. One day Frank asked his friend if he would pray with him to be baptised with the Holy Spirit. Somewhat taken aback the pastor said, 'I'll go away and pray about it.' Afterwards he confessed that he had not been too certain whether a Roman Catholic was a fit candidate! God saw differently and the pastor returned and prayed with Frank. There was joy in the café as Frank entered on a new adventure with Christ.

Many of our early experiences mirrored those of St Peter, when through a vision and a direct call from God he was led to share the Good News with Cornelius, the Roman Centurion. St Luke records the amazing and rather amusing incident in Acts 10. Peter was involved in a successful mission in the area of Lydda on the Mediterranean coast. Signs and wonders attended his ministry. A man who had been paralysed for eight years was instantaneously healed. Further down the road at Joppa a woman beloved by everyone for her works of mercy died. When Peter came and prayed for her she was raised from the dead. Then God presented Peter, a Jew, with possibly an even greater challenge. Would he go to pray with Commander Cornelius of the Italian regiment stationed at Caesarea? Overcoming his deep prejudices Peter obeyed. What happened next is one of the most important events to affect the whole story of the Christian church. Peter had only begun his address when God took over:

> While Peter was still speaking these words, the Holy Spirit came on all who heard the message. The circumcised believers who had come with Peter were astonished that the gift of the Holy Spirit had been poured out even on the Gentiles. For they heard them speaking in tongues and praising God. Then Peter said, 'Can anyone keep these

people from being baptised with water? They have received the Holy Spirit just as we have.' So he ordered that they be baptised in the name of Jesus Christ. Then they asked Peter to stay with them for a few days. (Acts 10:44–48)

Walls that seemed impossible to remove had come down, enemies became friends, old traditional moulds had been broken, long-standing prejudices had melted away in the fire of God's love. New possibilities, never before dreamed of, had opened up for the spread of the Gospel. And all because one man obeyed the voice of God that confounded his own judgment and overpowered his inherited prejudices.

We knew something of what Peter must have felt in leaving aside his cherished prejudices to embrace someone from the other side for so long regarded as the enemy. 'You're being naïve'; 'you are confusing the situation'; 'darkness and light cannot agree'; all the well worn slogans nursed over centuries of fear and division were hurled from both sides. When they were drummed out and voiced even by Christian friends it was sometimes hard to silence the doubts that arose in one's mind. Those of us born in Northern Ireland seem to be born with prejudice in our bloodstream. And it is not only those who live in deprived areas of our country who hold those prejudices. I have worked and mixed long enough with the most highly-educated people in Ireland to know that religious prejudice is not the preserve of one class.

When we are willing, the Holy Spirit can reach those roots of fear and prejudice that lie deep within. Only God can heal those deep wounds created by past hatred, injustice and mistrust. And we need constant treatment in the clinic of God's love to go on receiving his healing.

One of many such healings came to me in Enniskillen, the town where I was born and grew up. In 1973 the three main Protestant churches in the town, Church of Ireland, Methodist and Presbyterian, invited me to conduct a Youth Outreach in the town. It was an event that had been held annually for some years and involved speaking in schools and leading meetings over a period of several days. I said I would accept the invitation if they would allow me to bring a team of students, Roman Catholic and Protestant, from both Queen's and Dublin. To their credit they agreed and for the first time committed Christians from both traditions shared a mission in Enniskillen. Marie Duddy, a Sister of Mercy on the staff of St Mary's Teacher Training College in Belfast, was a member of the team. She was involved in the prayer group at the university and had made arrangements for some of the women on the team to stay at the convent in Enniskillen. During our time in the town we were all invited to take part in a short outdoor service near the convent in full view of the main road running through the town. A priest and the sisters were leading the service and we gathered round to share in the short liturgy. As I stood there I suddenly began to feel a great fear coming over me. I sensed that as the cars drove past many of my friends and relatives were looking at me. In my mind of fear I could see them rolling down the windows of their cars and shouting 'You are a traitor'. Then I had an almost physical sensation of a bullet being shot into my back. It was all so frighteningly real to me that I had to ask my brothers and sisters from both traditions to pray that I would be delivered from that fear.

Many times when we have been faced with protesters, opposed and abused, I recall that experience and quietly pray that we may all be released from that spiritual bondage that can hold us. I should say that at that time in Enniskillen, some who could not understand how it was possible to do what we were doing were themselves melted and touched by the love of Jesus, which they admitted was evident in the young people who accompanied me.

It seemed clear that in a land where distinctions are so clearly defined and convictions so strongly held God was demonstrating that he has no favourites. His love is without discrimination. The lesson that St Peter learned we too had to re-learn. When Peter began to speak in the house of the man he had perceived as an enemy he said, 'I now realise how true it is that God does not show favouritism but accepts men from every nation who fear him and do what is right' (Acts 10:34–35).

And then when Peter had to explain his actions before a critical gathering of churchmen he said:

> As I began to speak, the Holy Spirit came on them as he had come on us at the beginning. Then I remembered what the Lord had said: 'John baptised with water, but you will be baptised with the Holy Spirit.' So if God gave them the same gift as he gave us, who believed in the Lord Jesus Christ, who was I to think that I could oppose God? (Acts 11:15–17)

Come together in Jesus' name

In the early 1970s sectarian violence was increasing daily. The British army had been called to assist the local Royal Ulster Constabulary in keeping the peace. Despite a large army and police presence IRA bombs were making town and city centres virtual war zones. Hundreds of innocent people lost their lives in merciless murders.

Fear stalked town and county and it seemed increasingly likely that all-out civil war would ensue. While forces of evil were so obviously at work trying to drive people apart God was pouring out his Holy Spirit in saving and renewing power in a way that the people of Ireland had not experienced for many years.

One significant event that made a considerable impact at that time was the staging of a musical called *Come Together in Jesus' Name*, written by Jimmy and Carol Owens, two composers from the United States. It was performed in Britain and Jean Darnall in London believed it would be important to launch it in Northern Ireland. Harry Ferguson, John Kyle, Paul and Hilary Kyle and several others accepted the challenge and called together a choir of young people drawn from many different backgrounds. Some of them were students who had shared in the prayer group in the university, and they used the Church of the Resurrection at Queen's for rehearsals, often spending more time in prayer together than in practising the music and songs. Their talents, however, as singers and musicians were quite remarkable. For the first performance a small choir from the British tour, with Pat Boone as narrator and soloist, joined the local choir for a moving presentation right in the centre of Belfast. After that it was agreed that the local choir should continue the musical and bring its message to other parts of Ireland. I was asked to take Pat Boone's place as narrator. I was not sufficiently healed from my childhood singing failure to match Pat's voice and Paul Kyle very ably took over those solo singing parts! We travelled with the musical to over sixteen centres in Ireland, north and south, and thousands were deeply touched and many hearts and attitudes changed.

In one very divided town in the heart of Ulster old people wept with joy that so many young people should give up their time to carry such a message of love and peace throughout the province. When we took *Come Together* to a large concert hall in Dublin a young Jew left before the show ended. He said to his friends, 'If I stay any longer I fear I too will become a Christian.' Quite a number of young people from that choir are now in positions of leadership in the church at home and overseas. Some are making significant contributions towards building bridges of trust in Belfast through the Community of the King. Paul Kyle, author of the song which is used all over the world 'Lord Jesus we enthrone you', is one of the leaders of that community which joins together Protestant and Catholic Christians across the divides of the city of Belfast.

National renewal conferences

In January 1973 the university prayer group arranged a conference under the title 'Power for Christian Living' to which more than eighty came from north and south. Speakers included Sister Marie Duddy, Roy Millar and Jerome McCarthy, who was one of the leaders in the fast growing group in Dublin. In March, for St Patrick's day, we helped to arrange what must have been the first all-Ireland Conference on Charismatic Renewal held in Benburb, County Tyrone. The guest speakers were a Methodist minister, Joe Petree, and a Dominican priest, Jim Burke, both from the United States. Over two hundred people came from almost every part of Ireland. Following that gathering a National Service group was formed representing many different traditions. Our main concern was to provide more opportunities for those who were being renewed in the Holy Spirit to come together for teaching, fellowship and reconciliation.

Over the next four years national conferences were held, drawing people from all parts of Ireland, both Roman Catholic and Protestant. To each conference we invited two main guest speakers from abroad. In 1974 more than a thousand came to hear Bishop Joseph McKinney from the USA and Michael Harper, then Director of the Fountain Trust in England. Numbers increased to five thousand the next year when Cardinal Suenens and Tom Smail were the main speakers. The Royal Dublin Society showground was filled to capacity the following year when Ralph Martin from the USA and Canon David Watson from England addressed the assembly. Again in 1977 a full house heard challenging messages on unity, renewal and reconciliation from Bishop Langton Fox and Archbishop Bill Burnett from South Africa. In addition to the addresses from the main speakers each conference provided opportunity for a wide variety of 'workshops' where participants could meet in smaller groups to learn and share various aspects of personal and corporate renewal. Many for the first time in their lives were discovering the joy of praying with people from other Christian traditions.

At a time when news of bombings and killings was going out across the world from Ireland, the press and media were eager to report such an unusual coming together of Christians from all parts of our divided land.

The call to unity in the Body of Christ was a recurring theme in those conferences. Cardinal Suenens, a well-known leader who addressed conferences all over the world, expressed this call clearly. He said in 1975:

> The church of today is wounded because of the lack of visible unity. Let us pray together for that unity so that we may be one. I believe that the solution of ecumenical disunity will not finally be the result of a dialogue between the Church of Rome and the Church of Canterbury or the Orthodox Church of Moscow. It will not be a dialogue between the churches as such, but a dialogue between Rome and Jesus, Canterbury and Jesus, Moscow and Jesus.

The centrality of Jesus was a marked feature of such assemblies. A year later the well-known Anglican evangelist Canon David Watson was a speaker at the Dublin conference. In his autobiography, *You are My God*, he recalled some of his impressions:

> I had gone as the opening speaker, and was amazed to find 6,000 present, of whom 5,000 were Roman Catholic including many hundreds of nuns and priests, and the rest were Protestants of all denominations. It was an incredible conference. I was especially impressed by the God-centred, Christ-centred nature of it all. Every meeting began with a prolonged time of worship; it seemed that the people were not willing to listen to any speaker until they had first fixed their minds and hearts on God himself. It was the Lord whom they wanted to hear, not just some ordinary speaker! Equally obvious was their hunger for God's word: they loved to hear the Scriptures expounded. They were also profoundly aware of the difference between religion and the 'real thing'. It was astonishing for me to hear Roman Catholic priests from the platform saying to this vast crowd: 'It is not enough being born as a Catholic; you need to be born again by the Spirit of God. It is not enough to come to Mass each week; you need to

know Jesus Christ as your personal Lord and Saviour.'
It was almost like a Billy Graham evangelistic crusade![2]

All this was new for Ireland. People whose history and
religion had taught us suspicion, fear and mistrust of one
another were discovering a new fellowship in the Holy
Spirit. I have no doubt we were seeing an answer to the
prayers of God's faithful people in Ireland over many
generations. Many had sincerely prayed such prayers as
the one found in the Church of Ireland Prayer Book:

> O God, the Father of our Lord Jesus Christ, our only Saviour,
> the Prince of Peace; Give us grace seriously to lay to heart
> the great dangers we are in by our unhappy divisions. Take
> away all hatred and prejudice, and whatsoever else may
> hinder us from godly union and concord; that, as there
> is but one Body, and one Spirit, and one hope of our
> calling, one Lord, one Faith, one Baptism, one God and
> Father of us all, so we may henceforth be all of one heart,
> and of one soul, united in one holy bond of truth and
> peace, of faith and charity, and may with one mind and
> one mouth glorify thee; through Jesus Christ our Lord.

Many had been courageously working for that unity of his
people that Christ wills and for which he prays.

In 1964 during one of his frequent visits to Northern
Ireland the Revd Duncan Campbell, whom God had signally
used in the revival in the Scottish Hebrides, declared,
'Ireland will have riots and revival.' Andrew Woolsey, in
his biography of Duncan Campbell, *Channel of Revival*,
recalls a moving convention held in Lisburn when Duncan
described how God would visit the island through small
bands of praying people in the country districts.

Birth of the vision

The riots had certainly come. So also had the dew of God's
blessing with a foretaste of revival. In such an atmosphere of

'riot and revival' the vision for the Christian Renewal Centre was born. It came first to me, not in a blinding flash but as a growing conviction that God would call many people to share in praying and working for an Ireland united in Christ and in the power of his Holy Spirit. As the vision focused more clearly I saw the need for a place where people from all backgrounds could come together, not to argue or debate but in an atmosphere of prayer to meet Jesus and allow him to lead us forward in his purpose for his Church and for our land.

There was exhilaration in the thought but also an enormous challenge. From the Scriptures it is clear that many significant events in salvation history were inaugurated by visions of various kinds. And the one entrusted with a vision carries a great responsibility. All I can say is that, however much I tried to suppress it, the vision would not go away. Tremblingly I shared it first with Myrtle and then with some close and trusted friends, inviting prayer for guidance and direction. I have discovered how tender is the seed of a vision which God may entrust to any one of us. It needs to be carefully planted in the soil of prayer, constantly nourished by faith and exposed to God's loving judgment and direction. Fear can corrode the seed of vision, unbelief explode it and hasty action can abort it. I have learned that when God wants us to do something special for him he is always urgent about it but never in a hurry. 'Where there is no vision the people perish', the wise man in Proverbs reminds us (Prov. 29:18 AV).

I am convinced that God has given many visions to men and women of what he wants to do. One reason why they may never have been brought to birth is that they have been too quickly shared and exposed to withering unbelief, often expressed by Christian friends who should know better.

Over a year or more the kernel of the vision that I felt God had given did not change. As we submitted it to faith-filled brothers and sisters it gradually germinated and flowered until we knew the time for acting on it had come. It became clear that we were being called to establish a Centre for

Prayer, Christian Renewal and Reconciliation which would be staffed by a community of people, men and women whom God would call to share that ministry throughout Ireland. We knew the location should be in the south of the province near the border, to facilitate people from both sides to meet each other. The Centre would not belong to any existing denomination nor would we begin a new one: Ireland already has too many. The Centre would serve all God's people. It would be a work of faith depending totally on God's provision through his people, and it would be constantly supported by the prayers of those who accepted the vision for the work of renewal and unity.

God is consistent in the way He speaks and we sought direction from the Bible. There were two passages in Scripture that seemed to come very much to the fore. Ephesians 2, especially verses 14–18, and Isaiah 55. The words in Ephesians 2, 'For he himself is our peace, who has made the two one and has destroyed the barrier, the dividing wall of hostility,' became the foundation text for the Centre. Their challenge is constantly before us. Revealing their truth in the stubborn soil of Ireland is an urgent task.

The words of Isaiah 55 were a source of great encouragement over many months of waiting and discerning. While I was pondering these words and wrestling with the vision in June 1973, Father Jerome McCarthy and I attended the second European Conference on Charismatic Renewal. It was held in Schloss Craheim, a Christian Centre near the border with East Germany, run then by a Christian community led by a Lutheran pastor, Dr Arnold Bittlinger. Visiting the conference just for one day was Dr Vinson Synan from the United States. During one of the sessions as we waited together in prayer Vinson felt the Holy Spirit moving him to share something.

He said, 'I don't know why but God is urging me to share his word in Isaiah 55. I believe it is for someone here.'

He read the words and sat down. Immediately I sensed that God was confirming what he had been saying to us during the previous months and that he would work in ways that we could not understand with our human minds: 'For my thoughts are not your thoughts, neither are your ways my ways, declares the Lord. As the heavens are higher than the earth, so are my ways higher than your ways and my thoughts than your thoughts' (Isa. 55:8–9).

Over a year later when we moved to Rostrevor and looked out over the tree-clad mountains of Mourne verse 12 of Isaiah 55 took on a special meaning: 'You will go out in joy and be led forth in peace; the mountains and hills will burst into song before you, and all the trees of the field will clap their hands.'

Nor did we miss God's sense of humour in the rather personalised promise for us both in verse 13: 'Instead of the thornbush will grow the pine tree, and instead of briers the myrtle will grow.'

God's provision

A number of possible places to locate the Centre were considered. I remember Reg East was with us in the autumn of 1973 to preach in the Church of the Resurrection. Several years before Reg and his wife Lucia together with John Gunstone had founded a community to work for renewal in Whatcombe House near Blandford in Dorset. With Reg I visited a large house in Armagh which had just come on the market for sale. Having seen the building we sensed it was not the place. Reg said, 'Have no fear, God will lead you to the right place in his time.' Literally the next day I saw an advertisement in the paper: 'Large house for sale overlooking Carlingford Lough.' I contacted the estate agent and arranged to see the property. It was a cold November day when Myrtle and I set off on the fifty mile journey to Rostrevor. I think we had only been there twice before in our lives. As we walked up the path from the Shore Road to the house the prospect was not very inviting. Before us stood an empty, cold Victorian building that had obviously seen better days. A large guard dog patrolling the property did not add to the welcome. Our visit was brief, to be followed by a closer inspection at a later date. We came away with a sense that this might well be the place that God would use in furthering the vision he had given us.

Early in 1974 I made an appointment with my bishop, Dr Arthur Butler, to discuss the possible project with him and to talk about the future of the work in Queen's. Over the nine years that I had been Chaplain in the university we had developed a good relationship. The bishop was a frequent visitor, had a good rapport with students and was a constant encourager in the work we were doing. He listened carefully as I outlined the way that we thought God might be leading us and I mentioned the possibility of Rostrevor as a location for the proposed Centre. His initial response was deep concern for our family and the effect that such a step would have on them. He had been keen for me to move to a parish in or near the city so that I could continue the work of teaching in the Pastoral Counselling Course at the university. However as we talked his attitude changed. He said, 'I believe God is calling you to do this new work and I believe the place is right and the time is ripe.' Then we prayed together and the bishop led in a prayer that meant a lot to me at that moment:

> O God, who art the light of the minds that know thee, the joy of the hearts that love thee and the strength of the wills that serve thee; help us so to know thee that we may truly love thee, so to love thee that we may fully serve thee, whose service is perfect freedom in Jesus Christ our Lord.

Similar confirmation came from Bishop George Quin of Down and Dromore in whose diocese Rostrevor was. Both bishops had been actively involved in building bridges in our divided community and had encouraged their clergy in some very difficult areas where sectarian violence had occurred. Bishop George was engaged in a Diocesan Renewal Campaign which had a profound effect on many parishes in his diocese. He assured me of a warm welcome if we did establish the Christian Renewal Centre in Rostrevor.

We now knew that the next step was to submit the whole vision to a larger group of people whose judgment we trusted and invite them to pray with us. In February 1974 a group of eighteen accepted our invitation to our home for an afternoon to help us discern whether we should proceed. Having outlined the vision and shared what progress had been made so far we asked those present to pray, waiting on God to discern his will together. After the prayer it was unanimously agreed that this was a call from God which we needed to pursue and all present assured us of their prayers. Then someone asked, 'Where will the money come from?'

Tom Henderson, an Economics graduate of Queen's who had been an active member of the university prayer group, said, 'I believe God wants you to do this work and he will put it into the hearts of the right people to give the right amount at the right time.'

We did not realise how prophetic that word would prove to be in the years to come. Tom had not learnt it from his Economics textbooks, but it has remained the financial principle for the Centre ever since.

Now we were 'walking on the water'. We had to keep our eyes fixed on Jesus, the author and perfecter of our faith. The days ahead were times of great testing as God's purpose unfolded. Another visit to Rostrevor to see the house convinced us that the building had considerable potential and would be ideally situated as a Centre for Reconciliation, convenient both to Dublin and Belfast. The owner who inherited the property eighteen years earlier had divided the building into seven self-contained flats. The task of conversion and restoration of such a large building seemed daunting both practically and financially. Eventually the owner agreed to the sale with some furniture included for the sum of £16,000. It seemed very good value, but we did not have even £1,000. And so our walk of faith began in earnest and remembering God's word through Tom Henderson we started proceedings to purchase. Competition for the purchase was not a factor, we discovered. Few people wanted such a large house in an area where the IRA was active.

We drew up a simple brochure explaining the vision for the Centre and stating the financial needs for the purchase and running of the house. Especially we invited people to pray that God would be honoured in the entire venture. We sent out the news to friends we knew would pray for us and the response was an encouragement to our faith. Letters and messages came from people from all backgrounds with assurances of continued prayer for us as a family and for the project. Others, understandably, found it very hard to accept. Some thought we were crazy! Some could not understand why we wanted to leave a strategic ministry in the university to step out into the unknown.

Trial of faith

Many setbacks tested our faith to the limits. Legal difficulties over the deeds led to months of protracted negotiations; in order to make way for my successor to the post of Chaplain in the university I soon had to tender my resignation to the bishop. With hindsight we can see that all these testings were allowed by God so that we could trust him more fully in the greater testings that were to come.

In March 1974 our own commitment received a final test which cleared the ground for Myrtle and me. First I received a letter from our good friend John Taylor who was then General Secretary of the Church Missionary Society, and later Bishop of Winchester. He had been a guest in our home when he came to Queen's to give a series of theological lectures. He wrote asking me to consider the possibility of coming to London to take on an important post in the headquarters staff of the Church Missionary Society, a worldwide missionary agency. Then the Bishop of Down offered to put my name forward for nomination to be Rector of a large parish in the city. We were brought back to our knees again to check our discernment. We had close contacts with the CMS and had been interested in its work for many years but we both felt that God was definitely calling us to work in Ireland for the foreseeable future. The other decision was harder. I had been invited several times before to consider parish work and had not felt it right to accept although I had a great love for pastoral ministry. In the work of renewal I had always believed that the local church was the key to the renewal of the whole church.

I sought the help and advice of Bishop Arthur Butler. What he wrote to me confirmed what in my heart of hearts I knew to be right. He said:

> God has clearly called you to this work and given you the vision for it. Someone else will be able to undertake the work of the parish but if you do not do the work you feel called to it may never be done and the opportunity may not come again.

My colleague John Dinnen was appointed to succeed me as Chaplain. Our final monthly cheque would be paid on 31 August. The weeks were flying past and there was no news of the completion of the sale nor of a date for moving to Rostrevor. We had burnt our boats but the Lord was helping us walk through the waves. Meanwhile the vendor agreed that we should pay £10,000 before we moved in and the remaining £6,000 by the end of 1974. That seemed reasonable. The only difficulty was that the bank account for the project at the beginning of June stood at £8,000. To us it was a lot of money: it had come in small and larger gifts from all kinds of people, some of whom we had never met and a few who remained anonymous. We knew that each gift came with assured love and prayer. On 4 June three others joined Myrtle and me to pray about the whole situation. Walter Skelsey travelled over from England, Michael Frawley came from Dublin and Fanny Robertson from Belfast. Walter and Fanny by this time felt fairly certain that God was calling them to join us as initial members of the community.

In our prayer many of our questionings were answered by the sharing of a Scripture from Exodus 33:12–15. It really seemed to speak into our condition of anxiety at that time.

Moses said to the Lord, 'You have been telling me, "Lead these people," but you have not let me know whom you will send with me. You have said, "I know you by name and you have found favour with me." If you are pleased with me, teach me your ways so I may know you and continue to find favour with you. Remember that this nation is your people.' The Lord replied, 'My Presence will go with you, and I will give you rest.' Then Moses said to him, 'If your Presence does not go with us, do not send us up from here.' (Exod. 33:12–15)

Then quite simply in our prayer we told the Lord what he knew very well already. 'Lord, here we are with only a few weeks to go and we need another £2,000 for the first payment.'

The speed of his answer alarmed us. We had scarcely said 'Amen' when the telephone rang. It was the owner of the house in Rostrevor.

She said, 'You remember the arrangement we made that you should pay £10,000 before you move in and £6,000 at the end of the year. I have been giving the matter some thought and I wanted you to know that I would be quite happy if you pay £8,000 now and the other £8,000 on 31 December.'

The Lord had helped us over another hurdle but the legal difficulties over the deeds remained. Alan Hewitt, our solicitor, wisely advised us not to move into the house until everything was fully cleared up. It was back to prayerful waiting. In faith we began to pack and prepare for the move. We said our farewells. The other chaplains presented me with a print of a William Conor painting, a Belfast scene of a busy street outside a factory. I was grateful for the gift but found it hard to accept. Inside me the struggle over leaving the Belfast we loved had not been resolved.

It was some weeks later that God graciously spoke into that struggle. We were on holiday with the children in a cottage near Ardglass on the other side of the Mourne mountains from Rostrevor. On an early morning walk I was talking to the Lord and sharing the struggle I was going through. As I looked across to the mountains he spoke to me in an almost audible way. He seemed to say, 'Look across the Mournes. Right there high up in those mountains is the Silent Valley, the reservoir that supplies much of the water to the city. Silently every day it yields that essential supply. If you are faithful in what I have called you to do in Rostrevor rivers of living water will flow into many of those thirsty areas of Belfast.'

Literally at the last minute the legal difficulties were sorted out and we were free to go. Two nights before we left Belfast Alan and Ruth Hewitt invited us to their home. They were joined by our good friends William and Eleanor Fitch. Together they offered a prayer that comforted our trembling souls and gave us fresh courage. Their prayer was that every day we would experience the presence of God as Moses and the people of Israel did; that going before us would be 'a pillar of cloud by day and a pillar of fire by night'.

4

LIVING IN COMMUNITY

How good and pleasant it is
  When brothers live together in unity . . .
For there the Lord bestows his blessing,
  even life for evermore.

                                        Psalm 133

   *Christian brotherhood is not an ideal which we must
realise; it is rather a reality created by God in Christ in
which we may participate. (Dietrich Bonhoeffer)[1]*

Abraham left, as the Lord had told him . . . he took his
wife Sarah, his nephew Lot and all the possessions they
had accumulated and the people . . . and they set out for
the land of Canaan. (Gen. 12:4–5)

We had some fellow feeling for Abraham and his family
when we set out from Belfast on 22 August 1974! Maybe
we had accumulated less possessions and fewer people
but all our belongings were transported more speedily
than Abraham's as we travelled the fifty miles south to
Rostrevor: Myrtle and myself, our three children, Ruth,
David and Timothy, and Myrtle's father whom she had
just nursed through a serious illness. Fortunately there
were none of the oxen and asses that Abraham had to
take! With the delay over the legal difficulties we had
been unable to do any work of preparation on the house.
For the next year or more we were to face the prospect

of 'camping out' in a few rooms in the house while we tried to restore it to something of its former glory. The prospect was daunting to say the least, but we held on to God's promises. We realised how much we needed to be supported in prayer, and wrote to those who had already expressed an interest in the work. Many affirmed the vision and some contributed generously in money, furniture and equipment. Without that growing army of praying people it is doubtful whether we would have survived those early difficulties.

We quickly discovered that God was calling the right people to share the vision and work at Rostrevor. Patricia Moore, one of the university prayer group and recently graduated, felt God had called her. Stephanie Crowther from Nottingham, who had been a member of the Scargill Community in Yorkshire, also volunteered. Patricia and Stephanie bravely made their way to Rostrevor the day before we did and were there to welcome us. Walter Skelsey was one of the first to express an interest in joining us in the community. After a distinguished career as a British army officer in the Duke of Wellington regiment he became a life member of the Scargill Community. Deeply concerned about the conflict in Northern Ireland he felt that God wanted him to make a contribution to peace-making in Ireland. Generously the Scargill Community released him for two years during which he was a blessing to us and to many throughout Ireland. Fanny Robertson was enthusiastic at an early stage; she was Overseas Secretary of the Presbyterian Women's Association and had travelled widely at home and overseas. For a long time she had cherished a desire that God would use her to bring Roman Catholics and Protestants together to study God's word, and she saw the Centre as an opportunity for this to come to pass. And come to pass it did, for in the two years before she died Fanny led many into the gold-mine of Scripture and taught them how to enjoy the Bible. Scargill's generosity to Ireland was further extended when Keith and Nola Worsfold joined us. A delightful young couple, just married, they were an answer to prayer as Nola had an interest in cooking and Keith was a trained interior decorator.

We were learning the truth of God's word that 'he is secretly planning in love for us'. He knew the gifts and skills we needed. That was proved again when Lavinia was the next Community member to join us. She lived in the village with her mother Marjorie and sister Ann. A year before we came to Rostrevor Lavinia's father died and she was left to run the family business. When it was decided to close the business Lavinia not only came herself but brought all her office equipment with her! As one of the longest serving members her secretarial and book-keeping skills have been rich gifts to the community. By January 1975, to our great joy, we had grown to twelve including our own family.

Our primary identity

From the outset we knew that at the heart of our work there would be a community of people. Called by God from many different backgrounds we would pray and work for Christian renewal and reconciliation all over Ireland and wherever he called us. We had discovered in our own experience that unity is God's gift to all who believe in Jesus Christ as Saviour and Lord, all who are 'in Christ' by repentance and faith and through his grace are already made one. If you are 'in Christ' and I am 'in Christ' then, whether we acknowledge it or not, we are forever one in him. Jesus makes us brothers, not half-brothers. Thus I can never refuse to call him brother whom my Father has made his son. Even though we gratefully acknowledge the blessings which have been brought to us through the Christian traditions in which we have been nurtured, our primary identity is 'in Christ' as brothers and sisters. The greatest challenge to the church in Ireland and indeed all over the world is not only to believe and acknowledge that truth but to live it.

An army of ordinary people

Over the years more than sixty people have come at different times to share our life together, bringing with them an amazing variety of gifts and talents. Men and women, young and old, married, widowed and single, from many different Christian traditions, they have responded to God's call. Anglican, Church of Ireland, Roman Catholic, Methodist, Presbyterian, United Reformed, Lutheran, Free Church and Pentecostal reflect the varied tapestry of Christian confession united in Jesus Christ. Several nations are represented, Ireland north and south, England, Holland, Sweden, Germany, Taiwan, United States of America and Switzerland.

The New Testament uses extraordinarily extravagant language to describe the calling of the Christian Church. Jesus said, 'You are the light of the world . . . the salt of the earth . . . sons and daughters of his kingdom . . . a new creation'; we are called to 'shine as lights in the darkness' to be 'ambassadors for Christ', to reflect his glory and to be the bride of Christ, even to be the 'aroma of Christ'. Perhaps the most revealing is the language St Paul uses so often when he says: 'You (believers) are the body of Christ and each one of you is a part of it' (1 Cor. 12:27). Ordinary people like you and me God calls to represent him in the world. With all our weaknesses and failures he accepts us and makes us what he wants us to be.

Looking back it is fascinating to recall the various ways God has called people to the Centre. They have come from teaching, business, industry and nursing; or for a year between school and university; or after university or college. All have made sacrifices and no one has taken the calling lightly. David Gillett, who made a valuable contribution to the life and work of the Centre for three years, recalled the struggle which he went through in responding to what he knew was God's call. He was on the staff of St John's Theological College, Nottingham:

I spent a month of my sabbatical term in Northern Ireland and on the last day called into the Christian Renewal Centre at Rostrevor. I was only there for about three hours and at the end of my brief visit Cecil Kerr said, 'We are looking for someone like you to come and develop the teaching ministry of the Centre.' My reaction was something like, 'I would not dismiss such a thought straight away.' I flew back to England quite expecting Cecil to write to me in about eighteen months time – half hoping that by then I would be settled into a new job in England! In the event, I received a letter in about eighteen days inviting me to join them at Rostrevor. Curiously (perhaps providentially) I opened the letter when Harold Miller was having breakfast with me. Harold, a former student, was over from Northern Ireland where he was a curate, being interviewed for a job in college. (He was in fact my successor as Director of Extension Studies.) That was one possible pointer to me that the Lord was calling me to Northern Ireland for the next stage in my ministry. I then went to spend a week at Rostrevor just before Easter. My first reactions were definitely cool! Much as I liked the place and admired its work I could not get used to the idea of 'living by faith'. However, during the week, God made it plain that he was calling me there, and the idea of 'living by faith' far from being a burden, began to be a point of freedom. The words from Scripture that God used in my call to Northern Ireland are from Hebrews 13:13–14: 'Let us, then, go to him outside the camp, bearing the disgrace he bore. For here we do not have an enduring city, but we are looking for the city that is to come.' This spoke to me very powerfully of the situation in Ireland and of my own Christian discipleship and service. On returning to St John's I shared with the staff what I felt and asked what their feelings were. The general response was that this seemed to be a genuine and urgent call from God and that they would accept the responsibility of finding a successor, thus releasing me to go in the autumn.

Eric Mayer came with his wife Mabel for a short holiday at the Centre. They joined in the daily prayer of the community and I remember Eric prayed earnestly and with faith, asking God to call and equip his people to work effectively for healing the wounds of Ireland.

After the prayer time I said to him, 'Would you ever consider God might call you to be the answer to your prayer?'

Eric and Mabel were involved in a very effective ministry in a United Reformed Church in Warrington, Lancashire, where they had moved after Eric's work as a journalist with the Billy Graham Evangelistic Association. Over several months of prayer and discernment with their elders and prayer partners Eric and Mabel knew that God was calling them back to Ireland, where God's gifts of ministry in them have been greatly used.

Eugene Boyle first visited the Centre to spend time in prayer, seeking God's direction for his life after he had experienced a deep renewal of his faith. Returning frequently to offer his welcome skills of handcraft and carpentry he and his wife Una responded to the call to join the community. Eugene's training in theology and experience in teaching have been turned to fruitful work for the Kingdom of God. Una out of her experience with her own children felt God calling her to start the King's Kids, with the help of other members of the community. It has become a valuable ministry with children in the locality.

Gwen Tollerton had been a prayer partner for some years. Although she lived in England her husband was Irish and she shared the concern of many Christians for Ireland. After her husband's death she read in our newsletter of the need for someone interested in home-making and creating a place of warmth and welcome in the Centre. She knew that God was calling her and we knew she was the answer to our prayer at that particular time. Again and again we have witnessed God's faithfulness in sending those he is calling just at the right time.

Servants of the servants of God

It has to be a miracle of God's grace that people from such varied backgrounds and with such different personalities can live and work together. It was clear to us that it was not to be community for community's sake. Our calling was to serve God's purpose 'to bring together God's scattered people and make them one'. Our unity as brothers and sisters in Christ would have to demonstrate in practical ways the unity Christ desires for his people. That meant providing a place of welcome for all who came; an open house where people could find the Lord in each other. We are called to be 'servants of the servants of God'.

People often say after a weekend at the Centre, 'It must be wonderful living in a Christian community with opportunity for regular shared prayer and constant fellowship and contact with other people.' We have to say there is another side to it. We live in the real world of cooking, cleaning, washing up, preparation and all the mundane activities that make up daily life. It is not a dream world in which we live. Bring a group of people together from diverse religious, cultural and national backgrounds and you experience the real challenge of growing together as the family of God. The parody may be poor poetry but it expresses some truth.

> Oh to be one up above
> With the saints in love
> That will be glory
> But to be one down below
> With some of the saints I know
> That's quite another story!

Early in our experience of living and working together we learned from others who had gone the way of community before. Graham Pulkingham and his wife Betty established the Community of Celebration in England after moving from the Church of the Redeemer in Houston. Reg East and his wife Lucia with Canon John Gunstone lent encouragement from their experience in Whatcombe House. Walter Skelsey of the Scargill Community calmed many a storm in his gentle way. We remember community meetings when the going was difficult and Walter would quietly say, 'Tomorrow is another day.' Walter too introduced us to a book by the German pastor and theologian Dietrich Bonhoeffer. Written from his experience of close Christian community during the Nazi regime it is a treasury of wisdom and common sense. He states simply what we had begun to realise and have come to see more clearly as the years go by:

> Christianity means community through Jesus Christ and in Jesus Christ. No Christian community is more or less than this. Whether it be a brief, single encounter or the daily fellowship of years, Christian community is only this. We belong to one another only through and in Jesus Christ. What does this mean? It means, first, that a Christian needs others because of Jesus Christ. It means, second, that a Christian comes to others only through Jesus Christ. It means, third, that in Jesus Christ, we have been chosen from eternity, accepted in time, and united for eternity.[2]

From Bonhoeffer we learned what every group setting out on this way of community must learn quickly if the endeavour is to succeed:

> Innumerable times a whole Christian community has broken down because it had sprung from a wish dream. The serious Christian, set down for the first time in a Christian community, is likely to bring with him a very definite idea of what Christian life together should be and try to realise it. But God's grace speedily shatters such dreams. Just as surely God desires to lead us to a knowledge of genuine Christian fellowship, so surely must we be overwhelmed by a great general disillusionment with others, with Christians in general, and, if we are fortunate, with ourselves. By sheer grace God will not permit us to live even for a brief period in a dream world. He does not abandon us to those rapturous experiences and lofty moods that come over us like a dream.

God is not a God of the emotions but the God of truth. Only that fellowship which faces such disillusionment, with all its unhappy and ugly aspects, begins to be what it should be in God's sight, begins to grasp in faith the promise that is given to it. The sooner this shock of disillusionment comes to an individual and to a community the better for both. A community which cannot bear and cannot survive such a crisis, which insists upon keeping its illusion when it should be shattered, permanently loses in that moment the promise of Christian community. Sooner or later it will collapse. Every human wish dream that is injected into the Christian community is a hindrance to genuine community and must be banished if genuine community is to survive.[3]

Living in community and working through interpersonal relationships sheds light on a deeper understanding of the experience of our Lord with his disciples. Have you ever wondered why he did it the way he did? Who would have chosen the kind of men he did? And yet he welded those men, so different in their backgrounds, personalities and experiences, into a community of love, commitment and self-sacrifice. We can imagine some of the problems created for those men when Jesus added a group of women to his faith-sharing team! St Luke tells us:

After this, Jesus travelled about from one town and village to another, proclaiming the good news of the kingdom of God. The Twelve were with him, and also some women who had been cured of evil spirits and diseases: Mary (called Magdalene) from whom seven demons had come out; Joanna the wife of Chuza, the manager of Herod's household; Susanna; and many others. These women were helping to support them out of their own means. (Luke 8:1–3)

Minutes were not written of the community meetings of the apostles on their mission but the Gospels give many glimpses of the reality of their debates, their prejudices, petty jealousies and frequent disagreements. Yet Jesus did not dismiss them. He had chosen and called them. They had responded. The grace of God and the certainty of the clear call of Jesus held them together in the many storms through which they had to pass.

Many of us sincerely desiring to follow the Lord want him to mould us and fashion us and we say to him, 'Lord, do that work with just you and me together.' He turns round and says, 'I have other instruments I use to do my work of refining and fashioning you. I have given you brothers and sisters!'

The Celebrant Singers, a group of talented young musicians led by Jon Stemkoski, are dedicated to sharing the Good News all over the world in music and song. With so much travelling and sharing cramped accommodation in all kinds of conditions they learn about Christian community the hard way. Once when they were with us we had a mutual sharing of our experience of community living. We knew what they meant when one was introduced as 'Sister Sandpaper' and another as 'Brother Chisel'!

At first we used to feel condemned in difficult times of personal relationships or decision-making. Then we found people coming to the door or staying with us for rest or counselling who, to our amazement, said, 'We experience such peace in this place. We feel God's healing presence here.' God in his grace and patient love was reminding us, 'As long as your hearts are set on following me and being faithful to me and you are willing to work through those difficult relationships with love and mutual forgiveness I can stand here to bless those who come.' Only when we dig in our heels and refuse to forgive is the Spirit of God grieved and the whole ministry affected.

Growth in community

Myrtle was given the job of answering people's enquiries about joining the community. Her task was to explain the realities of our life and work, especially for those who might be seeing it, as we say, 'through rose-tinted spectacles'. At

the same time she conveyed the privilege of God's calling
to such work and the resources he makes available to us.
Her gentle pastoral skills and radiant faith have steered
many of us through turbulent times. Having acknowledged
God's continuous healing in her own life she has confidence
to believe that 'he is able to do infinitely more than we ask or
think' even in the most difficult circumstances. Through the
years no one in the Centre has been more closely identified
with the internal life and growth of the community than
Myrtle. What she shares out of her experience is both
illuminating and instructive.

'As I look back on the fifteen years Cecil and I have spent
as members of the community at the Christian Renewal
Centre my prevailing feeling is one of thankfulness to God.
I want to thank him for the way I have seen him work in
the lives of people around me, and in my own life, for the
ways he has cared for us as a family and as a community. I
have learned more than I can ever tell from those men and
women of God who have worked with us for a year or two,
or in some cases ten or fifteen years. However I must admit
it was in some trepidation that I personally said "yes" when
God called Cecil and me to start the community. My fears
stemmed from deep personal insecurity, which God has
been graciously healing as I have allowed his love to melt
my fears. It has not been easy, but God's grace has always
been there. He only asks us to be faithful and obedient.

'I knew enough about community life to be afraid of the
vulnerability one experiences in living and working with
other people. One is forced to grow in an unavoidable
way and that can be painful. I would have preferred to
protect myself from the pain involved in this growth; a
selfish reaction, I admit, especially as the Lord became
utterly vulnerable for us in dying on the cross.

'We can meet weekly in a church service or in a mid-
week fellowship, or even in a weekend conference or
holiday week without being challenged to grow in our
interpersonal relationships. We can even live together in
the same house and avoid the caring for one another that

makes us vulnerable. You can stay 'in your small corner' and 'I in mine'. If however we want to demonstrate the truth that 'By this shall all men know you are my disciples, if you love one another' (John 13:35) we must become involved with each other. That involvement is costly. It takes time, and it risks rejection. It was so costly for Jesus that he gave himself totally for us. Can it be less so for us who are his disciples?

'I don't mean that everyone is called to live in a residential community in order to discover what committed Christian love means. For most people this is not God's calling, and God will challenge us in family life and in church life to grow in loving and caring whether or not we belong to a residential community. A community like ours can be at best a kind of microcosm of what God wants for the Church, in the context of the purpose he has set before us, of prayer, renewal and reconciliation. He wants to teach us to love one another in spite of all our differences.

'Jimmy and Carol Owens, commenting on Jesus' words in John 13:35, wrote, "This love is the identifying mark of Christ's disciples, his body. We talk a lot about Christian love, but too often our 'love' disappears in a hurry when doctrinal differences arise. Too often love loses out to personal biases; external things such as race, age, social and cultural differences." Sadly how true this is in Northern Ireland, and sadly it is so in the Church. People outside the Church have a right to look for the love of God among us, and instead they often find bigotry, hatred, bitterness and pride. How we need the purifying fire of the Holy Spirit to burn up all these things in our midst and in our hearts, which prevent people finding the love of Christ!

'Jesus was utterly uncompromising in his insistence on forgiveness of one another. He went as far as to say in Matthew 6:15, "Your heavenly Father will forgive you if you forgive those who sin against you, but if you refuse to forgive them, he will not forgive you." Again he said, "So if you are offering your gift at the altar, and there remember that your brother has something against you, leave your gift there before the altar and go; first be reconciled to your brother, and then come and offer your gift" (Matt. 5:23–24 RSV).

'For us in the community at the Christian Renewal Centre the challenge of God's word comes to us daily, to allow his forgiving love to flow among us. Because we work closely with each other, and because we are all different in temperament and background we naturally hurt each other. These hurts may seem trivial and unimportant, but if allowed to remain in my heart unforgiven and undealt with, will cause real difficulty in my walk with the Lord, and real restraint in my relationship with the one who has hurt me, or whom I have hurt. It clears the air, and can become an occasion of growth with my brother or sister if I can go to him or her and explain why I was hurt, or if they can come to me when I have hurt them. I appreciate it when someone has the courage to come and tell me that I am hurting them in some particular way. I can remember on one occasion someone telling me my attitude to them was patronising. I am sure it was true, and I had to learn how to relate to that person in a better way.

'Unresolved hurt or interpersonal difficulties can clog up our ability to hear the Lord as a group. Whenever we come to seek him for direction in our common life, and perhaps about a particular project, He very often takes us back to the basic matter of loving one another.

'On one such occasion, when the community was grappling with some issue and not getting very far, one member went out and returned with a towel and a basinful of water. That prophetic action broke the log-jam and we proceeded to wash one another's feet, relationships being resolved amid tears and hugs. Then we were ready to receive individual words from the Lord through another member of the Community for each of us, personally.

' "Humble yourselves under the mighty hand of God, that in due time you may be exalted" is as relevant in our day to day life as it was in St James's time and it is a word of which the Lord often reminds us. If we fail to humble ourselves he is likely to allow circumstances to humble us.

'On the practical side, I have appreciated those who have had the courage to speak the truth in love.

'In the early days at Rostrevor a member of community, who was considerably younger than I, pointed out that we needed to spend more time with our young family. Trained as a teacher she was quick to notice insecurity in them because they never knew when Cecil or I would definitely be with them for an undisturbed time, taken up as we were with the ministry of the Centre. We accepted what she said and tried to make sure there was a time, usually in the early evening, when we would be available to them. Up until this we had been having our midday and evening meals with the other members of community and guests. Now, since a flat was ready for us in the main house, we decided to have our evening meal as a family with the children, still having lunch communally, as the children were usually at school until the afternoon. To start with, when we first went to Rostrevor, partly because there were very few rooms ready for use, and partly because we saw mealtimes as a good time for building us all together, we had all meals, including breakfast, together. This soon proved too much of a strain on our younger children, and once a living room and kitchen became ready we were able to have breakfast together as a family.

'Because Cecil's ministry has always meant him being away quite a lot I felt it important to stay with the children to give them a sense of security, so I seldom attended conferences away from the Centre and did not accompany Cecil on ministry abroad until 1981. While I must admit I was sometimes envious of what seemed a more exciting life for him, the positive side was that I knew the support of the other members of community in the day to day interweaving of our lives, and besides, through the children attending the local school, I made friends with other young Mums. Days off and holiday times became very important for us as a family, times when we could grow together and enjoy each other. We have happy memories of holidays spent in homes kindly lent to us in Edinburgh and York, and later in David Gillett's Rectory in Luton. For anyone in a caring ministry, particularly those who live in community, the use of someone else's home can be a real godsend.

'What was pointed out to me as a need in our children's lives, that is, time when we would make it a priority to be with them, is also true for us as a couple, and for the community itself. Cecil and I can only maintain a healthy marriage if we make time for each other, but if we do, what we have to give to others will be of more value. If we become so busy that we hardly see each other then there won't be much to share with anyone else. The quality and level of our communication as a couple or as a community will affect the health of our relationships, and will further or inhibit our effectiveness as a resource, under God, for the healing of others.

'Rostrevor is a wonderful place for walks, and much needed communication between us as a couple, or with one of the family, or a member of the community often took place on brief walks in the nearby park. Sometimes failure in communication could be a sore point with the family, like the time when one of the boys heard on a visit to the barber that Dad was going to England at the weekend, and we had forgotten to tell him!

'If our relationships are secure within the family, and within the community, and we are sure of each other's support and confidence, we can more readily reach out in a generous way to one another, or to the guests who come in need of help.

'This readiness to pray for or to counsel someone in need is a constant challenge. Most of the time the call is unexpected, so the temptation is to see it as an interruption. I may be preparing a meal, or Hoovering an upstairs room, but by the time I reach the phone I trust the Lord to give me the sympathy and faith needed to pray for the sick person or their distressed relative who needs reassurance at the other end. Once a very ill person telephoned and as usual I listened, and then prayed with her on the phone. As I prayed and spoke words of faith from Scripture to her there was then a long pause.

' "He's speaking to me myself", she said.

'I was able then to say goodbye quietly and leave her receiving a real blessing from the Lord.'

A servant heart

'You do not exist for yourselves. You are not here for your own comfort and enjoyment. I have a work to do in each one of you and in all together. It is not a superficial work. It is a radical work on behalf of my whole body.'

A word of prophecy which recalls us, as a community, to our primary task of serving the purpose of God in the healing of division in his body, the Church. On many occasions we have been brought back to the supreme example of Christ given by St Paul in the letter to the Philippians:

> If you have any encouragement from being united with Christ, if any comfort from his love, if any fellowship with the Spirit, if any tenderness and compassion, then make my joy complete by being like-minded, having the same love, being one in spirit and purpose. Do nothing out of selfish ambition or vain conceit, but in humility consider others better than yourselves. Each of you should look not only to your own interests, but also to the interests of others. Your attitude should be the same as that of Christ Jesus. (Phil. 2:1–5)

Jesus, who came not to be served but to serve, is to be the pattern for our ministry whether it is leading worship, cleaning the bathrooms, answering the telephone, typing letters or speaking to a conference or retreat. We do not wear any special uniform or habit; the servant heart emblazoned with faithfulness and love is to be our badge.

To be a servant is surely the hardest lesson of all to learn. Yet the daily round of household chores can give glory to God and teach us something in the process. Geraldine Griffin, a member of the community, asked the question in one of our prayer letters: can any reward be found in housework?:

> It is hard to describe some domestic activities in anything other than negative words and phrases – such as futile, wearing, tiring, will-have-to-be-done-again-tomorrow, frustrating, unfulfilling, unrewarding. These words and phrases come to our mouths readily when someone walks on the newly mopped tiles or flicks crumbs over the floor you have just Hoovered. Any feelings of pleasure we might feel from seeing crumbs being sucked up by a vacuum cleaner are shortlived, and any sense of satisfaction we might receive in polished glass doors and mirrors and fireplaces, lasts only until the next person pushes through them hands first or the wind drives rubbish down the chimney!
>
> Is there a lesson to be learned, a revealing point to be discovered in all this mindless activity? Can God really speak to us through this negativity? The answer is yes to both questions, for I am like the crumby floor, the marked glass, the dirty oven and the dusty shelves. My Father cleans me up, wipes me over again and again and never uses negative words or phrases to describe the process. If my sin is overcome today I may well fall again tomorrow and he will have to mop up once more or dust me down another time, but he does so cheerfully, tirelessly, positively, lovingly, and I am left amazed at his patience, resilience, dedication and joy at doing his housework on me.

Betty Claesson from Sweden described what it meant for her to be a servant for the Lord in a role that was so different from what she had trained to do:

> Mainly during my stay I have been working in the kitchen. That was a new experience for me, to cook for so many people and to serve in the background when we had groups and clergy days. Previously, working in a parish in Sweden,

I was the person attending the meetings, whereas this year I have been learning to serve so that others can join in. The Lord also taught me how life can be in a big family. That is very humbling! Not always to think of yourself first, but to be more aware of others.

A similar sentiment was voiced by Laura Hill from Belfast:

It took me a while to get used to community living. It wasn't always easy trying to live and work with so many different people, but often I found that the Lord used others to speak to me and humble me. I feel so enriched now as a result of sharing a year of my life with seventeen other people and learning from them.

Another means which God used in his refining process was the practical day to day work in which I was involved. Every community member was involved in at least one area of work around the Centre and mine was the cleaning and laundry area. The emphasis on service in the community helped me to realise that I was serving the Lord, however mundane the task, and this growing realisation changed my attitudes and made me more willing to work.

I feel so privileged to have spent a year at the Centre. Through it, I know that God has deepened my walk with him as I've allowed his healing love to fill more and more of my life. I feel now that the Lord has changed me in many different ways and I'm so grateful to him for my year at Rostrevor. This little poem sums up very simply what God has done in my life:

Thank you, Lord for this year
A time of pruning
A time of changing
A time of healing from every fear
As I allowed you to wipe away every tear.

Praise you, Lord, for your life within
A life so joyful
A life so peaceful
A life which is cleaned from all sin
As I allow your Spirit to enter in.

Encouragement

In our life together we are often reminded of a Greek word in the New Testament, *Allelos*, which is translated 'each other' or 'one another'. It rings like a clarion bell calling us to active service in the body of Christ. We are urged to 'love one another', to 'forgive one another', to 'honour one another', to 'serve one another', to 'bear one another's burdens' and to 'pray for one another that we may be healed'. That call was reflected in a picture which someone saw as she prayed for the community. It was of a dressing-gown woven in different colours to look beautiful but also to give warmth. In a community like ours every opportunity to build up and affirm each other needs to be taken. It is so easy to become discouraged, to see the gifts in others and despise ourselves. Learning that there are no useless members in the body of Christ and realising that each one is called by God for a special task is a defence against discouragement.

In community prayers one morning I was greatly encouraged and blessed when one of the members, Maureen Slattery, led us in an interesting meditation.

'Imagine your heavenly Father writing a letter to you,' she said. 'You can put your name at the top of the letter.'

Dear
My love for you, beside that of an earthly father, is as the warmth of the sun compared to that of a candle. Before you were formed in the womb I knew you. At your birth I breathed my own Spirit into you. I love you as you are – unconditionally.

My Son died so that you might have fullness of life. Won't you allow me to give you all that he has won for you? I want to pour my love into your heart and enrich your life. When you open your heart to my Spirit, and surrender to my direction, you will experience freedom and fulfilment. My love in you will overflow to others.

Do not focus on your own weaknesses, but rather on my limitless power and love. Accept yourself as you are, as a child does. I do not accuse or reproach; just trust me to strengthen and lead you. Guilt about the past is a useless burden, as is anxiety for the future. Be alive to the possibilities of the present moment. Allow my love to cast all fear from your life. I will never ask more of you than you are able to give.

Your heavenly Father.

Often in the community such encouragement will come as we pray for one another either in small groups or individually. Opportunity for such ministry is found also in the occasional days we set aside for retreat with time to pray for specific needs or for individual direction or guidance. We have been learning too from Brother Lawrence how to practise the presence of God in 'the daily round and common task' by creating a 'chapel in the heart'.

It is not needful always to be in church to be with God. We can make a chapel of our heart, to which we can from time to time withdraw to have gentle, humble, loving communion with him. Everyone is able to have these familiar conversations with God, some more, some less, he knows our capabilities.[4]

Gladys Swanton, who often leads us into God's presence with her gift of music and song, reflected those sentiments from the perspective of our life in Northern Ireland.

Sometimes our hearts can be discouraged by news reports or by what we see of the violence around us. We realise afresh the intensity of the battle in which we are all involved. It is wonderful how at these times God encourages us by his word as we meet together to worship and pray.

In worship we draw from him all the grace that we need to live each day, whatever form of service he calls us to. Worship is coming into the presence of One whose love never runs dry, and never gives us up. The love that flows from Calvary fills us and transforms us and takes us away beyond the boundaries that we often set for ourselves and others.

In Romans 12 we read that true worship is the offering up of ourselves as a living sacrifice, honouring him and obeying his word, allowing him to remould us; to give us his way of thinking. This work does not happen in our lives without our share of kicking and screaming but God is faithful and leads us on.

God's caretakers

Wednesday morning is an important stage in the week for us as a community. We begin the day by sharing Communion together, finding God's healing, and renewing our commitment to serve him. Following that we have our community meeting to review the work and witness of the past week and prepare for what is to come. First on our agenda is a time of thanksgiving for God's provision in the gifts that people have shared for the work of renewal and reconciliation at the Centre. We never cease to be moved by the way God has remained faithful to that early promise to us that 'he would put it into the hearts of the right people to give the right amount at the right time'. Our faith is often renewed by the amazing timing of the gifts that are made, exactly when they are needed, neither too early nor too late. It should not really surprise us that God is such a good economist. We read the names of those who have given gifts in money or in kind, committing them to God 'who loves a cheerful giver'. From time to time 'goodies' arrive for sharing among community members. We have many good friends in Switzerland and when their delicious Swiss chocolates arrive there is special joy.

We are always conscious of the great responsibility that God has entrusted to us in the stewardship of the Centre and we pray for wisdom to use what he supplies for the work of his Kingdom. We often say to visitors, 'You are welcome to God's house,' and that is literally true. Every penny to buy the house, to equip and run it is given by God's people who have been obedient to his prompting and faithful in their response. Every piece of furniture and equipment, every carpet, picture and curtain is an expression of God's love given through one of his servants. From the onset we decided that the Centre would be run as a charitable trust. David Baillie, Roy Darling, William Fitch, Larry Kelly, Peggy Martin, Bishop George Quin and I are the Trustees, the community for the time being holding responsibility for the day to day running of the Centre and its work. We realised the prime importance of our financial stewardship. Every gift is recorded and acknowledged, and the accounts of the Centre, audited annually, are available for inspection by any donor who may request them. When a person joins the community he or she is not asked to disclose any capital to the Centre. If a community member wishes to make a capital donation it is recommended that it should be done anonymously. We live by faith and community members do not receive salaries. Food, heating, lighting and all daily needs are met from the gifts to the Centre. Each member receives a small weekly allowance and an annual gift towards clothing and holiday. New members receive the same amounts as those who have been there a long time. Cars are not provided by the Centre and those who own them have to trust for their maintenance and replacement, although a mileage allowance is available for community business and ministry outside the Centre. Those of us who travel for ministry overseas do not draw on community funds but depend for resources on those who invite us or on gifts specially provided for each particular outreach. Work at the Centre is constant and demanding most of the time and it is essential to find some time for fun together. When we attended the induction of Willi and Ruth Stewart to their new parish of Naas in the south of Ireland someone there welcomed those who had come from the Christian RECREATION Centre! Farewell parties for those who are leaving the community are frequently occasions when hidden talents are revealed in impromptu sketches and songs. It is a special treat when gifts are provided to allow members to go on an outing or have a meal out together.

Joy and sorrow

Since members of the community do not make vows of celibacy at least six have met their spouses at the Centre during their time in community. We have shared in their joy.

But there have been times of sorrow too. Trials and tribulations draw us closer together and through them we learn and grow. Some of the most painful times have been those of deepest growth.

Soon after Fanny Robertson joined the community in 1975 she learned that she had cancer. It was a shock to us all and inevitably we asked the question 'Why'? We prayed earnestly for her healing, joined by thousands who knew her. In God's healing touch and through medical skills Fanny experienced a remarkable remission; and during that period she was a great example and blessing to those to whom she ministered. Sadly however complete healing was not granted and Fanny died on 6 July 1977. During her illness God had provided for Fanny and for us all. Anne Forde from Dublin, who had just joined the community, had experience of nursing someone through a similar illness; and Sister Mary Henderson returned from nursing in India and came to us for the three months which coincided with Fanny's last illness. It was a specially grace-filled time of reconciliation that Fanny, a life-long Presbyterian, should be looked after by two sisters in Christ who were both Roman Catholics. After quite a struggle Fanny came to terms with death and entered into Christ's victory, so that when she spoke to a large gathering at a Bible Week she was able to say: 'If in the next few weeks or months you hear that I have died do not grieve or be distressed. Rejoice for I will be with the Lord.' We knew it brought joy to Fanny when just before her death she was able to participate in a Festival of Praise in Church House in Belfast, where for an unforgettable weekend up to 1,400 Roman Catholics and Protestants from all over Ireland witnessed to the Lordship of Jesus Christ.

As we left the graveyard after Fanny's funeral emotions of sorrow and thankfulness mingled and we were encouraged by the words David Baillie shared with us for the whole community: 'Fear not, little flock, for it is my Father's good will to give you the Kingdom.'

Through the years over and over again we have received words of immense encouragement that keep us going in times of difficulty, and which, like the gifts of money, come just when they are needed. We can never fully express what these messages mean to us. From Hazel Dickson, a faithful prayer partner and founder member of the Cornerstone Community in Belfast (devoted to a similar ministry of reconciliation), came these encouraging words:

> Be my rainbow in this place
> Signalling hope,
> Signalling mercy,
> Signalling my never-failing promises
> Be my rainbow
> Spanning the divide
> Bridging the gap
> Linking this place to heaven.
> Be my rainbow
> My life shining through
> Shedding light in the darkness
> Heralding a new beginning.

And that's what we try, by God's grace, to be. Deeply aware of our own frailty and shortcomings we are more aware of the promise, 'The one who calls you is faithful and he will do it' (1 Thess. 5:24).

5

PRAYER

The earnest (heartfelt, continued) prayer of a righteous man makes tremendous power available. (Jas. 5:16 Amplified Bible)

> *Prayer is a shield to the soul,*
> *A sacrifice to God*
> *And a scourge to Satan.*
> *John Bunyan*

When the seven of us, including our three children, moved into the Centre we were absolutely certain of one thing, that prayer must be a daily priority on our programme. Looking back on all that we have been through there is no way we could have stayed together if we had not prayed together. We set aside two hours in the day, morning and evening, in which we prayed together, and which were not to be a substitute for times of private prayer.

In setting a priority on prayer we were entering into a rich heritage of the Irish Church since its beginning in the fifth century. St Patrick and those who worked with him in the early days of the Christian mission in Ireland were fuelled by a life of prayer and intercession. St Patrick's first coming to Ireland was as a slave on the barren hills of Slemish in County Antrim. Although brought up a Christian, he tells us, 'I knew not the true God.' Far from home and family and facing an uncertain future he had a real encounter with God that changed the course of his life and also the face of Ireland. After six years in captivity he escaped only to be called back as evangelist to the Irish nation.

In the lonely years of slavery on the Antrim hills he had learnt in the school of prayer. As he recalls:

> When I had come to Ireland I tended herds every day and I used to pray many times during the day. More and more my love of God and reverence for him began to increase. My faith grew stronger and my zeal so intense that in the course of a single day I would say as many as a hundred prayers, and almost as many in the night. This I did even when I was in the woods and on the mountains. Even in times of snow or frost or rain I would rise before dawn to pray. I never felt the worse for it; nor was I in any way lazy because, as I now realise, I was full of enthusiasm.[1]

His 'confession' reveals that Patrick was no stranger to praying in tongues or praying in the Spirit:

> On yet another occasion I saw a person praying in me. I was as it seemed inside my body and I heard him over me, that is, over the inner man. There he was, praying with great emotion. All this time I was puzzled as I wondered greatly who could possibly be praying inside me. He spoke, however, at the end of the prayer, saying that he was the Spirit. When I awoke I recalled the words of the apostle: The Spirit comes to help our inadequacy at prayer. For when we cannot choose words in order to pray properly, the Spirit himself expresses our plea with great emotion in a way that cannot be put into words. Again: The Lord who is our advocate expresses our plea.[2]

Fortunately that chain of prayer has never been totally absent since. It was obviously most clearly seen in the three centuries after Patrick's mission when the famous monasteries in Ireland drew thousands of committed Christians together for prayer and sent them out to share the Gospel throughout Europe.

We were novices, learners in the way of community prayer. In our human weakness we were conscious of our need to rely on God for everything. We were one with the disciples when they came to Jesus and said, 'Lord, teach us to pray.' We will never be 'experts' in prayer. It is the calling of a lifetime and is the one Christian activity that Satan will try again and again to demolish. As Samuel Chadwick declared, 'The one concern of the devil is to keep the saints from prayer. He fears nothing from prayerless studies, prayerless religion. He laughs at our toil, mocks at our wisdom, but trembles when we pray.'

Before we went to Rostrevor our friend Sheila Kenny gave me a book which is a veritable treasure. She wrote on the fly leaf, 'You won't be the same again after reading this book – I'm not.' In *Prayer the Mightiest Force in the World*, Frank Laubach says something which challenged and inspired our earliest efforts at prayer together:

> Prayer is likely to be undervalued by all but wise people because it is so silent and so secret. We are often deceived into thinking that noise is more important than silence. War sounds far more important than the noiseless growing of a crop of wheat, yet the silent wheat feeds millions, while war destroys them. Nobody but God knows how often prayers have changed the course of history. Many a man who prayed received no credit excepting in heaven. We are tempted to turn from prayer to something more noisy, like speeches or guns, because our motives are mixed. We are interested in the making of a better world, of course, but we also want people to give us credit for what we have done. Secret prayer for others all during the day is an acid test of our unselfishness. The highest form of communion is not asking God for things for ourselves, but letting Him flow down through us, out over the world – in endless benediction.[3]

We realised we could minister to the broken and needy only

when we had first met the One who, alone, can 'preach good news to the poor . . . bind up the broken-hearted . . . proclaim freedom for the captives and release from darkness for the prisoners' (Isa. 61:1).

In our kindergarten of prayer we have been re-learning the three elements of praise, worship and intercession which God's people have discovered through the ages.

Three elements

Praise has always been an important part of our prayer. St Paul encouraged the early Christians to 'Speak to one another with psalms, hymns and spiritual songs. Sing and make music in your heart to the Lord, always giving thanks to God the Father for everything, in the name of our Lord Jesus Christ' (Eph. 5:19–20). Even though there may be only a few of us together we use the Psalms and the hymns to adore and praise our wonderful God. Praise is the music of heaven and in our adoration we are joining with the hosts of heaven: praise is rehearsal for heaven. It is no accident that in times of spiritual revival and renewal new songs inspired by the Spirit are born. In our day it is hard to keep up with them. Many are ephemeral but others will endure and take their place alongside the great hymns of the Church.

It has been exciting to be present at the birth of a song given by the Holy Spirit during our worship in the Centre. Jonathan Kimber spent a year with us after school before going to university. One day as we were in worship the Lord gave him a new song which blessed us and many others who heard it:

> Seek my face, and I will reveal it to you,
> Seek my face, and I'll show you my truth,
> For I long to bring you my grace and my love,
> And I long to draw you much closer to me.

> Open yourselves, and I will come in and fill you,
> Humble yourselves, and know that I am God,
> For then I can use you to demonstrate my love,
> And I can empower you to live my good news.

On another occasion the Fisherfolk, a talented music group, were with us and used the Centre as a base for ministry in Ireland. In the quietness and peace of the place the Holy Spirit inspired one of them, Ruth Wieting, to write this song:

> Come, you weary ones, come and be refreshed;
> Lay your burdens down, let your soul be blessed.
>
> For I know your struggles, I feel the pain you bear;
> My heart aches with your heart, and in your grief I share.
>
> I know all your troubles, the depths of your despair;
> Let my peace surround you, for I have heard your prayer.
>
> I know the road you travel is not an easy one;
> I have gone before you, and victory I have won.
>
> Know that I am with you, whatever comes your way;
> With my love I will guide you, and with you I will stay.[4]

Worship comes from an old English word 'worthship' and means telling God what he is worth to us. In worship we also recover the sense of our own worth as creatures of a loving God, that we are precious to him and honoured in his eyes for he loves us. Often we might say to someone: 'Keep looking up, things may not be too bad.' Worship gives us the right perspective when we realise the truth of St Paul's words which in effect say: 'Keep looking down, you're seated in the heavenlies' (Eph. 2:6). Reading and sharing God's word daily enriches our life together and gives direction and depth to our ministry. On many occasions we experience what the two disciples discovered on the way to Emmaus: 'Were not our hearts burning within us while he talked with us on the road and opened the Scriptures to us?' (Luke 24:32).

'Love on its knees' is how intercession has been defined. It is another important ingredient of our daily prayer. It has been said, 'We should pray with the Bible in one hand and the newspaper in the other!' We bring before God the needs of our land and the nations of the world. We pray especially for those who have been bereaved through the violence. One of the members has the task of writing to bereaved families offering comfort and assuring them of our prayers. Many people write or telephone special requests for prayer for themselves or loved ones. When we hear of specific answers to prayer there is cause for rejoicing. Always we count it a privilege to bring others into the healing, loving presence of Jesus.

Prayer partners

From the beginning we knew we would need to enlist the prayer support of others who shared the vision for God's healing of our land. Now more than four thousand prayer partners are linked with us in a fellowship that spans the world and is still growing. When we travel abroad we are humbled to discover the prayerful concern that so many people have for Ireland. It is such an inspiration to know that even when we are asleep our brothers and sisters in Australia, New Zealand, Singapore and South-East Asia are upholding us in prayer. We know that many of our prayer partners remember us daily. In turn we have a rota of prayer for them included in our daily prayer. Even though we may not be able to get our tongues round some of their names we are made more aware of the rich variety in the worldwide family of God to which we are privileged to belong.

It is especially encouraging that some take responsibility for praying for individuals while others have a particular concern for the families. For years now a brother in Rome has sent regular and welcome postcards to each one of our children with an assurance of prayer for them. From time to time concern may be expressed in practical ways such as a gift that will provide transport; or help towards a holiday; or the offer of a home for a rest and refreshment. Myrtle shares how she was greatly blessed through the loving and prayerful concern of one of our prayer partners.

'In January 1980, the day after I had had an operation in Daisy Hill Hospital in Newry, I was conscious of my utter weakness. I had planned to catch up on my letter writing, but all I could do was just lie there and rest.

'Cecil came in with a letter for me, which he opened and read aloud. It was from a prayer partner in Lancashire, whom I had never met, and was written the day before my operation. She had no way of knowing that I was in hospital but she wrote: "Today I feel you need God's help in a special way, so I have been praying for you, and felt I should write a little note of encouragement, enclosing £5 for some flowers."

'That incident is very clear in my mind today because it spoke in an undeniable way of the love my heavenly Father has for me, that he would alert another of his children to my need and put it into her heart to write to me just then. It was as if that token of love came straight from the heart of the Father. In moments of anxiety or doubt the memory of it has encouraged me ever since.'

Changed lives

Soon after we moved into the Centre we knew we should open the doors and invite the local people to join us for regular meetings of praise and prayer. At first about twelve people joined us but the numbers quickly grew. After a few weeks of meetings we borrowed a hall in the village for a day of renewal. Canon John Gunstone came over from England and spoke about what it means to know Jesus personally and how we can open our lives to allow him to baptise us with his Holy Spirit. During that day a number of local people experienced the release of the Spirit in their lives and became valued and regular members of the weekly prayer group. During the years that followed numbers increased until the largest room in the house could not accommodate all who came. When the number moved towards two hundred Victor Henderson and our friends from the Presbyterian Church kindly allowed us to use their spacious hall in the village. Many of those who met the Lord in the Monday night meeting were hungry to learn more about life in the Spirit and growth in Christian living. They came on another night to share God's word and search the Scriptures together.

As time went on groups began to meet in other towns and villages; Warrenpoint, Kilkeel, Bessbrook, Newry, Hilltown and Newcastle. All of them were led by people who had been touched by God through the meeting in Rostrevor. Peter and Eileen Grant hosted the meeting in Warrenpoint. Their hotel had been bombed by terrorists. Only the bar area remained intact. That is where the weekly prayer meeting was held. It caused a considerable stir in the town. Even the *Reader's Digest* covered the story in a leading article, describing the evening when a passing British army patrol called to investigate who could be singing in a pub with no beer. The soldiers discovered sixty people praising God in the bar. When the officer enquired whether the bar was open a chorus of voices called out, 'We're open for prayer, you're welcome to come and join us.'

Hundreds who attended the Monday night meetings at the Centre witness to the radical changes God has made in their lives. Some have been healed from addiction to alcohol and drugs. Compulsive gamblers have been delivered. Broken marriages have been healed. People consumed by hatred, resentment and bitterness have been set free. Men and women of violence have been transformed by the power of Christ. Former enemies have openly embraced each other in moving acts of reconciliation. Not a few wounded and bereaved in the violence have found healing and comfort. Many have experienced remarkable physical and emotional healings. For others the weekly gathering has been a lifeline during personal and domestic tragedy or crisis. Praise, prayer, Scripture sharing, thanksgiving, testimony and teaching are regular features of the meetings. We are open to the leading of the Holy Spirit who works in infinitely varied ways. No two meetings are ever exactly alike. One evening a regular attender brought a friend who had never before experienced such a gathering. On his way home the friend observed, 'That's an ideal place for a pick-pocket. So much of the time they had their eyes closed and their hands in the air!'

The test of any work of God is the enduring change it brings in people's lives. We praise and thank God for the mighty miracles we have seen him do in the lives of so many people. To see hundreds of Roman Catholics and Protestants meeting regularly so close to the border, praising and worshipping God together, is itself a miracle. On many occasions they have travelled lonely and dangerous roads to be together in the fellowship. One young bank clerk who lived near the border had to walk the last two miles home along a road that was a haunt for terrorists. Asked if she was afraid she answered, 'Jesus is with me and I sing his praise and I am not afraid.'

Albert McElroy has been a regular member of the prayer group for many years. Although in his youth Albert attended church and Sunday school he drifted away completely from those early influences. From heavy drinking he gradually became a hopeless alcoholic and had to have hospital treatment. Added to that problem he became a compulsive gambler. His addictions were not only destroying his own life but threatening his marriage and family too. Albert was in a state of despair yet desperately seeking a way out when a friend invited him to the prayer meeting in the former bar in Warrenpoint.

'When I went in there,' Albert recalls, 'I saw something different about the people. They were all so obviously happy and at peace.'

As it happened a visitor from Italy was speaking that

evening. Dr Fred Ladenius, who had worked as a press officer in the Vatican, was sharing how he had experienced a personal encounter with Christ and been baptised in the Holy Spirit. When he finished speaking Dr Ladenius invited people to come forward for prayer. Albert will never forget that evening.

' "There is someone here suffering from a back problem," Dr Ladenius said. "Will that person please stand up. The Lord wants to heal you."

'At first my legs felt like rubber. I was frightened to stand up, but as the seconds ticked by I knew he was speaking about me. Finally I picked up courage, stood up and went forward for prayer. The pain left my back and has not returned. Later on that evening I knew God was speaking very personally and directly to me. Somehow I felt it was my last chance to respond. I decided to commit my life totally to God that night and finish with the life I had been living. Thank God I have never been the same since. I certainly know what St Paul meant when he said: "If anyone is in Christ, he is a new creation; the old has gone, the new has come!" (2 Cor. 5:17).'

Soon after his dramatic conversion I met Albert for the first time when he attended the prayer meeting at the Centre. Although a new man eager to rebuild his broken life, he was currently unemployed. A friend of the Centre who had seen the great change in Albert offered to pay his wages for six weeks for helping with maintenance work and gardening at the Centre. Those six weeks have turned into twelve years during which Albert has had a most remarkable ministry to people from all walks of life and especially those who suffer from his old addictions. All who knew the 'old' Albert recognise the change that has come over him. He boldly witnesses to people that Jesus can change even 'hopeless cases'. During the years he has been with us he has travelled with teams from the Centre to share the great miracle that God has performed in his life.

'The same Jesus who worked miracles in Israel, who died on the cross and rose again, is still alive today,' he says. 'If you are willing and have come to an end of yourself as I had, he can change your life just as he changed mine.'

Bernie O'Rourke lives in Warrenpoint. She with other members of her family are active in the prayer group and sometimes join the community in teams of outreach. Her sister Mary is a member of the community and Bernie joined a mission team to Nigeria led by Niall and Geraldine Griffin.

'You are not here tonight of your own choice but because God called you and drew you to this place,' were the words Bernie heard at her first meeting at the Christian Renewal Centre.

'It was the first time I felt God drawing me to him,' she said. 'People were obviously happy, singing, clapping, waving their arms and dancing. I worked in a bank in Derry and over the months I thought about that meeting. God reminded me of my behaviour at discos and parties when I would jump, dance, shout and wave my hands in the air. I asked God questions: "Why was I born?" "What was I to do with my life?" I prayed for a transfer to where he wanted me to be.

'One night the house where I lived was taken over by a group of gunmen. My friend and I were held hostage all night. I had never been so frightened before. I prayed that God would intervene so that no one would be killed and my prayer was answered. The IRA gang had planned to shoot at an army patrol that passed the house every morning. Mercifully that morning the patrol changed its route. The IRA took my car and it was later found and blown up by the security forces in case it was booby-trapped. Thank God nobody was hurt in the incident. After that I was moved to Armagh, Enniskillen and then to Newry. I was feeling shattered and very nervous. My life felt empty and I decided to go to the Bible Week at the Centre. Eric Mayer was speaking on the second coming of Christ and asked if we would be ready to meet him. That scared me. I felt like standing up and begging Eric to ask Jesus not to come that night.

'I decided, with great fear, to attend a group for beginners led by Niall and Geraldine Griffin. The first night I committed my life to Christ. I had never heard a more beautiful prayer than was prayed with me that night. I went home feeling just great. I kept going to the group and near the end of the course I was baptised in the Holy Spirit.

'I am slowly turning from a very negative person with a very low self-image into a very positive person. When I moved to my own house I asked God to use it for his glory and I have been amazed at the people he has led to me there and with whom I have prayed. My life has changed completely and I just don't know how I existed before without him.'

Victor Finlay was eighty years old when he attended his first prayer meeting. He and his wife Eileen became regular attenders both at the prayer group and the Bible study group.

'Ever since I retired from the Nigeria Police in 1950, I had been what I would call a church attender. In other words you would find me there each Sunday morning and on other special days, listening to what went on, but allowing the whole thing to wash over me with a minimum of penetration.

'I said my prayers pretty regularly, especially when I wanted something, but with little or no praise, although I did thank God when he was good enough to give me what I wanted.

'Life was pleasant enough although I found myself, bit by bit, becoming dissatisfied without really knowing why or about what. A friend with whom I used to play golf died suddenly one afternoon and I began to think more seriously about the future, and where I was heading.

'Up to that time I believed that in order to go to heaven I had to lead a good life and that would be sufficient, but how to do this? When I thought about the matter I seemed to be breaking some part of some commandment daily, and my life became a routine of don'ts or thou-shalt-nots.

'I was then sent a fairly serious heart complaint which

spurred me somewhat out of my semi-apathetic outlook and I searched around for someone to help me. I had by now arrived at the conclusion that prayers in church were for the congregation, and not for me, even though I was part of the congregation, and so I badly needed a personal Saviour who regarded me as someone special, and to whom I could talk and pray for any guidance.

'It so happened that my son and his wife who lunched with us said on leaving that they wanted to call at the Centre to get some books. I enquired as to what the Centre was, and decided that I would if possible attend on the following Monday. My wife and I did so, but it happened to be a night on which a large number of people from Newry attended and the meeting had to be held in two adjoining rooms with the doors between left open. It was not very satisfactory as the speakers had to face both ways in turn, and their words were partially lost. However we had seen and heard enough to want to come again.

'After a few of these Monday meetings I began to have a new outlook on life, and the don'ts began to be replaced by the do's. The Lord spoke plainly to me through Cecil Kerr and I realised that God's gift of eternal life really was a gift through Jesus, and that all I had to do was to repent of my sins, and accept humbly and gratefully this wonderful gift.

'The whole thing became crystal clear to me one Tuesday morning when I was digging in my garden. It hit me suddenly and I had the most wonderful feeling of happiness. There and then I thanked my Lord and ran in to tell my wife. At that moment I firmly believe I was born again, and I have never since ceased thanking God. I have had my dull spots since, and as a sinner will no doubt have more, but now I am free.'

Victor and Eileen lived a very full life for the next four years. Bible study and prayer became their daily pattern and they shared a special concern in praying for prisoners. I remember Victor once saying how he would like to meet the Lord when his time came. An imposing figure, Victor stood erect in military style and said, 'When the Lord calls me I want to be able to say, "Ready, Sir." ' One day at the age of eighty-four he came in from working in the garden. He explained to Eileen that he was feeling tired and would rest a little. That night he slipped quietly away to salute the Lord he had come to know and love so much.

When we obey him

'Call to me and I will answer you and show you great and mighty things which you have not known.' God spoke those words to Jeremiah in the turmoil of his surroundings long ago. This has been a word of comfort and encouragement for us as we try to be obedient to God's call. When we began the work there were no precedents to follow. We had to come to God in our emptiness, seeking his guidance and direction. Each day is a walk of faith. But it is faith in a loving and faithful God. Before we left Belfast a friend encouraged us with words from Psalm 25:10. Translated in the Living Bible paraphrase it reads: 'And when we obey him every path he guides us on is fragrant with his loving kindness and his truth.' We knew we could trust him to guide us even in the small and practical details, in the enormous challenge of repairing the rambling house and finding the finance to support the community as well as to pay for the builders and materials. We often prayed:

> Lord, help us not to go ahead of you and lose the way;
> Lord, help us not to stay so far behind you that we fail to
> find you. Lord, help us to follow closely by your side that
> through us your will be done, your kingdom come and your
> glory be revealed to the world you love and long to save.

God had graciously provided for the first payment on the house. The remaining £8,000 had to be found by 31 December. Could we believe it would come in time? Would there be enough to keep us in food in the meantime? God was teaching us to walk by faith and not by sight. Little by little the money was coming in and 'the barrel of meal' did not run out nor the cruse of oil fail! By Christmas 1974 there was £6,000 in the account. I remember going to the bank with some gifts and speaking a word of faith to the clerk. I said, 'You know, there will be £8,000 in that account by the end of the year.' Over Christmas several larger gifts came in and on 31 December a gift of £5 came from a prayer partner in Scotland which brought the total in the bank account to £8,001.61. How faithful God was. We paid the final instalment on the house and rejoicing set our hearts on the new challenge ahead of us.

The first winter in the house was a cold one. There was no central heating and we could not afford electric fires for the thirty rooms in the building. Several open fires became popular gathering places. Mysteriously, bags of coal began to arrive from time to time in the back yard. Another answer to prayer. Delivered by a local coal merchant they had been ordered and paid for by the Sisters in the local convent of the Poor Clares. Walter Skelsey became an expert in heating management. His years in Africa had given him the habit of early rising but had not acclimatised him to the cold winter winds blowing off the Irish Sea. For someone who had been a District Officer in Kenya and accustomed to servants doing the work for him, it was a special labour of love that he had fires prepared each day and a warm room ready for our morning prayers.

As we debated whether we should install central heating, we did not know that again the Lord was already secretly planning in love for us. In the autumn of 1974 we had a letter from 'Wilde Ganzen', the Wild Geese, in Holland. Mrs Manassen the secretary explained:

We are a fund-raising programme of the Dutch Reformed Church. In the meeting of our board last week we decided to tell our listeners on radio and viewers on television about your Centre and ask for their financial assistance. We do not know yet when this goose will fly, but as soon as we have the proceeds in hand we will remit the money to your bank.

Before Christmas they phoned to say their appeal had raised twice as much as their normal weekly amount and they were sending it on. It was almost enough to meet the £5,000 needed to install full central heating. Someone had reminded us that God's work done in God's way never lacks God's supply.

Over the years we have learned more about God's ways of guiding. Often by not listening or by going our own way we have had to learn from our mistakes, ask his forgiveness and try to stay closer to him the next time. Discerning God's will over the programme we should plan both in the Centre and outside is a constant challenge. In his busy earthly ministry our Lord only did what his heavenly Father told him to do. Among all the good things finding God's best is what we have to seek. With increasing numbers coming to the Centre our Trustees and others often suggested that we should consider extending the accommodation and building a larger meeting room. When we knew that this was not just a good idea but that God was prompting us we faced the biggest financial challenge to our faith so far.

Enlarge the place of your tent

Early in 1982 I had been invited to New Zealand to speak at a series of summer schools run by Christian Advance Ministries, an interdenominational group committed to renewal in the Church. On my way home I was graciously hosted by our friends Boon Yew and Alice Chua in their lovely Christian hotel in Singapore. After an exceedingly busy programme in New Zealand I had a welcome few days to rest. In prayer my attention was drawn to Isaiah 54:2–3. I sensed the Lord was speaking clearly to me about the Centre. 'Enlarge the place of your tent, stretch your tent curtains wide, do not hold back; lengthen your cords, strengthen your stakes. For you will spread out to the right and to the left.' That word came again several times as a word of encouragement and challenge to us all in the community. As we asked God what it meant we believed that it referred not only to an increase in the work and witness of the Centre but also to an extension of the building.

Then there came a clear word of prophecy which we discerned was from the Lord:

> You are my children whom I love and cherish. I will do a new thing through you and you will see my glory. My work is done not only through you and it is not just for your land. My work is for all the earth. I am giving you a new vision and a new way. I will pour out my Spirit on you and strengthen you for the task.
>
> > Build a place of worship
> > Build a place of worship
> > Build a place of worship.

As you can imagine such a word took our breath away. However it was followed by a strong word of encouragement:

> > Do not be afraid. I will be with you.
> > I will give you the place.
> > I will give you the power.
> > I will give you the protection.
> > I will give you the money.

As we spent many hours in prayer over the course of several months God clearly spoke to us about the physical building which he wanted us to erect. First it was to be a place of worship, not in the sense of a denominational church building, for our vision is to serve the whole body of Christ and not to develop another branch of the church. The primary purpose of the new extension was to be a place where people could come from all denominations and give honour and glory to Jesus Christ who alone is the head of his living body, the Church. In worshipping and adoring Christ together we would be brought nearer to each other.

The Lord showed us that the worship building would be like fingers pointing out to pierce the darkness of this land. Behind the fingers was the hand to support. God showed us that behind and above the worship area would be bedrooms to accommodate those who would come to pray and to intercede and give support to the work of worship.

God also showed us that in the coming years many who are in Christian work in Ireland and are wounded in the spiritual battle would come for help and healing. Strengthened and renewed they would return to the battle.

Building began in January 1986 and a beautiful new extension with seating in the worship area for more than three hundred and accommodation in bedrooms for a further twenty guests was completed in the autumn of that year.

Wednesday, 22 October was a great day of rejoicing in Rostrevor. The sun broke through from a wintry sky and poured into the lovely new house of praise. Friends had come from the four corners of Ireland to give glory to God and to pray for the future witness of the Christian Renewal Centre. Some had come from overseas and we were conscious of concerts of prayer for the Centre around the world on that day of dedication.

Archbishop Robin Eames, and priests Pat Collins and Jim Burke, ministers David Baillie and Stanley Ross, and the clergy of the four churches in the village brought greetings. The prayers of many had been answered in some very remarkable ways. The building was completed in record time. In a year when many building projects had to be postponed and even abandoned because of terrorist threats the work went on without interference. It was too a sign of reconciliation that workers from all sections of the local community, Roman Catholic and Protestant, shared in building the house of praise and worship. Not least of all the miracles was the fact that soon after its completion the total sum of £326,000 had come in as gifts from God's people all over the world to pay for the building, and to God be all the glory.

6

SPIRITUAL WARFARE

I want men everywhere to lift up holy hands in prayer, without anger or disputing. (1 Tim. 2:8)

There are two equal and opposite errors into which our race can fall about the devils. One is to disbelieve in their existence. The other is to believe, and to feel an excessive and unhealthy interest in them. They themselves are equally pleased by both errors and hail a materialist or a magician with the same delight. (C. S. Lewis)[1]

Spiritual warfare can be defined as coming against Satan, the enemy, with the supernatural weapons that God has provided for the Christian Church. In spiritual warfare we are using God's long range weapons to go behind enemy lines. Through faith-filled prayer we can reach into the most difficult situation in the world. In the prayer which Christ taught us we, his followers, are given incredible authority. With him we are invited to pray to the Father: 'Your kingdom come, your will be done on earth as it is in heaven.' Prayer has changed the course of history and it still does if we are willing to persevere. St Paul was writing to Timothy, a young leader in the infant church in the first century. Christians were a small and frequently despised minority in a pagan society ruled by the Roman Emperor. Yet Paul urged Timothy to encourage the Christian communities to pray earnestly for politicians and those in leadership.

I urge, then, first of all, that requests, prayers, intercession and thanksgiving be made for everyone – for kings and all those in authority, that we may live peaceful and quiet lives in all godliness and holiness. This is good, and pleases God our Saviour, who wants all men to be saved and to come to a knowledge of the truth. (1 Tim. 2:1–4)

Amazingly Paul wrote those words while he was imprisoned on a trumped up charge in a Roman gaol. Paul knew from his own experience the power of faith-filled prayer. The prayer of forgiveness uttered by Stephen, as Paul and his friends stoned the first Christian martyr to death, had no doubt touched him deeply and was a factor in his remarkable conversion. Through prayer Paul had, on countless occasions, escaped death and been delivered from all kinds of dangers. Even prison doors were opened miraculously when he and Silas prayed and sang praises to God after they were almost beaten to death and thrown into the high security wing of the Philippian gaol. Paul knew from Scripture that God is 'the Lord of the kings of the earth'. As Daniel acknowledged hundreds of years before, God 'changes times and seasons; he sets up kings and deposes them. He gives wisdom to the wise and knowledge to the discerning. He reveals deep and hidden things; he knows what lies in the darkness, and light dwells with him' (Dan. 2:21–22).

Why is it that as Christians we so often neglect this great gift of prayer? Visiting churches all over the country and in different parts of the world, it is revealing to discover what priority is given to prayer. Apart from the Sunday services, it is a great shame to admit that a vast majority of churches in Ireland have no times of meeting for consistent, concerned prayer. I believe it is only when this priority is recovered that we shall see real renewal of spiritual life in our land or indeed in any other.

Some years ago when Bill Burnett was Archbishop of Cape Town he quoted in *Good Hope*, his Diocesan newsletter, these wise words written by Raymond Raynes of the Community of the Resurrection in 1943:

There is grave danger, in the face of the appalling social disorders and injustices of our time, of imagining that we can produce some kind of new order which is called Christian, and having forced it upon society by legislation or revolution, consider that we have planted firm foundations upon which will arise a temple of the Holy Spirit . . . This is an idle dream because it overlooks the fundamental fact that the heart of all our problems is the heart of man . . .

Writing during the Second World War he goes on:

Speak to an audience of soldiers or working men of the new world after the war in terms of economic justice and equality of opportunity attained by the application of Christian principles to national affairs, and they will listen. Speak to them about the life of prayer and faith which is the very heart of the Christian religion, and their interest flags. Why? Partly because inner religiousness has no economic value, but also because social preaching implies that sin does not lie in them, but in the structures of society. Under the Christian flag they can fight for a better world without the necessity of themselves having to become better men. Very comforting, but very untrue.

William Cowper the poet says:

> When nations are to perish in their sins
> Tis in the church the leprosy begins.

'Judgment begins at the house of God' was a clear word frequently proclaimed by the prophets of the Old Testament. At a time of terrible crisis in the land of Israel Ezekiel the prophet exposed the faithless religious leaders and the injustice and violence that was rampant: 'The people . . . practise extortion and commit robbery; they oppress the poor and needy and ill-treat the alien, denying them justice.' And he voices the pleading of God's heart for even one person who would stand in the gap:

I looked for a man among them who would build up the wall and stand before me in the gap on behalf of the land so that I would not have to destroy it, but I found none. So I will pour out my wrath on them and consume them with my fiery anger, bringing down on their own heads all they have done, declares the Sovereign Lord. (Ezek. 22:29–31)

Praying against violence

In the crisis that faced Ireland we felt sure God was calling more Christians 'to stand in the gap' if any real advance was to be made against the forces that were destroying our land. In 1979 we began to hold regular days of prayer for Ireland and encouraged people in different parts of the country to engage in similar gatherings for prayer and spiritual warfare.

Our usual pattern for these gatherings begins with praise and worship, building faith in God's power and presence, which leads to an attitude of humility and total dependence on God. Frequently it brings us to deep repentance and confession of our own sins and failures. Next we share God's word of encouragement and some teaching from the Scriptures on prayer and intercession. Often we will spend a prolonged time waiting in silence so that God may reveal specific areas into which we should pray. It may be that God by his Holy Spirit through the gifts of wisdom or knowledge will reveal particular plans of violence which are being prepared. With the authority that Christ has given his people through his victory on the cross over the powers of evil we can 'bind' those forces of destruction. A remarkable example of such an action is recorded in the Old Testament in the ministry of Elisha the prophet. In 2 Kings 6 we read about a war that was raging between Israel and Syria. The King of Syria made detailed secret plans with his officers about where he would establish his camp:

But the man of God sent word to the king of Israel, 'Beware that you do not pass this place, for the Syrians are going down there.' And the king of Israel sent to the place of which the man of God told him. Thus he used to warn him, so that he saved himself there more than once or twice. And the mind of the king of Syria was greatly troubled because of this thing; and he called his servants and said to them, 'Will you not show me who of us is for the king of Israel?' And one of his servants said, 'None my lord, O king; but Elisha, the prophet who is in Israel, tells the king of Israel the words that you speak in your bedchamber.' And he said, 'Go and see where he is, that I may send and seize him.' It was told him, 'Behold, he is in Dothan.' So he sent there horses and chariots and a great army; and they came by night, and surrounded the city. When the servant of the man of God rose early in the morning and went out, behold, an army with horses and chariots was round about the city. And the servant said, 'Alas, my master! What shall we do?' He said, 'Fear not, for those who are with us are more than those who are with them.' Then Elisha prayed, and said, 'O Lord, I pray thee, open his eyes that he may see.' So the Lord opened the eyes of the young man, and he saw; and behold, the mountain was full of horses and chariots of fire round about Elisha. (2 Kings 6:9–17 RSV)

The amazing sequel is that the war was ended without bloodshed. On Elisha's advice the King of Israel entertained the Syrian officers to a lavish feast before they returned to their king. Obedience to God's word of knowledge and the gift of faith led to reconciliation and peace. Have we the faith to believe that it could happen more often today?

During one weekend of prayer and spiritual warfare when the whole gathering gave a day to fasting and prayer, we experienced a similar revelation through the operation of supernatural gifts of the Holy Spirit. We were encouraged to listen to God in silence and then share anything we felt God was saying to us. One man described a detailed picture which he saw as we prayed. It was a stone bridge over a wide, dark river with densely wooded banks. He explained that it was near an island on Lough Neagh in

Northern Ireland. He sensed that there were explosives hidden there but he could not see them in his vision or picture. We took time to pray into that situation, whatever it might be; taking authority over any plan of violence or destruction. Together we prayed that any plans of evil would be exposed and brought to the light without causing any loss of life or destruction. You may imagine our joy five days later when we heard on a BBC news bulletin that the security forces had safely defused 750 pounds of explosives found underwater near the bridge where the river Blackwater flows into Lough Neagh. The news report added: 'Through extreme vigilance on the part of the security forces this bomb was discovered and a major tragedy averted.'

As we learn more about this aspect of spiritual warfare we encourage people to pray this 'Prayer against violence':

> Lord Jesus Christ, we thank you
> That through your death on the cross
> You disarmed the powers of evil.
> Help us, we pray you,
> To enter into your victory
> And to stand in your authority
> Against all evil.
> Lord, send forth your light and your truth,
> Bring to light the deeds of darkness
> And let plans of violence
> And murder be revealed.
> By the power of your Holy Spirit
> Convict those who have allowed
> Their minds to be dominated by evil.
> Lead them, O Lord to true repentance
> That they may receive your new life
> And rejoice in your forgiving love.

Praying like this is hard work yet it is inspiring to find that many more are taking up the challenge. The violence that continues to cause so much suffering and death in our land is carried on by a relatively small number of committed terrorists. They work in tightly-knit groups, preparing with precision their deeds of murder and destruction. Mobilising more people to pray is an urgent task and a most effective weapon against the onslaught of evil (for a framework for individual or collective prayer, see Appendix).

Shortly after we began the days of prayer for Ireland the Lord encouraged us through a picture. We saw a long line of sand dunes miles along the seashore. In each sand dune we could see a group of people gathered. There was no obvious physical communication between the groups. Then we observed that the people in each group were looking up and listening. We believed the Lord was showing us that he was gathering groups of people all over Ireland who were looking to him and listening to his voice. Their prayers were being heard and because they were all listening they would all hear his call to come together in his time.

Only heaven will reveal the power for good that has been released into the world by people who were faithful to the lonely and demanding task of prayer according to the mind of Christ. We meet many of these warriors. They may never be seen on a platform or in a place of importance but their work is vital. Glenn Clark's parable of the 'fanner bees' quoted in Frank Laubach's book on the Lord's Prayer, provides a good illustration of such saints:

> There arose from the beehive a sibilant note . . . not unlike the sound of sea waves. 'They are fanner bees,' whispered the old beekeeper. 'It's their job to keep the hive sweet and fresh. They're standing with their heads lowered, turned towards the centre of the hive. Their wings are moving so rapidly that if you saw them you would think you were looking at a fray mist. They are drawing the bad air out through one side of the entrance, while the pure air is sucked in on the other side.' The old beekeeper stepped to the hive, holding a lighted candle in his hand. Instantly the light was extinguished by the strong current. The old man said, 'The fanners draw out the bad air and let in the fresh.' Isn't that how people who call themselves Christians ought to act?[2]

Born into battle

Every Christian is born into battle. Most baptismal services for children or adults make that abundantly clear. In many liturgies there is a prayer of deliverance or exorcism from evil powers or influences. In all there is a clear call to die to sin and rise to a new life of walking in obedience to God. The one who is baptised is signed on the forehead with the cross, 'in token that hereafter he or she shall not be ashamed to confess the faith of Christ crucified, and manfully to fight under his banner, against sin, the world, and the devil; and to continue Christ's faithful soldier and servant unto his or her life's end' (Book of Common Prayer).

Jesus warned the early disciples on many occasions about the powers of evil they would encounter. The Gospels record the clash between evil and the power of good in the temptations Jesus endured in the wilderness after his baptism in the Jordan. Jesus met the powers of darkness 'head on' when they emerged in the form of 'possession' of people or the demonic domination of authorities civil and religious. Behind the manifestation of those evil forces Jesus saw the malevolent force of Satan, the devil, the adversary, the prince of this world. 'The thief comes to steal and to kill and to destroy,' said Jesus, 'but I am come that you might have life and have it more abundantly.' Everywhere we see stealing, killing and destruction, there we see the power of the devil at work. In his last instructions to the disciples before his crucifixion Jesus left them in no doubt that in the world they would have tribulation and went on to add, 'but be of good cheer, I have overcome the world'. 'The prince of this world is coming. He has no hold on me,' Jesus confidently declared. And amazingly that same confident power was passed on to all who believe in Jesus and acknowledge him as Saviour and Lord. The early church lived in the experience of the tribulation and the triumph. St John reminded his readers, 'The reason the Son of God appeared was to destroy the devil's work' (1 John 3:8) and went on to encourage them, 'the one who is in you is greater than the one who is in the world' (1 John 4:4).

How sad that in many parts of the church today it is hardly recognised that there is a battle on. The pervasive influence of secularism and the glittering bauble of materialism have blinded our eyes. Many even in the churches scoff at the idea of a devil and dismiss it as an outmoded fable of a past age. I remember some years ago a group of theologians signed their names to a letter in a leading British newspaper disclaiming the existence of the devil. I felt like inviting them all to come and live in Northern Ireland for a few weeks and explain the origin of so much destruction that is going on. Over the years even the secular media have been increasingly describing many of the terrible atrocities here as 'demonic'.

Thankfully in the renewal of the 'charismata', the grace gifts of the Holy Spirit, Christians are becoming more aware of the struggle we are in and the resources which God has made available to us to fight and to overcome. One of the many restored gifts of the Holy Spirit being experienced in the church is the 'gift of discernment of spirits'. It is the ability, under the direction of the Holy Spirit, to distinguish the spirits of evil which influence and often dominate people, causing them to act in violent and unsocial ways.

I remember the first time I met with a team to minister in Crumlin Road prison in Belfast. Men who have committed some atrocious murders are there. Some are serving several life sentences for multiple murders, the gruesome details of which emerged in their trials. I recall thinking on the way to the prison, 'It will be easy to pick out those who have committed such terrible murders, they are bound to look depraved.' As more than a hundred men filed into the chapel for the service, however, they seemed the same as the people we mingle with every day on the streets of Belfast and elsewhere in Northern Ireland. I realised they were ordinary people like you and me who had given themselves over to the devil's work of killing, stealing and destruction. And I realised 'there but for the grace of God go I'.

How can we come against this insidious power of evil which is so evident in the world today? The battle is not peculiar to our times. Writing to the Christians in first-century Ephesus St Paul made clear the nature of the spiritual warfare in which the Christian Church is engaged:

> In conclusion be strong – not in yourselves but in the Lord, in the power of his boundless strength. Put on God's complete armour so that you can successfully resist all the devil's craftiness. For our fight is not against any physical enemy: it is against organisations and powers that are spiritual. We are up against the unseen power that controls this dark world, and spiritual agents from the very headquarters of evil. Therefore you must wear the whole armour of God that you may be able to resist evil in its day of power, and that even when you have fought to a standstill you may still stand your ground. (Eph. 6:10–13a Phillips)[3]

After more than twenty years of the recent hostilities in Ireland army experts have declared that there is no military solution to our conflict. The battle is on another front, for the minds and hearts of Irishmen and Irishwomen. Christians hold the key to victory in this battle. The 'powers' of which St Paul speaks have emerged under many different guises in the twentieth century. With hindsight it is easy to observe their vicious power and vice-like grip on the hearts and minds of people.

In world terms one of the most obvious examples is the rise of Communism, demanding people's total allegiance, subjecting everything to the ideology which spawned it, and causing the deaths of countless millions of innocent people. Another is Nazism. In his revealing book, *Christ and the Powers*, Hendrik Berkhoff the Dutch theologian describes his own experience of the subtle power of Nazism in its early blossoming in Germany:

When Hitler took the helm in Germany in 1933, the powers
of Volk, race, and state took a new grip on men. Thousands
were grateful, after the confusion of the preceding years,
to find their lives again protected from chaos, order and
security restored. No one could withhold himself, with
utmost effort, from the grasp these powers had on men's
inner and outer life. While studying in Berlin in 1937 I myself
experienced almost literally how such powers may be 'in the
air'. At the same time one had to see how they intruded as a
barrier between God's word and men. They acted as if they
were ultimate values calling for loyalty, as if they were the
gods of the cosmos.[4]

Dietrich Bonhoeffer and many with him in the Confessing
Church clearly discerned the power of evil that motivated
such an ideology, but sadly a larger proportion of the church
in Germany was blind to it.

The detection of such destructive powers nearer home
is often more difficult to see. They hide under many
cloaks of accepted cultural and even religious guises. They
masquerade under the covers of secret societies and exclu-
sive 'orders' with high-sounding names. To unmask such
'powers' takes spiritual discernment, deep humility and
great courage in a society where they have ruled without
much interference for centuries.

The ingredients of Irish history, so closely intertwined
with Britain, have provided fertile soil for the seeds of
evil to grow. Injustice, deliberately imposed by a colonial
power, bred resentment and bitterness. Deep fears festered
both in the oppressors and the oppressed, creating mistrust
and suspicion. Pride of religion and race, perpetuated from
generation to generation, have built almost impenetrable
barriers. Prejudice, fed by a thousand myths and lies, has
led to bitterness and hatred. Add to that the bigotry and
religious apartheid sometimes practised by the churches in
Ireland, and you have the elements for the violent explosions that have occurred so frequently in recent history.
The effect of such distortion is reflected in the slogans that
are assumed by the para-military groups. On the one hand

the Ulster Volunteer Force carries the motto 'For God and Ulster' and on the other the Irish Republican Army has openly equated the deaths of Irish patriots with the death of Christ on Calvary. Such principalities and powers which manipulate people today need to be exposed. Christians need urgently to unite under the power of Christ's name to pull down those strongholds.

Such spiritual warfare is beyond human endeavour, as St Paul reminds us: 'For though we live in the world, we do not wage war as the world does. The weapons we fight with are not the weapons of the world. On the contrary, they have divine power to demolish strongholds' (2 Cor. 10:3–4).

In June 1986 some of us from the Christian Renewal Centre were involved with other Christian leaders in drawing up a Declaration of Faith and Commitment. It was signed by Christians from many churches, Roman Catholic and Protestant, and widely distributed. In the introduction we stated:

> Murder, arson, bombing, threats and violence of deed and word are every day increasing tension and spreading fear throughout the whole population of Northern Ireland. Sectarian activists and false gods of party are demanding from our respective communities a total loyalty that belongs only to Christ. Followers of Christ, living together in this land, must re-assert His sole Lordship. At this time of choice, we make the following declaration of our faith and commitment.

In the first of five points we confessed:

> We believe that all our land belongs to God: not to Unionists or Nationalists. All of us have to live in it and share it together. We believe that all human life is sacred. All Christians must recognise that murder is evil by whomsoever and for whatsoever reason it is committed. The sin of murder is shared by those who co-operate in it whether before, during or after its execution. We believe that for us obedience to Christ is more important than

Nationalism or Unionism. We believe that all of us without exception share in the blame for our present troubles and for the failure of our communities to live together in peace and mutual respect. Our differences are no excuse for refusing to seek reconciliation with God and with each other.

Finally we pledged ourselves 'to obey God's will and word rather than give unqualified support to any political leader whether Nationalist or Unionist'.

This statement, similar to the Barmen declaration drawn up by the Confessing Church in Nazi Germany, was used as a basis of discussion in churches. It continues to challenge the hard line attitudes which are sadly so deeply rooted.

The work and the weapon are one: praise

In undertaking spiritual warfare we have been learning more about the importance of power-filled praise. It is an aspect of spiritual warfare mentioned on many occasions in the Old and New Testaments. During a particularly difficult period in Belfast in 1977 over a thousand Christians from all parts of the province came together for a Festival of Praise. During our time of praise, prayer and worship a prophecy was shared which has encouraged us on many occasions since.

Behold I am doing a new thing. You are the first fruits of an army I am raising up in this land. But it is an army such as this land has never seen before because it is a spiritual army that moves together in the Spirit. It is an army that puts on the Lord Jesus and moves forward together under the banner of love. It is an army that moves forward together in obedience to the word and with a two-edged sword of the Spirit in its hand. It is an army to which I have given a most important work and my most powerful weapon. The work and the weapon are one, they are praise.

At the festival we sang with great conviction a new song by Ron Wilson of Belfast:

I hear the sound of rustling in the leaves of the trees;
The Spirit of the Lord has come down on the earth.
The Church that seemed in slumber has now risen from
    its knees,
And dry bones are responding with the fruits of new birth.
Oh, this is now a time for declaration.
The word will go to all men everywhere.
The Church is here for healing of the nations.
Behold the day of Jesus drawing near.

My tongue will be the pen of a ready writer,
And what the Father gives to me I'll sing.
I only want to be his breath
I only want to glorify the King.

And all around the world the Body waits expectantly.
The promise of the Father is now ready to fall.
The watchmen on the tower all exhort us to prepare,
And the church responds – a people who will answer the
    call,
And this is not a phase which is passing.
It's the start of an age that is to come.
And where is the wise man and the scoffer?
Before the face of Jesus they are dumb.

A Body now prepared by God and ready for war.
The prompting of the Spirit is our word of command.
We rise, a mighty army, at the bidding of the Lord;
The devils hear and flee for their time is at hand.
And children of the Lord hear our commission,
That we should love and serve our God as one.
The Spirit won't be hindered by division,
Through the perfect work that Jesus has begun.[5]

This song is now sung all over the world and has inspired
faith, courage and hope in many people in similarly difficult
situations. Many centuries ago Ignatius of Antioch wrote to
Christians in Ephesus with this advice:

Do your best to meet more often to give thanks and glory
to God. When you meet frequently the powers of Satan
are confounded and in the face of your corporate faith

his malevolence crumbles. Nothing can better a state of peaceful accord, from which every trace of spiritual or earthly hostility has been banished.

On many occasions as a community we have proved how true his words are. And we have seen it work in some very difficult circumstances. Once when a local town was threatened with sectarian conflict we gathered with some local Christians on a hill overlooking the town. In the early morning we sang God's praise, proclaiming the power and authority of the name of Jesus over the town and asking God to protect life and confound any plans for violence. We rejoiced greatly when we heard later that all the demonstrations passed off peacefully.

A bleak railway station near the border was another early morning venue for a sortie of praise and prayer. At a time when almost daily the IRA were threatening to blow up the main line between Belfast and Dublin, or had already planted bombs there, we felt it was right to proclaim God's power in that place. It was a rare sight for the driver of the first train from Belfast to be confronted with a group of people breaking the dawn with praise and prayer. He greeted us warmly when we explained that we were praying for him and others who had to do such difficult and dangerous work. 'Someone would need to be praying,' he called as he pulled out of the station.

Pentecost praise

Over the years we have been involved with Christians of different denominations in organising special gatherings at Whitsun, the birthday of the Church. In cathedrals, parks and public halls thousands have come together to celebrate and pray. On Pentecost Sunday 1983 members of the community were closely involved with a unique gathering in Dublin. For the first time in its thousand-year history as many as eight thousand Christians celebrated for several hours in the city under a common banner proclaiming 'Jesus is Lord'. Ireland's cities and towns are familiar with parades and processions. Many of them are notorious as protest marches or expressions of sectarian triumphalism. This one was different. It was a joyful march of praise that made its way through the city. Patrick Nolan, the Religious Affairs correspondent of the *Irish Times*, describes the scene:

> 'Religion is joyful' was one of the messages of the celebration, which was organised by the Dublin Inter-Denominational Charismatic Committee. Mr Kerr reminded us that joy is a mark of the presence of the Holy Spirit. It was a reassuring occasion. First it was a moving manifestation of faith. Second it showed that, in spite of highly publicised differences, Christians of several denominations have much in common and are often ready to worship happily together. 'Jesus is Lord', 'Jesus rules OK' and 'Jesus loves our family', proclaimed some of the larger banners near a float at the head of the procession. Thousands of smaller banners showed a white dove on a red background, symbol of the Holy Spirit, or simply bore the word 'Love' or 'Peace'. Among them were streamers indicating where groups had come from – Downpatrick, Mullingar and Clonmel, for example. About 1,000 came in special buses from Northern Ireland, many of them Protestants. All the main churches and most of the smaller ones were represented among the southern contingents. The singing was perhaps the most notable aspect of the celebration. It had the vigour, volume and special ardour that appear to have become typical of charismatic gatherings. The hymns began before the procession started to move slowly from the west side of the green. The singing continued all along the way and it was resumed, seemingly with more fervour and conviction, when the crowd assembled in the cathedral two and a half hours later.[6]

Along the route the procession of praise stopped at three points. Prayers were said for those in leadership in public life at Leinster House, the seat of the Irish Parliament; at the General Post Office, scene of the Easter Rising in

1916, there was a call to renounce the spirit of violence and bloodshed; and at the City Hall we prayed for the city and the nation.

When the marchers crowded into St Patrick's Cathedral, with thousands gathered in the nearby park, there was renewed joy in the praise that filled that ancient building. We were reminded by the Dean, Victor Griffin, that on that site over 1,500 years ago St Patrick had preached the Gospel. No doubt St Patrick would have been pleased to hear the witness given that afternoon by two former terrorists. Mary from the south of Ireland and Billy from the north, ex-members of opposing para-military organisations, told how Jesus had miraculously healed them in body and changed their hearts, replacing hatred with love and violence with a spirit of reconciliation. Together from north and south, Roman Catholic and Protestant, we prayed, pleading forgiveness for the sins that divided us. We turned to the Lord Jesus Christ in a new commitment to serve him and prayed for a new Pentecost in Ireland. Something special happened in Dublin that day. God's glory rested on those who rejoiced together and reclaimed Ireland for Christ. A new hope was born in many hearts.

7

RENEWAL

When I think of the wisdom and scope of his plan I fall down on my knees and pray to the Father of all the great family of God – some of them already in heaven and some down here on earth – that out of his glorious, unlimited resources he will give you the mighty inner strengthening of his Holy Spirit. (St Paul in Eph. 3:14–16 Living Bible)

Come Holy Spirit,
Restore our lives, which without you are as dead.
Kindle our hearts, which without you are cold and dull.
Fill the church, which without you is an empty shrine
Through Jesus Christ our Lord.

'All over the world the Spirit is moving' are words in a song we often sing. They echo the message of the prophet Habakkuk 600 years before Christ came. He lived at a time of great upheaval when his country was under threat of invasion. Yet as he worshipped the eternal God he caught a vision of a day to come when 'the earth will be filled with the knowledge of the glory of the Lord, as the waters cover the sea' (Hab. 2:14). With his physical eyes he saw impending doom but with the eyes of faith he saw God's purpose being carried forward to the day when the glory of God would be revealed in the person of Jesus, God's Son.

The early Christians on the day of Pentecost entered into that vision too when they believed the promise of Jesus, 'You will be baptised with the Holy Spirit . . . and you will be my witnesses in Jerusalem, and in all Judea and

Samaria, and to the ends of the earth' (Acts 1:5,8). To men and women who had scarcely travelled more than a few miles beyond their places of birth the challenge must have seemed staggering.

Today we are entering into that great promise. It is being unfolded before our very eyes. The Good News of the Gospel is now reaching almost every part of the earth. Over the past twenty-five years we have witnessed what must surely be the most universal outpouring of God's Holy Spirit the world has ever seen. In Africa, Asia and Latin America this century has seen a remarkable growth in the Christian Church. Despite fierce persecution from Communism, the churches in China and the Soviet Union have grown both numerically and spiritually. Even the sleeping Church in Europe is beginning to waken as the fresh wind of God's Spirit blows into our complacency and selfish materialism.

Thank God, Ireland has not been overlooked. Alongside the tragic conflict that is all too evident to the watching world, the Spirit of God has been moving in power, bringing personal renewal of spiritual life to many and challenging the spirit of hopelessness and despair.

Restoration

God is the one 'who makes all things new'. Countless men and women would joyfully endorse what St Paul wrote to Titus:

> At one time we too were foolish, disobedient, deceived and enslaved by all kinds of passions and pleasures. We lived in malice and envy, being hated and hating one another. But when the kindness and love of God our Saviour appeared, he saved us, not because of righteous things we had done, but because of his mercy. He saved us through the washing of rebirth and renewal by the Holy Spirit, whom he poured out on us generously through Jesus Christ our Saviour, so

that, having been justified by his grace, we might become
heirs having the hope of eternal life. (Titus 3:3–7)

Renewal is God's work in our personal lives and in the
Church. In his *Synonyms of the New Testament* Archbishop Trench reveals the richness of the rare Greek
word *Anakainosis* which St Paul used: 'It is that grad-
ual restoration of the divine image, which is ever going
forward in Him who, through the new birth, has come
under transforming powers of the world to come.'[1] The
word, Trench suggests, is derived from the world of art,
describing the restoration of the beauty originally intended
and created by the artist. What has disfigured, defaced or
obscured the original beauty is removed so that the glory
may shine through again. That process is often painful in
our personal lives and in the Church. But God desires a
glorious Church without spot or wrinkle.

Dr John Armstrong, Archbishop of Armagh and Primate
of the Church of Ireland in 1980, was someone who entered
joyfully and whole-heartedly into the renewing work of God's
Holy Spirit in our country. Commending the first Church of
Ireland Renewal Conference held in Dublin he wrote:

> Renewal in the Church must flow in two directions if it
> is to proclaim the greater glory: firstly, in the individual,
> the renewal must be felt and expressed in life and action;
> secondly, in the Church, by a deeper and more telling
> spirituality which will force those outside the Church to
> recognise that we have been with Christ. People must see
> in us that we are in the Church because we have seen his
> glory and are satisfied.

When I pray 'Lord, renew the Church' I must always add
'and begin with me'. In the Anglican service of Confirmation
when the bishop lays his hands on the head of the candidate
he prays this marvellous prayer: 'Defend, O Lord, this thy
servant with thy heavenly grace, that he or she may continue
thine for ever; and daily increase in thy Holy Spirit more and
more, until he or she come unto thy everlasting kingdom.'

You shall receive power

Infilling and daily empowering with the Holy Spirit is the Lord's desire for every believer. If the apostles and early disciples of Jesus needed that, how much more do we. After his resurrection and before his ascension Jesus commanded them: 'Do not leave Jerusalem, but wait for the gift my Father promised, which you have heard me speak about. For John baptised with water, but in a few days you will be baptised with the Holy Spirit' (Acts 1:4–5). Those people who had believed in Jesus, and received his Holy Spirit when he breathed on them in the Upper Room on the evening of the resurrection (John 20:22) were to experience a release of that same Holy Spirit in their lives that would send them out fearlessly to proclaim the Good News to the ends of the earth. Jesus explained, 'You will receive power when the Holy Spirit comes on you, and you will be my witnesses' (Acts 1:8).

The word used there for power in Greek is *Dunamis*, from which we derive our word dynamite. In warning them to wait for this experience Jesus knew how vital it would be for his mission through them. It was too dangerous for them to confront the world, the flesh and the devil in their own strength. They needed 'power from on high'. It was not enough that these men and women had witnessed the resurrection of Jesus from the dead, the greatest miracle that had ever happened. They needed to be baptised in the Holy Spirit to continue the work he commissioned them to do. In faith and obedience 120 of them waited prayerfully and expectantly in the Upper Room and the promise of Jesus was fulfilled:

When the day of Pentecost came, they were all together in one place. Suddenly a sound like the blowing of a violent wind came from heaven and filled the whole house where

they were sitting. They saw what seemed to be tongues of
fire that separated and came to rest on each of them. All of
them were filled with the Holy Spirit and began to speak in
other tongues as the Spirit enabled them. (Acts 2:1–4)

Many refer to that explosion of power as the birthday of
the Christian Church. The Acts of the Apostles, or more
accurately the Acts of the Holy Spirit through them, records
the amazing consequences of that mighty revolution. Those
men and women, who before had been inhibited and fearful,
went out with boldness and courage to proclaim what they
had seen and heard. When they emerged from the Upper
Room they were so inebriated with joy that sceptical
onlookers taunted, 'they have had too much wine'. How
many observers would make the same mistake today if they
saw us coming from church on a Sunday? I find it really
amazing that in the first sermon Peter preached on the day
of Pentecost he had to convince his hearers that he and his
friends were not drunk! Three thousand people responded
to his preaching of the Gospel and were baptised that very
day. We are convinced that this birthday gift is God's desire
for the Church in every day and age. As St Peter said, 'The
promise is for you and your children and for all who are far
off – for all whom the Lord our God will call' (Acts 2:39).

In his illuminating book, *The Household of God*, Lesslie
Newbigin underlines one factor which undoubtedly in-
hibits Christians today from entering into the fullness
of Pentecost:

Theologians today are afraid of the word 'experience'.
There are some good reasons for this, and also some
bad ones. But I do not think it is possible to survey this
New Testament evidence, even in the most cursory way
. . . without recognising that the New Testament writers
are free from this fear. They recount happenings which
we would subsume under the head of religious experience,
and do not hesitate to ascribe them to the mighty power of
God and to give them right of way in theological argument
over long cherished convictions. They regard the gift of

the Holy Spirit as an event which can be unmistakably recognised, and they treat it as the determinative and decisive thing by which the church is constituted. The living Spirit incorporates us in Christ, and where He is, there is the life and power of God.[2]

In Acts 19:2–6 St Luke records St Paul's visit to Athens where he found a group of people who had believed in Jesus through the preaching of Apollos:

Paul asked them, 'Did you receive the Holy Spirit when you believed?' They answered, 'No, we have not even heard that there is a Holy Spirit.' So Paul asked, 'Then what baptism did you receive?' 'John's baptism,' they replied. Paul said, 'John's baptism was a baptism of repentance. He told the people to believe in the one coming after him, that is, in Jesus.' On hearing this, they were baptised into the name of the Lord Jesus. When Paul placed his hands on them, the Holy Spirit came on them, and they spoke in tongues and prophesied.

Clearly we as believers in the Lord Jesus Christ today are meant to experience in our personal lives what it is to be baptised in the Holy Spirit. Bishop Newbigin goes on to comment:

(St Paul's) modern successors are more inclined to ask either, 'Did you believe exactly what we teach?' or 'Were the hands that were laid on you our hands?' and – if the answer is satisfactory – to assure the converts that they have received the Holy Spirit even if they don't know it.[3]

Personal renewal

At the very heart of the renewal is this personal experience of Jesus as Lord and Saviour and baptiser in the Holy Spirit. This vivid encounter with the living God is accompanied by a restoration of the 'charismata', the grace gifts of the Holy Spirit that God has given to Christians to build up the Church and extend the Kingdom of God in the world. In our work at the Christian Renewal Centre an important part of our ministry is to encourage individuals and churches to enter into the full inheritance that Christ has won for us. To this end we arrange regular days of renewal, retreats, conferences and Bible weeks to help people to understand and appropriate what God has promised. We are also invited to churches and fellowships all over the country to share the message of renewal. Teams from the community, frequently supplemented by members of the Monday night prayer group, go out for weekends of renewal and festivals of faith which may last for a week or more. Often the invitation may be for a single meeting.

Our ministry is always to exalt the Lord Jesus, to do as John the Baptist did. Pointing to Jesus he said, 'Look, the Lamb of God, who takes away the sin of the world . . . he who will baptise with the Holy Spirit' (John 1:29,33). Today the Lord Jesus issues the same invitation that he gave to the thousands of people who crowded the streets of Jerusalem at the Feast of Tabernacles:

> Jesus stood and said in a loud voice, 'If anyone is thirsty, let him come to me and drink. Whoever believes in me, as the Scripture has said, streams of living water will flow from within him.' By this he meant the Spirit, whom those who believed in him were later to receive. Up to that time the Spirit had not been given, since Jesus had not yet been glorified. (John 7:37)

Baptism in the Spirit

Jesus is now glorified, seated at the Father's right hand and longs to pour out his Spirit on all who are thirsty. Only the Lord Jesus can baptise us in the Holy Spirit. It is his sovereign work alone. Others can support us and pray with us just as those early disciples prayed for each other in the Upper Room. What did Jesus mean when he promised that we would be baptised in the Holy Spirit? The word 'baptise' in the Greek language means to soak, to saturate, to immerse, to fill to overflowing, to inundate. When St Paul prayed for the Christians in Ephesus he used similarly extravagant language 'that you may be filled to the measure of all the fulness of God' (Eph. 3:19).

In counselling and praying with those seeking to be baptised in the Holy Spirit I find it helpful to bring them to a picture or vision which was given to the prophet Ezekiel and recorded in chapter 47 of his book. In the vision a man leads Ezekiel to the door of the Temple. From beneath the altar of the Temple springs a river that flows out into the arid desert. Wherever the river flows life is restored and the desert blossoms. Even the waters of the salty Dead Sea become fresh. Fruit trees of all kinds grow on both banks of the river. Their leaves do not wither nor their fruit fail. They bear fruit every month because the water from the sanctuary flows to them. Their fruit serves for food and their leaves for healing. In the vision the man leads Ezekiel into the river. First the water is over his ankles, then over his knees, then it reaches his waist and after that it becomes too deep to walk through. It was a river to swim in. In the beautiful line drawings of the Swiss artist Annie Vollaton, used to illustrate the Good News Bible, she has a telling picture to accompany this passage. A figure with a staff, so obviously the Lord, is leading another figure into the water. It is the Lord who leads me into that river of the life of the Holy Spirit. Therefore I need have no fear. He who invites will never force me nor push me in. When I accept his invitation he takes me by the hand and leads me ever deeper as I yield to him every part of my body, from the soles of my feet to the top of my head. The water comes over my feet as I yield the direction of my life to him – not my way but yours, O Lord. As the water comes over my knees I am bowing to him – not my will but yours, O Lord. As the water comes over my waist I am yielding to him all my powers of procreation – not my desires but yours, O Lord. When the water reaches my heart I am yielding to him my emotions – not my love but yours, O Lord. As my shoulders go under the water I am yielding to him my physical strength – your strength not mine, O Lord. Finally the water is too deep and my head must yield giving him all my powers of intellect – a mind renewed, O Lord.

'God has poured out his love into our hearts by the Holy Spirit, whom he has given us' (Rom. 5:5). In the gentle flow of his love, fears which may have haunted me and bondages that held me begin to lose their power. What Jesus promised he provides. What he provides I claim by faith with thanksgiving, remembering that 'Every good and perfect gift is from above, coming down from the Father of the heavenly lights, who does not change like shifting shadows' (Jas 1:17). Thanksgiving is at once an act of faith and the key to receiving. Receiving brings joy, often expressed in tears, and frequently releasing the gift of tongues in which, like a little child, I am able to look up with confidence to my Father and cry 'Abba', 'Daddy'.

Praying in the Spirit or praying in tongues is that simple and glorious gift of the Holy Spirit that allows my spirit to commune with the Spirit of God within me in a way that bypasses my thought-processes but does not override my mind. It is a pre-verbal language of the Spirit which facilitates communion with God and builds faith and confidence in his power. I suppose the clearest illustration of this gift is the obvious communication of a baby with a mother. There is real communication and deep communion through sounds that are meaningless in terms of ordinary language. The psalmist reflected this: 'I have stilled and quietened my soul; like a weaned child

with its mother, like a weaned child is my soul within me'
(Ps. 131:2).

In the record of believers being baptised in the Holy
Spirit in the Acts of the Apostles, speaking in tongues
was almost always a consequence. Joy accompanied a
new sense of freedom in sharing the good news of the
saving love of Jesus. Personal assurance of salvation gave
confidence in the fatherhood of God. A variety of emotions
accompanied the experience, not the ecstatic expression of
religious fervour but an overflow of praise, which C. S.
Lewis has described as 'inner health made audible'. The
Holy Spirit is poured out not worked up. The significant
thing is that God was working through those ordinary
men and women in miraculous ways to bring release
and healing to broken victims of sin and disease. With
our intellectual mind-set and theological pride it is so
easy for us to ignore or dismiss the reality of such vivid
experiences of God's presence and power. In a graphic way
Lesslie Newbigin explains the important place of such lived
experience.

I believe that when a prospector first strikes oil there is
often a violent eruption of the oil which sometimes bursts
into flames and burns for many days before it is brought
under control. Later on there will be no room for such
displays. The oil will all be pumped through pipes and
refineries to its destination, and a desire to go back to
the early fireworks will be rightly regarded as infantile.
But the early displays did at least prove something: they
proved that oil was there; and without this all the pipes
and refineries in the world are merely futile. My illustration
is a crude one, but it will serve well enough to make the
point that what I have called the Pentecostal Christian has
the New Testament on his side when he demands first of
all of any body of so-called Christians, 'Do you have the
Holy Spirit? For without that all your credal orthodoxy and
all your historic succession avails you nothing.' To quote
again the blunt words of St Paul: 'If any man have not the
Spirit of Christ, he is none of his.'[4]

The Christian Renewal Centre, 1990

View over Carlingford Lough from the Centre

1974: the Centre, and the Kerrs with Timothy

Easter praise on Centre lawn, 1979

Cross community group of young people from Enniskillen at the Christian Renewal Centre

BE STILL AND KNOW

After a bomb in Belfast

Devastation after a
terrorist attack

March for Jesus, Dublin, in which 10,000 from North and South took part

Going through the narrow gate in Belfast's 'Peace' wall on a walk of witness

Above: Summer helpers at the Centre with
Fr Jim Burke

Right: Albert McElroy

Below: 'King's Kids' meet at the Centre

Cecil Kerr with Sir Harry Secombe, the Executive Producer, Bill Ward and Assistant Producer, Ron Cass after filming ITV's 'Highway' at the Centre

Cecil Kerr receiving a People of the Year Award, pictured with the other recipients and Dr Garret Fitzgerald

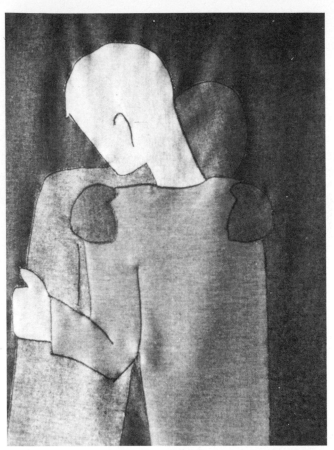

Banner of
Reconciliation in
Upper Room at the
Centre

Cecil and Myrtle Kerr

We have had the joy of praying with thousands of people for such a release of the Holy Spirit in their lives. Each one can tell a different story of how they came to that point, some out of desperation, others through aspiration. Surprised by joy, like the early Christians, they are glad to tell what 'they have seen and heard'. In her testimony Fanny Robertson, one of the foundation members of the community, spoke of a bondage often experienced especially by clergy and those involved in Christian work.

Being baptised in the Holy Spirit came to me as a great release of the Spirit. I had been a Christian for over forty years. As a schoolgirl I asked the Lord Jesus into my heart. I was well taught, and I knew a lot about the Holy Spirit. As a student and then a member of staff of a Bible college I had experienced his working in my life. But for twelve years I had been conscious of a very big lack. I was bound up inside, fettered, a prisoner. Someone laid hands on me and prayed that I might be baptised in the Holy Spirit but nothing happened that I was aware of. Why? Because I was not willing, I didn't want to be free, I was afraid to be free. I had an interesting, worthwhile job in Christian service, and I was happy and busy in it. If I allowed the Holy Spirit to set me free, what on earth might God want me to do? I might upset my committee – now I must say the members of my committee were wonderful people; I was on very good terms with them; I had a splendid relationship with them, and I wanted to keep it that way! I had lots of opportunities of speaking at church services on the missionary work of our church. Would this make the Ministers afraid to let me into their pulpits, and so on and so on! For four miserable years I resisted every attempt of the Holy Spirit to set me free.

I have a very strong defence mechanism, and it very soon went into action. Every objection anyone has ever voiced to this experience I had too. I majored on tongues! I read every book on the subject, I read and re-read 1 Corinthians 12–14. Then one day someone said to me, 'Forget about tongues. Put it right out of your mind for a bit.' Well, I did just that, but then I began to ask another question: 'Is this sound?' 'Sound' is a very important word in Northern Ireland. I was specially disturbed when I heard of Roman Catholics being involved in this movement. Now, this was strange, for I was never prejudiced. My best friend is a Roman Catholic, and I had real Christian fellowship with her, but I was disturbed about this development, especially as priests and nuns were involved. I got some comfort when a Minister assured me this was not for him, nor for me, for he and I were 'not the type' – we were too well-balanced!

But God is faithful. The subject came up time and time again. I could not get away from this message. To cut a long story short at last I yielded.

'My chains fell off, my heart was free.'

Then I wondered why on earth I had wasted four precious years. 'Where the Spirit of the Lord is, there is liberty, emancipation from bondage, freedom.'

This is absolutely tremendous.

But it didn't end there. I was learning a new lesson. My college Principal used to say it is easier to get Satan out of your heart than your grandfather out of your bones! It is easier to get out of prison than to get the prison out of you! It is not easy to adjust to freedom after a long time. I had a mental picture of a prisoner, free but with bits of chains on his ankles and wrists. He was free but hampered and could not move quickly. God was saying to me, 'You have release and I can remove the last vestige of captivity when you allow me.' At a Charismatic Summer School in Swanwick my release was completed. During a time of 'worship in the Spirit' I found myself singing in tongues. At the same time I lost a wrong reserve and found myself free to lift my hands in prayer and praise as prompted by the Holy Spirit. Now I know what St Paul meant when he exhorts us: 'It is for freedom that Christ has set us free. Stand firm, then, and do not let yourselves be burdened again by a yoke of slavery' (Gal. 5:1).

Some months after arriving in Rostrevor I was invited to speak at a weekend meeting in Benburb Priory near Armagh. I remember my immediate inclination was to decline the invitation. It was a cold and wintry time of the year and we were exhausted by our efforts in restoring the house. But God's timing is perfect and I am glad I decided to go. An eager and expectant group of people had assembled and they wanted me to speak about personal renewal in the Holy Spirit. Obviously this was a time prepared by God. One of those attending that weekend conference was Father Pat Collins, a Vincentian priest who was born in Dublin. Since that evening when I first met Pat we have become close friends and have often ministered together in many parts of Ireland. Someone has said that the longest journey to travel is from the head to the heart. That may be especially true of those of us who have had academic, theological and philosophical training. Pat had just returned from further study in Rome. Intellectually nourished, he felt spiritually hungry and thirsty. He recalls that evening in Benburb.

After my ordination in 1971, I knew a lot about Christ, but I didn't know him in a personal way. To me he often seemed distant and unreal. I found it hard to pray or read the Scriptures with fervour. I wasn't happy with the situation. I began to have a great desire for an outpouring of the Holy Spirit and a spiritual awakening in my life. For nearly two years I prayed for this grace. Eventually divine providence led me to an ecumenical weekend in Northern Ireland. I heard Cecil Kerr preaching about Jesus as the source of our peace. He spoke with extraordinary eloquence and conviction. His Spirit-filled words sent shivers down my spine and brought tears to my eyes. I wanted to know the Lord in the way that this man did. I approached him and told him of my desire. We talked a little. Then he read the following words of St Paul:

I pray that Christ will make his home in your hearts through faith. I pray that you have your roots and foundation in love, so that you, together with all God's people, may have the power to understand how broad and long, how high and deep, is Christ's love – although it can never be fully known – and so be filled with the very nature of God. (Eph. 3:17–20) Good News Bible).

These verses jumped alive off the page into my heart. They expressed exactly what I longed for at that point in my life. It was than that Cecil placed his hands on my head and prayed. Something happened. The Spirit fell upon me. I was flooded with a sense of God's love. Jesus became intensely real. It was as if he had walked through the walls of my body to live within me. From that moment on he was my most intimate friend, my second self. I could identify with the words of poet Tadhg Gaelach O Suilleabhain:

> The light in my heart, O Saviour, is thy heart,
> The wealth of my heart, Thy heart poured out for me.
> Seeing that Thy heart, Love, filled with love for me
> Leave Thy heart in keeping, hooded in mine.

Local church renewal

Sadly in many parts of the Church the Holy Spirit seems to be the forgotten person of the Trinity. I remember speaking to a prominent leader of the Dutch Reformed Church in South Africa. We were discussing the need for the Church to be radically renewed in the power of the Holy Spirit.

As we reflected together he said to me, 'You know in our Church we are so secure in our theology and institutional life we hardly need Jesus.'

How easy it is to run the Church on 'man power' instead of 'God power'. It is significant that when St John the Divine wrote his letters to the seven churches of Asia at the end of the first century he reminded each one of them 'to hear what the Spirit is saying to the churches'.

Speaking at the Assembly of the World Council of Churches in Uppsala, Sweden in 1968 Metropolitan Ignatias of Latakia made this statement:

> Without the Holy Spirit,
> God is far away,
> Christ stays in the past,
> The Gospel is a dead letter,

The Church is simply an organisation,
Authority a matter of domination,
Mission a matter of propaganda,
The Liturgy no more than an evocation,
Christian living a slave morality.

But in the Holy Spirit:
The cosmos is resurrected and groans with
The birth pangs of the Kingdom,
The Risen Christ is there,
The Gospel is the Power of Life,
The Church shows forth the life of the Trinity,
Authority is a liberating service,
Mission is a Pentecost,
The liturgy is both memorial and anticipation,
Human action is deified.[5]

Before Pentecost Jesus made this astounding promise to his disciples:

I tell you the truth, anyone who has faith in me will do what I have been doing. He will do even greater things than these, because I am going to the Father. And I will do whatever you ask in my name, so that the Son may bring glory to the Father. You may ask me for anything in my name, and I will do it. (John 14:12–14)

After Pentecost those men and women proved those words true. In the name of Jesus and through the power of his Spirit working in them they raised the dead, healed the sick and preached the Good News of Jesus wherever they went, even though it cost them suffering, persecution, imprisonment and even death. With Jesus the Kingdom of God has come in power. Believers in Jesus are heirs of that Kingdom. The same Holy Spirit who was with the apostles is in the Church and with his people now, if only we will allow him to do his work in his way. How poignant are the comments in the Gospel story where, even in the ministry of Jesus, in his home town 'he did not do many miracles there because of their lack of faith' (Matt. 13:58). Unbelief and unwillingness to move with God are major obstacles to the work he wants to do in every local church. The comment, 'we've never done it this way before', bondage to precedent and fear of change are real barriers to progress.

Working alongside ministers and priests in Ireland over the past fifteen years we have witnessed the courage often required to lead local churches forward in renewal. Vested interests of all kinds emerge. Centuries-old traditions are difficult to dislodge. Fear of change looms very large, but there can be no renewal, either in our personal lives or in the Church without change. Some people who regard their local church as dead and through desperation or sheer impatience are tempted to move somewhere else, we encourage to look again at the vision of Ezekiel. Led by the spirit into a valley of dry bones Ezekiel is asked:

'Can these bones live?' I said, 'O Sovereign Lord, you alone know.' Then he said to me, 'Prophesy to these bones and say to them, "Dry bones, hear the word of the Lord! This is what the Sovereign Lord says to these bones: I will make breath enter you, and you will come to life. I will attach tendons to you and make flesh come upon you and cover you with skin; I will put breath in you, and you will come to life. Then you will know that I am the Lord" ' . . . So I prophesied as he commanded me, and breath entered them; they came to life and stood up on their feet – a vast army. (Ezek. 37:3–6,10)

To those who may be tempted to despair and pass a sentence of death I often say, 'Stay around, have faith and pray. It is more fun to raise the dead than to heal the sick.'

God is giving fresh vision to many leaders and we rejoice to have had a share with them in seeing what he can do when they are willing to take a risk in response to his call. In a wide variety of churches in towns and cities and in the country north and south we have been privileged to see the fresh wind of the Spirit blowing, bringing new life and vitality to apparently moribund parishes and congregations, often through renewal events in which we are invited to participate.

We like to make preparations well in advance, calling the leaders together to pray about the needs of the area and to endeavour to catch the vision of what God is wanting to do.

Prayer is a vital ingredient. We invite those in the congregation to commit themselves to prayer, and through our network of prayer partners the whole venture is covered in prayer. Frequently there may be very few in a congregation who come together to pray, and even when they do they may be suffering from considerable discouragement. In a country parish in the north of Ireland where the rector invited us to lead a week of renewal there was only one man who met him to pray for the festival of faith. They prayed faithfully against all discouragement and opposition.

Having read Jackie Pullinger's book, *Chasing the Dragon*, where she recounts the remarkable miracle which God did among the drug addicts in Hong Kong, Eric McGirr the rector decided to follow Jackie's example by praying in tongues for half an hour every day. You can hardly imagine the impact of that week in the parish. Several people were healed of potentially serious illnesses. Some whose hearts had been bound in hatred and bitterness found deliverance. Many came to personal faith in Christ and were baptised in the Holy Spirit. Where before the festival there were two praying, afterwards more than forty men and women, young and old, were meeting, hungry to pray and grow in their faith and to study God's word. The influence for good was not only felt in the locality but many of them carried their witness further afield. One young married man who is a skilled builder volunteered, with the full support of his wife, to join a work party to do essential repairs to a hospital in Uganda.

In another country parish in the south, where John Neill the rector with a few faithful people had prayerfully prepared, others were sceptical and some rather hostile.

Prayer was answered in spite of the opposition and many were transformed in the experience of meeting the Lord in a new way. One young woman's life was radically changed by that weekend. Gladys Swanton went on to take a degree in Biblical Studies at Trinity College, Dublin. For six years she has been a most valuable member of the community at the Christian Renewal Centre where she has shared her gifts in many similar campaigns since. Writing after the weekend John, the rector, explained something of the impact of what God had been doing. In their first weekly meeting after the renewal weekend he said:

> The Lord was telling us very strongly that we had to learn the meaning of service. Then the meeting was disturbed by a crash in the porch. I went forward and found a young man there at the point of collapse and despair, who also had had rather a lot to drink. I brought him into another room and he wanted to talk about some trivial matter. I said to him after a few moments that his problem was of no great importance, but what did matter was what Jesus meant to him. Whereupon he broke down and said that he had lost what was most dear to him, the faith that he had received as a child with the London City Mission. I suggested that this was a matter for prayer, and we would if he liked join ten other people who were praying to Jesus in another room. He came in and without any warning the group welcomed him, accepted him, even slightly the worse for drink, and ministered to the very needs that he had laid bare privately to me. He ended up praying himself, and thanking the Lord that somebody still loved him, and learning more of the love of the Lord. This to me was the greatest sign I have ever seen in the parish, not of individual ministry, but of the church alive in the power of the Spirit.

Happily many such events are open to all denominations to attend. We are glad when local churches find it possible to co-operate in a particular area and give expression to their unity in the body of Christ. On many occasions we have witnessed the powerful effect of a team of Christians, both Roman Catholic and Protestant, sharing the ministry together. The strength of working as a team is obvious too. Various gifts and talents are shared and the mutual support in prayer and ministry is invaluable. Personal witness both in public and in the homes of the people is also a most important feature.

Change

Fire, water and wind are symbols frequently used in Scripture for the working of the Holy Spirit. He comes as the fire to burn up in us and in the Church all that is unworthy and a hindrance to his purpose. God will never deny in the present what he has done in the past. Neither will he take responsibility for what he never put there in the first place. 'Every plant that my heavenly Father has not planted will be pulled up by the roots' (Matt. 15:13) were the words addressed by Jesus to the conceited Pharisees bound by their man-made traditions.

Water symbolises the cleansing of God's Holy Spirit, renewing, refreshing and making real for us those elements of faith and worship that endure. When we open the sails of our faith to the fresh wind of the Holy Spirit then we will move purposefully in the path that God has charted for his Church, no longer depending only on precedent to guide us.

Local churches that have opened to this work of God are experiencing a spring time. Such growth is exciting but carries with it all the problems and challenges presented by rapid growth. There is perfect order in a graveyard but when the dry bones come together and manifest life then we know how much we need God to direct that growth. In the restored 'charismata', gifts of the Holy Spirit, we are learning again how the Church builds itself up in love and is equipped in power to change the world. These gifts are not toys but tools, given by God to do his work in his way in his world. Careful study of the Scriptures is needed to uncover these essential gifts, dusting off the neglect of generations and recovering what God has given, without recall, to his Church. Long neglected passages of Scripture such as 1 Corinthians 11 to 14, Romans 12 and Ephesians 4 yield treasures of inestimable worth in understanding the purpose of Christ for his Church. Through the gifts of the Holy Spirit his power is manifest; through the fruit of the Holy Spirit his life is revealed; through the ministries of the ascended Christ, Apostle, Prophet, Pastor, Teacher and Evangelist, his body is governed and sanctified.

Ministering to the ministers

Clergy and leaders in the Church are a special concern for us in our ministry at the Christian Renewal Centre. With the continuing violence and all its terrible consequences those in leadership need every encouragement in the work that God has called them to do.

Many come for private retreat, availing themselves of the opportunity to 'come aside and rest awhile'. Others come for times of private prayer and reflection when major decisions have to be made. One such was Brian Herd, who with his wife Norma had returned from many years of missionary work in Uganda. Shortly after the Centre opened he came to pray about the invitation he had received from the diocese of Karamoja to return there as bishop. He posted his acceptance from Rostrevor and he and Norma made a significant contribution to Uganda at a critical time in its history, finally escaping under Idi Amin's threat of death.

Some leaders will come specifically for prayer counselling or ministry. All churches face the very real question – who pastors the pastor? We welcome those who come for whatever reason, and, if they wish, they are free to join with the community in our daily times of prayer.

Since the beginning of the Centre we have set aside special times when we invite clergy from all denominations to come together. Wives of clergy too and lay leaders are welcome. We always have a problem in announcing these special events.

In the days of renewal for leaders we begin with an informal greeting over a cup of coffee, giving people the opportunity to meet each other. After a time of praise and worship, when all are encouraged to participate, there follows an address from a visiting guest speaker or a member of the community. After lunch we always have a time of ministry with prayer for one another. These 'Emmaus times' are especially appreciated by people. During these days of renewal and clergy conferences many have experienced the release of the Holy Spirit or have known God's healing in their bodies. Deep friendships have been formed and fellowship built which has led to some fruitful areas of shared ministry.

Dr Michael Kennedy is rector of a parish on the South Armagh border, an area notorious for some of the worst violence of the past years. He has had to minister to families bereaved in some horrendous terrorist atrocities. A regular visitor to the Centre, with colleagues from that area, he reflects on what the fellowship at the Centre has meant to him over the years:

My first contact with the Christian Renewal Centre was in the autumn of 1978 when I attended (with some others) a Monday night prayer meeting in the Presbyterian Church Hall in Rostrevor and found a large number of lay people, both Roman Catholic and Protestant, worshipping the Lord together in a most spontaneous manner. As a lifelong ecumenist I was deeply impressed to see actually happening something that one had imagined only to be possible in the distant future, even if then! I was struck by the freedom and the evident joy of the participants, and by the way in which the Scriptures were being used to convey a message which was of direct relevance and applicable to the circumstances of people's lives. Following this I began to attend monthly days of renewal for clergy and other church workers, and, slightly later, special days of intercession for peace and reconciliation in Ireland where one was able to witness the divisions being overcome in front of one's eyes. I can remember, even from those early days, a former IRA woman activist and a member of the RUC praying out loud for each other in front of all present; and the testimony of a former member of the (Protestant) Ulster Defence Association who had once gone about with a gun in his pocket and murderous hatred in his heart, and who now sought to have friendship in Christ with some of the very people he had once wanted to kill. The message of spiritual renewal was one that was very applicable to me personally; and it was not long before another rector from Armagh diocese and I sought ministry from Cecil Kerr for spiritual renewal in our own lives. This did mark the beginning of a new stage in my own ministry.

I can see the effect of the renewal ministry in Rostrevor in several ways that have involved me personally. One of these was in the coming into being of a clergy prayer group for renewal in Armagh diocese (which now includes several readers and other lay workers), called 'Oasis'. Initially one other clergyman and I met monthly for prayer and praise, and continued for the first eighteen months without any addition to our number. Then the Lord seemed to add the right people at the right time, and a fellowship developed which still continues and is a source of help and strength to all its members, who are able to share their faith together at a level which is not usually possible even for clergy. Secondly, I have been involved in leadership of an ecumenical prayer group whose membership is Roman Catholic and Church of Ireland, several from the troubled area of South Armagh. The reconciling power of the love of Christ is very evident at its meetings. Once, at a time when there was very great tension in the community, we met in a farmhouse belonging to one of the members only a few yards from the political border between Northern Ireland and the Irish Republic. As we prayed and praised God together and shared the Scriptures we experienced a complete feeling of unity in Christ in the power of his Spirit. Thirdly, it has been possible to have a small prayer meeting for renewal in my own parish (Lisnadill and Kildarton) although not all one's parishioners are receptive to spiritual renewal. I think it should be said on the basis of experience of the past twelve years that renewal does not automatically mean 'success' in one's ministry. There have been times when we have been looking for a Pentecost and have been given instead a cross to carry, and there can be a deep-seated resistance to the wind of the Spirit which blows where it wills. On the other hand, for those who stay open to the Spirit and try to respond to his prompting there is a real blessing. There is no doubt that the obedience and faith of those who set up the Rostrevor community has led in all sorts of ways towards changed attitudes in the Church and indeed in the province at large.

Jeremy Mould is a young man in training for the ministry, who received his vocation through a day of renewal at the Centre. He explains:

I came to Belfast from England in 1985 to work as a Careforce volunteer in a hostel for ex-offenders on the Antrim Road. I found it very hard going, especially in regard to Christian fellowship. My main source of fellowship was in fact the Wednesday morning Bible Study led by Sister Carmel at the Lamb of God Community in Duncairn Gardens in North Belfast, a community with close links to Rostrevor and involved in similar work. I think it was my mother who encouraged me to go to the Christian Renewal Centre in Rostrevor. It was a clergy day and the main speaker was the Revd. Willi Stewart, a young minister and then with his wife Ruth a member of the community at the Centre. Not knowing who he was, and the very thought of becoming a minister never entering my head, I thought, 'I would like to do what he does.' That week I was praying and fasting to find out exactly what God wanted me to do. I mean, exactly, because I had already applied to do a social work course at university. I went to bed having forgotten that I had no clearer idea and heard a still small voice say: 'Be my servant in my church in Ireland.' This was the funniest thing I had heard in my life. The last two things

I wanted to do was to become a minister and in Ireland! The Renewal Centre is in many ways a light in Ireland that gives me hope and has encouraged and uplifted me.

We rejoice in the many young people who have responded to the call of Christ to serve him in full-time ministry through the witness of the Centre. Some are now working very effectively for the Kingdom of God in difficult and challenging places throughout the world. Tom Leyden is a priest of the Divine Word Missionaries whom we have welcomed as a brother in Christ, and who by his presence has enriched our lives. He is involved in the training and formation of men for ministry overseas. Over a number of years he has come with a group of students to share in the life and witness of the community:

> For me Rostrevor is a place of the Resurrection, a true experience of living unity in diversity. I believe it is a great blessing and a deep healing for me and I hope and pray that it is a very meaningful moment in the lives of the young men who travel with me each year.
>
> Hope and vision are fundamental dimensions to life. While these are almost intangible, they are real and are visible when we meet them. Each time I return I enter a place of vision and hope and my own spirit is refreshed. It is simply the people who are there who give witness to that hope and reveal the vision. It is likewise the experience of community that comes through. As an individual who lives in community, I greatly value such a graced way of life but I'm also acutely conscious of the challenge it offers.
>
> It is my bounty that in Rostrevor I live among people who have taken our fragmented island to their hearts. To willingly take on such intercessory involvement is a sign of deep sincere love. It is also, because of the implications of love, a risky business.
>
> Rostrevor challenges me to move on and it is a constant invitation to me to change.

8

RECONCILIATION

Peacemakers who sow in peace raise a harvest of right-eousness. (Jas 3:18)

Reconciliation is the grace which outlasts the anger. (A black South African Christian)

'If the characteristic mark of a healthy Christianity be to unite its members by a bond of fraternity and love, there is no country in the world in which Christianity has more completely failed than in Ireland.'[1] That humiliating observation was made by the historian Leckey more than a hundred years ago. Many events since then, not least the awful conflict of these past years, have proved considerable truth in his comment.

Ireland, once known as 'the island of saints and scholars', has become a dark blot on the map of the Christian world and a real stumbling block to those who would seek to share the basic message of Christianity in an unbelieving world. Some time ago a friend told me about a large poster he saw prominently displayed in the centre of Moscow. Photographs of street violence in Northern Ireland, so familiar in the world's media, were enlarged; over the pictures were the words 'Northern Ireland' and beneath was written in large letters, 'See how these Christians love one another!'

Over the past fifteen years I have been invited to minister and speak in many parts of the world. Almost invariably I am asked to try and explain how a nation that professes so much allegiance to Christianity is so torn asunder by strife, hatred and violence. The question is a particularly painful one in countries where the Good News was first preached by Irish missionaries. Writing about the same time as Leckey, an equally devastating observation was made by the famous London preacher C. H. Spurgeon:

> Of all the stories of the nations the story of Ireland must be the hardest to tell. All the tragedies are comical and all the comedies are tragical. The road through Irish history is made up of lanes which wind about, and never come to an end till they twist into pathways that never begin. When a man conquers he becomes a victim and when he is beaten he goes on beating someone else. Ireland has never been at peace except during a great war and it has never been united except in the agreement to divide and upon that it was never of one mind.[2]

It is easy to see why many people despair of finding a peaceful way forward. Nor is it surprising when observers so often equate Northern Ireland with Lebanon and Belfast with Beirut, seeing little hope of finding solutions for ancient animosities, supported by modern methods of guerrilla warfare. Thousands of books and pamphlets have been written analysing the present situation of conflict in Ireland. Countless reports have been debated. Endless agreements have been proposed. Some of the best brains have devoted dedicated skills and energies towards finding solutions. All of these efforts are important but people are left asking the question, 'Are things really improving?' During more than twenty years of the violence almost three thousand people have been killed, many more maimed and injured. In human terms the tragedy is impossible to quantify. Long ago the vocabulary for the language of condemnation has been exhausted, with very many people being innocent victims of man's inhumanity to man.

Yet there is hope if the people of Ireland return to Christ in true repentance, receiving from him the power to love and forgive. Only he can heal us of the attitudes which we have carried over from past centuries of hatred and bitterness. Political solutions are important and we should constantly pray for and encourage those who endeavour to find such ways forward. But if we had the perfect solution tomorrow we would still be left with the basic problem. For the heart of the problem is the problem of the human heart. People's hearts need to be changed. Many are working for a new Ireland. But a new Ireland can only be created with new Irishmen and Irishwomen and only God can make us new in the reconciling love of Christ through the power of the Holy Spirit. Significantly, after practising the teaching of Marx, it was the revolutionary leader Che Guevara who wrote before his death, 'No matter how much you change society, no matter how much you restructure it, unless you create a new man, it all ends up in greed, lust and ambition.'

Only when we come together to the cross of Christ will we really understand the true nature of our conflict and find the way to overcome it. Through the perfect sacrifice of Christ on the cross of Calvary and through his resurrection God has provided for all time the way to resolve conflict, overcoming hatred with love and meeting violence with forgiveness. To many such a suggestion will seem naïve. They will rightly point out, 'But isn't the problem caused in large measure by religion?' Precisely. Even a casual reading of the Gospels will reveal that Jesus was hounded to an unjust death by corrupt religious prejudice combined with scheming political methods. Ostensibly the crucifixion of Christ was a victory for 'religion' on the one hand and for 'law and order' on the other. Throughout history the collusion between religion and politics has often provided a highly destructive mixture. Years ago Dr G. B. Newe, a Roman Catholic layman who made a significant contribution to reconciliation in Northern Ireland, commented, 'We have secularised our Christianity and sacrilised our politics.' The devil, as a fallen angel, is an expert in religious systems. He is a past master in the art of insinuating his demonic viruses into the very heart of religious structures.

A kingdom not of this world

The subtle interweaving of religion and politics which for many centuries had been a feature of Irish life was given added impetus at the beginning of the twentieth century. Indeed it can be said that a particularly virile poison was introduced which has produced so much of the cancer of hatred and bloodshed that has characterised this century of Irish history. In the period between 1912 and 1914 the British government proceeded to legislate for Home Rule for Ireland. The move struck desperate fear into the hearts of most of those of the Unionist and Protestant persuasion especially in the north of Ireland. An active campaign of opposition to Home Rule was mounted, supported in large measure by the main Protestant churches. There were those who expressed misgivings, suggesting that it was blasphemous to claim that 'God was on our side'. Such arguments were swept aside by the fears of Protestants that in Ireland 'Home Rule would mean Rome Rule'.

Professor Finlay Holmes recounts: 'On Easter Tuesday 1912, 100,000 men paraded at Balmoral on the outskirts of Belfast in an impressive show of strength which began with a religious service led by the Church of Ireland Primate and the Moderator of the General Assembly.'[3] In July 1913 the influential Presbyterian weekly newspaper, commenting on 12 July demonstration by Orangemen that year, wrote:

How could men die better than facing the forces of Rome for the faith and liberty of their fathers, for the life and liberty of their children. There may be some who think this wanton and wicked. We would say that anything else is weak, cowardly and traitorous. We hope that history will never have to level these charges at the people of this generation who represent such a noble ancestry.[4]

Professor Holmes goes on to record:

> The climax and supreme demonstration of the Ulster Prot-
> estants' determination to resist home rule was the signing
> of the covenant on 28 September 1912, known as Ulster
> day. The text of the covenant was largely the work of the
> Presbyterian ruling elder Thomas Sinclair, and recalled the
> historic Scottish covenants which occupied a hallowed place
> in Presbyterian memories and imaginations . . . It pledged
> its signatories:
>
>> humbly relying on the God whom our fathers con-
>> fidently trusted . . . to stand by one another in
>> defending for ourselves and for our children our
>> cherished position of equal citizenship in the United
>> Kingdom, and in using all means which may be found
>> necessary to defeat the present conspiracy to set up a
>> home rule parliament in Ireland.
>
> Preacher after preacher at services throughout the province
> insisted that it was a religious, rather than a political,
> occasion. They emphasised that they bore no enmity
> towards their Roman Catholic fellow countrymen but they
> opposed any establishment of a Roman Catholic ascend-
> ancy in Ireland.[5]

'The issue,' continued Holmes, 'might be regarded as religious but its implications were clearly political. It was
becoming clear, also that if they could not stop home rule for
Ireland, the Ulstermen would divide the country. 237,368
men signed the covenant and 234,046 women a parallel
document.' To support their threat of armed resistance,
if it proved necessary, the Ulster Volunteer Force was
formed and thousands of weapons were illegally smug-
gled from Germany and secretly distributed throughout
the country. International events were to overrule. In
1914 Britain was at war with Germany and thousands
of those Ulster Volunteers were to die in battle, shot by
weapons similar to those they had stored in their homes
back in Ireland.

While the religious and political web was being woven in the north a similar process was taking place in the Nationalist community. Ancient Irish mythology was being mingled with Christian symbolism to produce a potent mixture of 'religious' nationalism which, like its Unionist counterpart, claimed a total allegiance from its loyal subjects.

Patrick Pearse, with others, was a leader of the rebellion of 1916 known as the Easter rising. Pearse, a schoolteacher, repeatedly called the nationalist people to armed resistance against the British colonial power as others had done before him. To that he added a more sinister dimension urging that a blood sacrifice was needed to rejuvenate the land of Ireland.

'The canon of Irish history,' a most revealing study of this development and the part played by Pearse and his colleagues, was written in 1966 by Francis Shaw, a Jesuit scholar and Professor of Early and Medieval Irish at University College, Dublin from 1941 until his death in 1970. It is significant that Professor Shaw wrote the article in 1966, when the fiftieth anniversary of the Easter rising was widely commemorated. The fact that it was not published until 1972 is partly explained in his introduction:

One of the commonest occupations in the Ireland of today is the plying of sleeping dogs with tranquillisers. In this study of the Easter Rising in relation to Irish history an accepted view is challenged, a canon of history which has come into being, has been carefully fostered and was newly consecrated in the massive State-inspired and State-assisted Commemoration in 1966. The final seal on the Easter Rising is to be seen today on the walls of our schools in which the proclamation of Easter Monday is presented as the charter of our freedom and of our State.[6]

In a careful examination of Pearse's poems, plays, and speeches, Shaw exposes his notions of the 'sanctity of nationalism, especially of Irish nationalism' and 'the sacredness of warfare and blood-shedding':

> The idea that dedication to one's country is a good thing, a Christian duty is a commonplace, but Pearse introduced a new idea, a startling one: the idea that patriotism and holiness are the same, that they are convertible concepts. This idea is most unambiguously expressed by Pearse in the oration at the grave of Tone in Bodenstown in 1913:

>> We have come to the holiest place in Ireland; holier to us even than the place where Patrick sleeps in Down. Patrick brought us life, but this man died for us . . . He was the greatest of Irish Nationalists; I believe he was the greatest of Irishmen. And if I am right in this I am right in saying that we stand in the holiest place in Ireland, for it must be that the holiest sod of a nation's soil is the sod where the greatest of her dead lies buried.

There is no ambiguity here; nationalism and holiness are identical.

Pearse's solemn and alarming words at Bodenstown were not due to oratorical exaggeration. We find the same sentiment again and again in his writings.

But it is even more disturbing to find that consistently and deliberately and without reservation Pearse equates the patriot and the patriot-people with Christ. I accept without question the sincerity and the subjective reverence of Pearse in this matter, but one has to say that objectively this equation of the patriot with Christ is in conflict with the whole Christian tradition and, indeed, with the explicit teaching of Christ. The prayer of Pearse:

> O King that was born
> To set bondsmen free,
> In the coming battle,
> Help the Gael!

is aggressively unorthodox. In the sense in which Pearse uses the words they are false. Christ was not born to set bondsmen free from any chains other than those of sin. In the Judea of his day, Christ was set down in

a situation comparable to that of the Ireland of 1916.
Christ made it unmistakably plain that he was not a
national saviour, and his words to his disciples on the
day of the Ascension expressed his sorrow that those
who knew him and who loved him could continue so
long in error.[7]

Such distorted doctrines of 'religious Unionism' and 'religious Nationalism' have taken deep root in the fertile
fields of fear in Ireland. Such poisoned roots have produced
the fruits that are evident today in the conflict that yields
no rational explanation. How much those old-established
attitudes affect our land today is to be seen re-enacted
by the terrorists on both sides who are supported by
sections of the population, who are bound by the same
ancient fears.

Evidence abounds of how deep-rooted those doctrines are
in the minds of many people, expressed in the almost endless marches of commemoration and celebration of ancient
and modern confrontation. Significantly in 1981, at a time
of great tension when ten young Nationalists died on hunger
strike, Dr Ian Paisley gathered thousands of Unionist people
for a re-enactment of the Ulster Covenant of 1912. Of note
too is the fact that the most vicious 'Protestant' terrorist
organisation today is called the Ulster Volunteer Force,
with its motto 'For God and Ulster' tattooed on the arms
of its volunteers.

When the IRA initiated the hunger strike of its members
in prison 'to break the yoke of English rule', Bobby
Sands was the best known and the first of the ten to
die. As these men died their photographs were posted
up in public places, often very obviously depicted in the
way that classical paintings portray Christ's death on the
cross. One American priest at the commemoration of the
death of Bobby Sands referred to the fast of Jesus in the
wilderness and compared his death to that of Jesus on
the cross. The origin of such distortion was expounded
by someone reared in a Nationalist community in Northern

Ireland who said: 'We came very early to our politics. One learned quite literally from one's mother's knee that Christ died for the human race and Patrick Pearse for the Irish part of it.'

Such extreme sentiments are not peculiar to Ireland. Similar blind loyalties fuel conflicts in many other countries and between nations. The shame for us is that such sentiments are articulated in the name of the Christian faith.

Cahal Daly, the Roman Catholic Bishop of Connor whose diocese includes the city of Belfast, has made a courageous and consistent stand against such corruption of Christianity. I was present with him at a representative gathering of Church leaders from Britain and Ireland in 1985 when he addressed the subject 'Northern Ireland: risk and opportunity for the churches':

> Politics is indeed an arena of vital concern for the Christian. Christ's Kingdom is not of this world, but it has immediate and imperative consequences for the behaviour of men and women in this world and for the way they organise their corporate living and structure their society in this world. To find the right relationship between the Christian faith and political action, or between the Church and the State, is one of the great and recurring tasks of the Church in every age. It is a great preoccupation for the Catholic Church in Ireland, and it is a particularly delicate task for Churchmen in Northern Ireland at this time. It is for the good both of religion and of politics that the spheres of both be clearly distinguished and their relationship with one another clearly defined. It is not good for religion and it is not good for politics in Northern Ireland that to be born in the Protestant faith should automatically mean being born into a unionist or a loyalist political party, and that to be born in the Catholic faith should automatically mean being born into a nationalist or a republican political party. The term 'captivity' has been used by Dr John Morrow to describe the manner in which the Churches have become interlocked with political party allegiances. I wonder how many of us, Catholic or Protestant, have ever found ourselves instinctively feeling that a Catholic

or a Protestant has betrayed the Church or compromised
the faith when he or she chooses, if a Catholic, not to be a
nationalist, or, if a Protestant, not to be a unionist? If this
be so, have we not been dangerously confusing the things
that are Caesar's with the things that are God's?

Bishop Cahal Daly went on to outline a principle which he
has articulated in many of his public utterances:

> The Church cannot identify itself with any political com-
> munity. A Christian preacher speaks to the whole people
> of God, and not to members of the unionist party or the
> nationalist party. The Gospel is for all men, and not just for
> a politically homogeneous group. The Kingdom of God is a
> universal kingdom, not a political faction. When Churchmen
> say 'our people', they must not confine the phrase to people
> of one political persuasion. Indeed, I am convinced that our
> ministry of reconciliation summons all of us churchmen in
> our political situation in Northern Ireland to try to speak
> across the denominational divides and to address ourselves
> to both communities. We must never assert the right of one
> community without also affirming the rights of the other
> community. In matters where the faith touches on political
> and social responsibilities, we must not speak out of or to
> 'our own people' only; we must try to speak for and to the
> other community as well. To work to reconcile the two
> communities is our bounden duty as servants of God's
> universal Kingdom of justice, forgiveness, brotherhood,
> love and peace.
>
> There are many churchmen in Northern Ireland who in
> this time of turmoil and tension have spoken this prophetic
> word and have been listened to with respect by many in their
> own community and beyond it. They deserve the admiration
> and gratitude of all for their courage and integrity. They
> deserve the support of all for their Christian leadership.
> One does not exaggerate in comparing their witness to that
> of the Confessing Church in Hitler's Germany.

At the cross of Christ the demonic elements in religion and
politics are exposed for what they are. They are unmasked
or, as St Paul expresses it so succinctly, Christ 'having

disarmed the powers and authorities, he made a public spectacle of them, triumphing over them by the cross' (Col. 2:15).

The Jesus manifesto

Reconciliation is the very heart of the Gospel. Christ, long foretold by prophets as the Prince of peace, the suffering Servant, the Saviour, came in the fullness of time. He came so that 'whoever believes in him shall not perish but have eternal life'. 'For God did not send his Son into the world to condemn the world, but to save the world through him' (John 3:16,17).

Christ came into the world and lived among men in a land not unlike what we have just described. He lived among people who were subject to the fears and prejudices that are familiar features of the Irish landscape today. The little land of Israel, no stranger to conflict in its long history, was subject to the all-embracing power of the Roman Empire. Herod, the despot and puppet king, ruled in Rome's name. Only months after the birth of Jesus, Mary his mother and Joseph had to flee as refugees to Egypt to escape the massacre of children which Herod had commanded to stifle the paranoid fear he had over the news of 'a king being born'. Returning to Nazareth Jesus shared the life of humble villagers, making a daily living in the carpenter's shop, and felt the pain of a politically oppressed people. As a boy and a young man growing up in Nazareth he was familiar with the suffering caused by the Roman overlords and their Jewish collaborators.

Equally he was fully aware of the fierce and violent nationalism that gripped the hearts of many of his contemporaries. Some of them no doubt joined the terrorist guerrilla fighters of the Zealot movement, men who took up arms and used every opportunity to attack the hated oppressor Rome. They persisted with zealous commitment although they had little hope of victory over the superior might of the

Roman army. There was no press or television to cover the news of the atrocities. An even more sinister visual reminder was provided. Along the public roads the bodies of guerrilla fighters were crucified by Roman soldiers and left for days as a grim warning to others who would try the same thing on.

Sharing the pain of those among whom he lived, Jesus nourished in his heart the vision of justice, peace and salvation which he had come to bring to our broken, hurting world. His purpose was to reveal the love that was in his Father's heart, a love that is without distinction or discrimination.

In his three years of public ministry Jesus took every opportunity not only to speak about that unconditional love but to demonstrate it in all his deeds. In the first recorded public address in the synagogue at Nazareth, his home town, he deliberately announced the manifesto for his Kingdom, reading the words written about him 700 years before by Isaiah the prophet: 'The Spirit of the Lord is on me, because he has anointed me to preach good news to the poor. He has sent me to proclaim freedom for the prisoners and recovery of sight for the blind, to release the oppressed, to proclaim the year of the Lord's favour' (Luke 4:18–19). St Luke reports that 'all spoke well of him and were amazed at the gracious words that came from his lips'.

Then he had the audacity to use two illustrations from Jewish history when God had obviously showed mercy and love towards people of other races than the Jews. He mentioned a woman from Sidon, a despised Gentile region, and Naaman the Syrian army officer, a long time enemy of Israel. A race riot broke out and the people in the synagogue who had come in as respectable citizens rushed for Jesus as an angry mob. He had touched the nerve of their deep-seated religious and political prejudice and they tried to lynch him.

All the people in the synagogue were furious when they heard this. They got up, drove him out of town, and took

him to the brow of the hill on which the town was built,
in order to throw him down the cliff. But he walked right
through the crowd and went on his way. (Luke 4:28–30)

Such a public declaration was a signal for what was to
follow as Jesus revealed God's love for all men and his
desire that all should come into his Kingdom. The men
who responded to his call to follow him could hardly have
known what that would entail. Fulfilling Christ's manifesto
in the hard religious and political soil of Israel would be no
easy work. The group of men he chose to share the task
were themselves to be a symbol of the reconciliation he had
come to proclaim. We can imagine how difficult it must have
been to weld together such a diverse band of individuals;
men with such different personalities and backgrounds, and
varied hopes and aspirations. Simon the Zealot, a former
guerrilla fighter, working alongside Matthew the tax collec-
tor, the 'traitor' who had collaborated with 'the enemy' by
collecting taxes for them. James and John nicknamed ap-
propriately the 'sons of thunder', fervent Nationalists. Peter
the blustering man of action who carried his dagger under
his cloak and even used it in a heated moment of danger.
    To such men Jesus imparted a message that would change
the world and turn upside down their long cherished sectarian attitudes and lesser loyalties. In the synagogue of
Nazareth Jesus had issued his manifesto. On the mountain
above the Lake of Galilee for all to hear he issued his
mandate in the Beatitudes:

> Blessed are you who are poor,
>   for yours is the kingdom of God.
> Blessed are you who hunger now,
>   for you will be satisfied.
> Blessed are you who weep now,
>   for you will laugh.
> Blessed are you when men hate you,
>   when they exclude you and insult you
>   and reject your name as evil,
>   because of the Son of Man.

Rejoice in that day and leap for joy, because great is your reward in heaven. For that is how their fathers treated the prophets.

> But woe to you who are rich,
>   for you have already
>   received your comfort.
> Woe to you who are well fed now,
>   for you will go hungry.
> Woe to you who laugh now,
>   for you will mourn and weep.
> Woe to you when all men speak well of you,
>   for that is how their fathers treated
>   the false prophets. (Luke 6:20–26).

Those words may have seemed strangely impossible but what was to follow must have appeared utterly impracticable. Jesus said, 'But I tell you who hear me: Love your enemies, do good to those who hate you, bless those who curse you, pray for those who ill-treat you' (Luke 6:27–28).

Agape was a new word coined in the Greek language to describe the kind of love that Jesus was talking about. 'It is a gracious, determined, and active interest in the true welfare of others, which is not deterred even by hatred, cursing, and abuse, not limited by calculation of deserts or results, based solely on the nature of God.'[8] In his commentary on St Luke's Gospel at this point Professor G. B. Caird explains:

Jesus did not tell his disciples to fall in love with their enemies or to feel for them as they felt for their families or friends. The men who were bidden to love their enemies were living in enemy-occupied territory, where resentment was natural and provocation frequent. They were not just to submit to aggression, but to rob it of its sting by voluntarily going beyond its demands. To those who believe in standing up for their individual or national rights this teaching has always seemed idealistic, if not actually immoral. But those who are concerned with the victory of the kingdom of God over the kingdom of Satan can see that it is the only realism. He who retaliates thinks that he is manfully resisting aggression; in fact, he is making an unconditional surrender to evil. Where before there was one under the control of evil, now there are two. Evil propagates by contagion. It can be contained and defeated only when hatred, insult and injury are absorbed and neutralized by love.[9]

Jesus said: 'By this all men will know that you are my disciples, if you love one another' (John 13:35). For all time and in all circumstances that is the distinguishing mark of the followers of Christ. He did not say 'People will know you are my disciples by the wonderful books you write; by the marvellous buildings you erect in my name; by the beauty of your liturgy or the soundness of your doctrines and wealth of your teaching.' Important as all these are it is by his agape, love shining through us, that the world will recognise Jesus. The greatest need in Ireland and indeed throughout the world is for Christians not just to talk about love but to show it. In the Church we spend so much time and energy on secondary things and neglect what is primary in the Lord's heart – allowing his love to be reflected through us in all his simplicity, truth and power. With the authority of her own example, Mother Teresa of Calcutta gave this resounding challenge when she spoke to six thousand priests from a hundred countries in Rome in 1984: 'Give the world Jesus. Teach us how to love Jesus. Teach us how to pray. Teach us how to adore Jesus.'

Communities of the new commandment

An urgent need in our land is to create what our good friend the Revd Ken Newell has called 'communities of the new commandment'. Open places, where people will be able to meet each other in an atmosphere of prayer in the presence of Jesus the Reconciler. Sadly some of our church buildings over the years have become fortresses that separate us from each other rather than places of meeting and sharing the love that Jesus gives. This was illustrated for me in 1980. At a time of great tension in late 1980 the leaders of the four main churches in Ireland gave a clear lead in calling people together for a week of prayer at the beginning of 1981. They asked that, where possible, people from many different traditions should come together in each other's churches. I remember asking one of the Church leaders what they were going to do to initiate the week of prayer. He said: 'we are finding it difficult to agree on a suitably neutral venue.' And I thought how sad it is that as Christian people we have spent millions of pounds on lovely church buildings and instead of being houses of prayer for all, they are tribal shrines where others may not feel or be made welcome.

I remember during our first few weeks in the Centre as we were working to restore the building some people called and we were showing them around. As they saw us taking down the dividing walls that had been erected to create self-contained flats one of the visitors suddenly exclaimed, 'Don't you see the parable in what you are doing. In the physical you are doing what God has called you to do in the spiritual; to remove the walls that were not there in the first place!'

Because the Centre is literally the Lord's house, open to all and not belonging to a particular denomination, people feel it less threatening than going into the unfamiliar church building of another denomination. Even so the fears on coming through the door are real, reflecting the conditioning process of centuries of 'religious apartheid' that has been practised in our land. People from the Protestant community often find it hard to come because they perceive us as 'Catholic' and equally some Catholic people perceive the place as 'Protestant'.

I remember a Roman Catholic priest arriving in the Centre. He was suffering from a painful stomach ulcer and he wanted prayer. Graciously the Lord healed him and he went away rejoicing. On a later visit he told me how he had walked up and down on the road outside the Centre filled with apprehension and fear at the thought of entering a 'Protestant' place! I can also recall a Protestant man coming to a Monday night prayer meeting. He had to leave his job as a salesman because of a severe attack of colitus. After the meeting we prayed that God would heal him. He did not return and I enquired from some of his friends who told me the man had been healed but would not come back to share in such 'mixed company'!

It is for us a constant joy to witness the powerful experiences of reconciliation which have taken place both in the Centre and in many of the conferences and gatherings in which we have participated throughout Ireland. Father Pat Collins is involved in Evangelism all over Ireland and is a frequent speaker at conferences abroad. He recalls what such sharing has meant to him:

> Over the years I met Christians from every denomination at the Christian Renewal Centre. Like myself they had come into a new experience of the Lord and His gifts through the power of the Holy Spirit. Together we prayed and shared. We also witnessed and ministered to the many visitors who came to the conferences, prayer meetings and Bible weeks organised by the Centre. This kind of outreach brought renewal to many people while nurturing and deepening my own Christian life. It also fostered a number of personal convictions.
>
> I have often heard Cecil say that there is no real renewal without reconciliation. I'm sure that's correct. But if renewal and reconciliation are to take place in, and between the churches, a change of perspective is called for. Instead of focusing on the experience of religious authority as heretofore, we should pay attention to the authority of religious experience. A proud preoccupation with doctrinal differences tends to divide, as the sad history of Northern Ireland has shown. However, at the Centre we have discovered that mutual recognition of the activity, gifts and fruits of the Spirit in all the denominations tends to reconcile. I saw this in my own life and in the lives of many men and women who came to Rostrevor. The scales

of religious prejudice fell from our eyes when we saw how God could use the ministry of a Christian from another church as the answer to our heartfelt desire to be filled with the Spirit or to be healed in body, mind or soul. Not only that, we found that when we ministered together in the light of this mutual recognition, our ministry seemed to be blessed in a special way. For example I can remember how a number of us who had met at the Renewal Centre went to Coleraine for a day of renewal. David McKee, a Presbyterian, preached the sermon. Afterwards he invited Larry Kelly, a Catholic layman; Harry Woodhead, a Church of Ireland minister; and myself, a Roman Catholic priest, to join him in praying for people. As we did so many of them began to fall under the power of the Spirit. It was the first time that I had witnessed anything like it. There they were, Catholics and Protestants alike, resting in the Spirit on the floor! When the meeting was over, David called me aside. 'That's the first time I have ever seen people being slain in the Spirit. Why do you think it's happened today?' 'As far as I'm concerned,' I replied, 'there can be only one answer. God is honouring our united witness to him, by blessing our ministry in a special way.'

I explained earlier how Christians from different backgrounds had met for the first time at the large renewal conferences in Dublin in which we shared active participation. In his autobiography Canon David Watson describes the blessing he experienced during one of those conferences at which he and his wife Anne were speakers:

Most moving of all was the Service of Reconciliation on the Saturday night. Led by a small group of Protestant and Catholic leaders, we saw, from a good exposition of Ephesians 2, that the cause of our divisions in home, church and society is always sin in the heart of man. Through simple drama enacted in front of a huge empty cross, we saw that the only place for reconciliation is at the foot of the cross. When we come to the cross, we come not as Protestants or Roman Catholics but as sinners; and when we put our trust in the one Saviour who died for our sins once for all, God accepts each one of us as 'my son, my daughter', and this means that we should now say to one another, 'my brother, my sister'. We were then all invited to go to anyone within that huge hall, to ask for forgiveness for anything we had said or done in the past that grieved the Spirit of God. I was at once surrounded by a large crowd of nuns and priests asking for forgiveness from me, as a representative Protestant, for things that they had said and done that were not right; and of course I reciprocated. Then we embraced one another as brothers and sisters, experiencing at a deeper level than I had ever known before what it means to be 'one body through the cross'. If we belonged to Christ, we belonged also to one another; and what God has joined together through the death of his own Son, let not man put asunder.[10]

Healing from prejudice

Coming to that place of recognising one another as members 'together in the body of Christ', especially when it involves those whom we had before perceived as enemies, is not such an easy matter for many of us. Nor was it for the Apostle Paul. Brought up and educated as a strict Jew, Paul's heart was filled with prejudice towards the early Christians. 'I persecuted them to their death, arresting both men and women and throwing them into prison,' he said; and in a letter written years later to his fellow-worker Timothy he wrote: 'I was once a blasphemer and a persecutor and a violent man' (1 Tim. 1:13). With fanatical zeal he had supported the murder of Stephen, the first Christian martyr. Then he had an encounter with the living Christ and was baptised in the Holy Spirit when one of the Christians he had come to persecute laid hands on him and prayed. The dramatic story of that meeting, recounted in Acts 9, demonstrates the power of God to change the hardest heart and dissolve the deepest prejudices.

It seems to me that what St Paul experienced is a healing we need in Ireland in an ever increasing way. Like Paul we need that encounter with Christ that makes us new and the mighty infilling of God's love. It is significant that God used a man St Paul had perceived as his enemy to be the agent of his healing. The story has direct application to us in Ireland as we reach out across the fear-filled chasms that separate us from each other. God gave Paul a new heart, and through the loving ministry of Ananias he received his sight. The filaments of fear and prejudice were melted away in the love of God mediated through the loving hands of a brother in Christ. Ananias is one of my heroes in the Acts. The courage it took for him to obey God's call! The faith he had to believe that such a 'hard case' could be converted. And the love he showed in reaching out and saying to his enemy, 'Brother Saul'. It surely must rank Ananias as one of the patron saints of reconcilers!

Yet nothing less than this is the calling of all who follow Christ today. St John says: 'We love because he first loved us. If anyone says, "I love God," yet hates his brother, he is a liar. For anyone who does not love his brother, whom he has seen, cannot love God, whom he has not seen.' (1 John 4:19,20). St Paul himself explains the Christian standing and his calling. Writing to the Christian Church in Corinth he says:

Therefore, if anyone is in Christ, he is a new creation; the old has gone, the new has come! All this is from God, who reconciled us to himself through Christ and gave us the ministry of reconciliation: that God was reconciling the world to himself in Christ, not counting men's sins against them. And he has committed to us the message of reconciliation. We are therefore Christ's ambassadors, as though God were making his appeal through us. We implore you on Christ's behalf: Be reconciled to God. (2 Cor. 5:17–20)

'A persecutor and a violent' man was how St Paul once described himself. Now an ambassador of Jesus Christ he became the great apostle who carried the Good News through the Mediterranean world of his day. We have witnessed that same transformation taking place in the lives of men and women who were once dedicated to violence. The Revd Eric Mayer, a member of the community at Rostrevor, has written of eight such people in his book *Hands Free of Violence*; those who, like the Zealots, were consumed by hatred and caught up in the violence of para-military groups. During the period when David Jardine was Chaplain in Crumlin Road prison in Belfast, teams from the Centre were invited to address the prisoners. During some of those visits when many people were praying for us we witnessed God's Holy Spirit move in mighty ways to change hard hearts and heal broken lives. One man who was serving a life sentence came to faith in Christ, and a young teacher from Bangor who was on our team befriended him, visiting him regularly in prison. In conversation our friend discovered that the prisoner's wife had decided there was no future in their marriage. In course of time our friend made contact with the estranged wife and children, invited them to attend his Christian fellowship where she too came to a personal faith in Christ. The prisoner's wife decided to visit him again and their marriage was restored. The members of the Christian fellowship were able to arrange for a three-day parole when the couple were reunited in a public Christian service of recommitment to each other as man and wife.

Once when we were ministering in the prison church I was reluctant to share with the congregation a word of knowledge which I sensed the Holy Spirit had given me. With considerable hesitation I finally spoke the word, which must have sounded strange in such unlikely surroundings.

I said, 'I believe that God is speaking to at least one man here who is going to become an evangelist, who will win many people to Christ.'

Soon after we had to leave the prison. A few days later I had a letter from David Hamilton, one of the prisoners sentenced for armed robbery as a member of a loyalist terrorist organisation. In prison he had repented and committed his life to Christ and was an active member of the fellowship group led by David Jardine. In his letter he told me that two people in the fellowship group had already spoken to him along similar lines to the word of knowledge. He explained how weak and unworthy he felt but if God called him he would be willing to serve him. The word I spoke had been a real encouragement and confirmed what he was already hearing.

When David came out of prison he shared the Gospel with many of his friends. I met him about five months after his release and he had led seventy people to personal faith in Christ. James McIlroy the Director of Prison Fellowship, invited him to work with that organisation, ministering to prisoners and their families. During several years there David's witness and ministry touched the lives of thousands of people and now he is working full-time as an Evangelist with Teen Challenge.

Liam McCloskey served a sentence in prison for arms offences and involvement in a Republican terrorist group. It was during the hunger strike of 1981. As one prisoner after another died on the hunger strike his turn came. On his fifty-fifth day without food he was blind and on the point of death and decided to end his hunger strike. After many weeks recovering in hospital, at the point of a nervous breakdown, he called out to Jesus:

> This crushed reed, he did not break. This smouldering wick he did not put out, that long sought rest was received. From being drained both in mind and in body I was revived. I had decided to end my links with republicanism and try to follow the way of Jesus, the way of love rather than hate, the way of reconciliation rather than bitterness and the way of forgiveness rather than vengeance. The Lord Jesus has drawn close and I have experienced more joy, beauty, depth and love than I ever knew existed. My mind often reflects on what happened to Saul of Tarsus on the Damascus Road and suspect that early Christians praying for him moved God to change him from one of the

main persecutors of Jesus to one of his main defenders. Perhaps if the people of Northern Ireland decided to pray for their enemies instead of hating them, it would transform this land.

The remarkable sequel to those two stories is that David and Liam, who before were sworn enemies, are now brothers in Christ and have often shared the same platform to witness to the transforming power of Christ.

Sons of thunder

'Blessed are the peacemakers, for they will be called sons of God,' was part of the mandate which Jesus passed on to his first disciples. They did not find it any easier to practise than we do. Their fears and prejudices were as real as any felt in Ireland today. It was no accident that James and John were called 'sons of thunder'. St Luke in his Gospel gives us a glimpse of the critical lesson that Jesus had to teach the two brothers. It was approaching the time of his crucifixion and Jesus deliberately decided to travel south along the west bank of the river Jordan, passing through Samaria on his way to Jerusalem. It was not the most popular route with Jewish travellers. A centuries-old feud with racial, political and religious undertones caused suspicion, hatred and division between the Jews and Samaritans. On their way through Samaria Jesus sent some of the disciples into a village to find food and lodging. The people in the village did not welcome Jesus, Luke records. We are left to imagine the comments that were made by the villagers to these despised pilgrims on their way to Jerusalem. When James and John saw what was happening their deeply held prejudices erupted. They exploded 'Lord, do you want us to call fire down from heaven to destroy them?' 'Burn them out' was their violent response, one very familiar in the North Irish context. But Jesus turned around and rebuked them with some searing words: 'You do not know what kind of spirit you are of, for the Son of Man did not come to destroy men's lives but to save them' (Luke 9:55).

The remarkable thing is that those two men had just shared with Jesus on the mount of transfiguration a most profound spiritual experience. And now Jesus had to say to them, 'You are being motivated by another spirit than mine'. 'You are listening to the thief who comes to steal and to kill and to destroy.' 'I am come,' Jesus had said, 'that men (Samaritans as well as Jews) might have life and have it in all its fulness.'

James and John had seen Jesus touch the eyes of the blind and make them see but their eyes were so clouded by the filaments of prejudice that they were prepared to inflict suffering and death on a whole village of people who had been made in God's image. In a moment of racial, political and religious anger they had forgotten how often their Master had reached out to the despised Samaritans and offered help and healing and salvation; the ten lepers he had healed together and only the Samaritan returned to express his thanks; and the famous parable in which it was the Good Samaritan who was commended.

When the group of disciples and Jesus were thrown out of the town 'they went to another village'. I wonder what the conversation centred on that night before James and John went to sleep. Or did they have a sleepless night wrestling with what Jesus had said to them? The interesting fact is that Jesus did not dismiss them at that juncture. He did not say, 'Men, you've failed the test. Go back to Galilee. I'll have to leave you out of my programme.' No. He took them with him through Gethsemane, through Calvary to the resurrection and on to Pentecost. I believe it was in the Upper Room, when the fire of God fell, that the prejudice was burnt out of their hearts. It is significant that St Luke records in Acts 8 that when Philip the evangelist went down to Samaria there was a great revival. Many turned to Christ, were healed and delivered from evil spirits. When news reached the Apostles in Jerusalem that revival had broken out in Samaria, guess who they sent down there to join Philip in the ministry? 'They sent Peter and John to them. When they arrived, they prayed for them that they might receive the Holy Spirit . . . Then Peter and John placed their hands on them, and they received the Holy Spirit' (Acts 8:14–17). St Luke notes that, as they completed their mission, 'Peter and John returned to Jerusalem, preaching the gospel in many Samaritan villages' (Acts 8:25).

I can easily imagine John coming back to the village where before he had felt such rejection. Previously his fists had been clenched in self-righteous anger, now his hands were open to minister the healing, reconciling love of Jesus. When I visit other countries I am sometimes asked, 'Why do we so often hear the Gospel from Northern Ireland preached in such harsh and strident tones?' I think of James and John. As for them, so we too have to allow the Holy Spirit to burn up in us those pockets of resistance to the love of God that reserves the right to act out of our inherited prejudices. It was from deep personal experience that years later James wrote these words:

Likewise the tongue is a small part of the body, but it makes great boasts. Consider what a great forest is set on fire by a small spark. The tongue also is a fire, a world of evil among the parts of the body. It corrupts the whole person, sets the whole course of his life on fire, and is itself set on fire by hell . . . With the tongue we praise our Lord and Father, and with it we curse men, who have been made in God's likeness. Out of the same mouth come praise and cursing. My brothers, this should not be. Can both fresh water and salt water flow from the same spring? My brothers, can a fig-tree bear olives, or a grapevine bear figs? Neither can a salt spring produce fresh water. Who is wise and understanding among you? Let him show it by his good life, by deeds done in the humility that comes from wisdom. But if you harbour bitter envy and selfish ambition in your hearts, do not boast about it or deny the truth. Such 'wisdom' does not come down from heaven but is earthly, unspiritual, of the devil. For where you have envy and selfish ambition, there you find disorder and every evil practice. But the wisdom that comes from heaven is first of all pure; then peace-loving, considerate, submissive, full of mercy and good fruit, impartial and sincere. Peacemakers who sow in peace raise a harvest of righteousness. (Jas 3:5–6, 9–18)

The narrow Nationalist hopes that the disciples inherited disappeared after Pentecost as the Holy Spirit led them into a new world of brotherhood never before seen on the earth. A fellowship of the Holy Spirit was born, transcending all the barriers of nation, race, colour, class and sex. The Kingdom of God began to grow; a kingdom not of this world but firmly planted in it. An everlasting kingdom whose subjects owed first and full allegiance to the King of kings but lived to be a benediction in the passing kingdoms of this world.

Over the years in Ireland we have witnessed the unmistakable signs of that Kingdom breaking through when we deliberately come together, climbing over the man-made fences of our history. In times like these, in small and large gatherings, we have felt in tangible ways the glory of God come down and 'the sun of righteousness arise with healing in its wings'. One such occasion was a gathering which we arranged in the centre of Belfast. With the Revd Ken Newell and members of Fitzroy Presbyterian Church, we invited Christians of all denominations to meet together for a night of prayer. For twelve hours we gathered from many parts of the city and beyond. As we joined in prayer, praise and intercession for our land we sensed the very real presence of Jesus among us. During the night God spoke many words of encouragement and hope in war-torn Belfast. Ken shared this word prompted by the Holy Spirit which expressed what God was doing among us:

> We are a people made one by
> The love of Christ our Saviour and Lord
> We have been changed as people by the grace
>   of our Lord Jesus Christ.

Gone is the pride that desires to dominate;
Gone is the anger that wants to undermine.
By his Holy Spirit we want to listen to
    each other's hurts and fears
And build together a community fit for us all to live in
Furnished with the generosity, justice
    and compassion of Jesus Christ.

9

FORGIVENESS

He who cannot forgive others breaks the bridge
over which he must pass himself.
For every man has need to be forgiven.
George Herbert

For if you forgive men when they sin against you, your
heavenly Father will also forgive you. But if you do not
forgive men their sins, your Father will not forgive your
sins. (Matt. 6:14–15)

C. S. Lewis wrote, 'Everyone says forgiveness is a lovely idea until they have something to forgive.' When Jesus taught the disciples the now familiar words which we call the Lord's Prayer the request 'forgive us our trespasses as we forgive those who trespass against us' must have sounded strange in their ears. 'An eye for an eye and a tooth for a tooth' was what they had known as the law of retribution and it seemed reasonable. And when Jesus went on to say that this forgiveness extended to enemies it sounded really impossible.

Yet in the moment of deepest testing the Lord proved those words true. As he hung in agony on the cross his words were, 'Father, forgive them for they do not know what they are doing' (Luke 23:34). In the face of the terrible injustice of his trial and in the experience of excruciating pain he asked his Father in heaven to forgive the perpetrators of this foul deed. How strange it must have sounded in the ears of those who stood by the cross. The words he had spoken to the disciples in the flower-covered fields of Galilee were not the words of a dreamer or starry-eyed idealist. There on the cruel cross of Calvary Jesus revealed the Father heart of God – a heart of forgiveness and love. A whole new world had dawned, where mercy would triumph over justice.

Would such action be possible for Christ's followers in the real world of injustice and hatred? Very soon they too were to prove the theory true. Stephen the first Christian martyr cried out, 'Lord do not hold this sin against them,' as a hate-filled angry mob stoned him to death on trumped-up charges supported by lying witnesses. Countless millions of Christians in all the centuries since then have followed that way with words of love and not hate on their lips.

Here in Ireland over the many years of terror and tears we have seen that same spirit of forgiveness expressed by many innocent victims of hatred and cruel violence. Through our ministry both in the Centre and outside we have been privileged to meet and share with those who have received the supernatural power to forgive in the most terrible circumstances. In the face of violence that has destroyed the lives of their loved ones or caused permanent disablement to themselves they have given back love instead of bitterness and resentment. The beautiful Mourne countryside where the Centre is situated has witnessed its share of atrocities. In the nine miles between Rostrevor and Newry, our nearest town, more than thirty people have been murdered by the IRA in the years of violence. Hundreds of families have had to face the harrowing news of the sudden and unexpected death of a loved one.

Meta was one of those. It was during a conference at the Centre that she came and asked some of us to pray with her. Only a week before her brother, a policeman, had been ambushed and killed by terrorists when he and his colleagues came to investigate a false report of a break-in at a garage in Warrenpoint, two miles from Rostrevor. Meta had loved her brother dearly and the grief she felt was intense. She had travelled the road which her brother had gone that fatal night.

'My heart was filled with bitterness and hatred for those who had carried out this attack,' she said. 'As a Christian I knew this was not right, yet despite knowing this I could not help myself. A friend suggested I should pray for the gunmen but at the time that seemed impossible. How could I pray for someone who had killed my brother?'

Together we brought Meta into the loving presence of Jesus the Healer. While we prayed the miracle happened. Some time later I heard Meta speak at a gathering of people in Dundalk. With remarkable calm and peace she said, 'As Christian brothers and sisters prayed for me, in a wonderful way the love of God filled my heart and I received a great peace. I could now pray and say, "Father, forgive them."'

Harry McCann is a regular traveller along that same road from Warrenpoint to Rostrevor where he often comes to join us for special days of prayer and renewal. In a specially adapted car he drives right up to the Centre door. Easing himself out of the car he stands upright using two walking sticks. Slowly but resolutely he makes his way into the house on two artificial legs. His cheerful presence always encourages and inspires us. He is another victim of blind hatred and violence. One morning as he was going to work, when he switched on the ignition on his car a booby-trap bomb exploded, blowing him into the air. He was rushed to hospital seriously injured. As he travelled in the ambulance he was still conscious. He explained: 'I could hear myself saying, "Father, forgive them," and I knew it was not my voice speaking. Another voice was speaking in me.' The skill of the surgeons and medical staff was able to save Harry's life but both his legs had to be amputated at the thighs. Long months of pain and years of adjustment to a whole new way of life had to follow for him, his wife and family. Harry, a Catholic, has travelled all over Ireland to witness to the love of Jesus. On a number of occasions he has joined with us as a member of a ministry team and witnessed to God's gift of forgiving love. 'Don't let hatred and bitterness hold you,' he said. 'Don't allow thoughts of resentment or revenge destroy you. Only God's love can heal this troubled land.'

Karen's victory

In September 1982 a headline in a Belfast newspaper caught my attention: 'Tribute to ex-pupil who fell victim to killers'. At the school prize day the Headmistress of Carolan Grammar School paid tribute to Karen McKeown who was head girl two years before. Karen, twenty years old, had been at an evening service in her church in East Belfast. As she closed the door of her car a gunman walked out of the shadows and shot her in the neck at point-blank range. This demonic act on an innocent girl was apparently claimed as retaliation for an attack in the area the previous day. Karen was rushed to hospital where she lived for three weeks in the intensive care unit, totally paralysed. She was a committed Christian who had chosen her university course so that she could be a probation officer and help those in need.

Yet the hatred that gripped the man who shot her could not destroy the priceless treasure that Karen held in her heart – her sure faith in God and her unfailing hope in him. I was deeply moved when I read what her Headmistress had said about Karen: 'We rejoice in having known Karen's warm personality, self-giving attitude and marked sense of service . . . It was typical of Karen that in the three weeks she survived, when she was alert mentally and strong in faith, she bore no grudge and showed concern for those around her.'

We were to learn later from Pearl, Karen's mother, how God's forgiving love had shone through that young girl. In total weakness and great pain she ministered to her parents the grace of forgiving love. Shortly before she died Karen said to her mother, 'Mum, think of the mother of the man who shot me. How must she feel? I'm sorry he did it, but I am more sorry for him.'

On the night Karen was shot she had been singing to her friends a song she really loved:

> I will enter His gates with thanksgiving in my heart
> I will enter His courts with praise.

On the evening of 16 October Karen slipped peacefully through those gates into the nearer presence of the Lord she loved. She had won the victory over hatred through the grace of forgiving love and passed on a rich treasure to many others. I spoke to a nurse who had often cared for Karen in those three weeks, and she told me that many of those who had come into that ward had experienced the benediction of the love of Jesus shining through Karen. On the night she died a young man in England who had heard her story committed his life to Christ.

He said, 'Karen's parents know that she has gone to be with God. I'm the same age as Karen. If I had died before tonight my parents would not have known where I had gone.'

During the years since Karen's death it has been our great privilege to come to know her mother and father. Pearl knows the awesome cost of such forgiving love and makes no secret of the struggle that she had to go through. For all those who have to travel that lonely road the walk is not easy. Their painful pilgrimage is captured in these words written by Bishop Michael Hare Duke:

> Yet love does not take away the pain,
> It gives a purpose to the holding on
> Till you can say, 'It's finished, victory's won;
> Scarred hands receive my spirit.'
> So sorrow becomes luminous joy.
> The mourner claims his blessing and is comforted
> With Glory which opens midnight windows on Eternity.
> Love waits to show himself without disguise
> Our anguish stands between and blinds our eyes.[1]

Through the unfailing grace of God that sustained her daughter, Pearl has been given a rare ministry. Working with Prison Fellowship she meets some of the people who, like Karen's murderer, have allowed their lives to be dominated by the power of evil. With the authority of forgiving love she is able to meet them face to face and speak to them in a way that few others can.

Grief knows no distinction of race or creed. Bernadette Power is another precious sister in Christ we have come to know and love. Bernadette and Michael her husband had every reason to be proud of their three lovely children. Their joy was deepened as they came into a new awareness of God's love when they were both renewed in the Holy Spirit. Outside their home and family and Michael's job as a taxi driver, they were involved in the life of their local church in Poleglass, a large housing estate on the west of Belfast. They enjoyed sharing in prayer and studying Scripture with other Christians as they grew in their new-found love for Jesus. Then one Sunday morning their happy world was shattered. As they drove to church in their car eight-year-old Michelle was beside her father in the front, young Gary was with his mother and baby Emma in the back seat. When they came to the crossroads another car drew alongside, a gunman opened fire and shot Michael at close range and sped away. One may imagine the horror of that awful moment. Bernadette prayed in anguish all the way to the hospital and with Michael as he died in her arms shortly after. Then she had to comfort Michelle whose eyes were badly damaged by flying glass, and console Gary and Emma who fortunately had escaped injury.

The so-called Ulster Freedom Fighters, a Protestant terrorist group, admitted responsibility for the murder, claiming retaliation for the murder of a soldier by the IRA the day before. Soon after the tragedy Bernadette was asked by a reporter to comment. She explained the faith in God that sustained her. She said, 'I would not like another person to be sitting here the way I am left today with a new baby of just three months. Whether it is a man, woman or child, soldier or policeman it doesn't matter – it just can't go on.'

In the three years that have passed since then Bernadette has known much of that 'anguish that stands between and clouds our eyes' but she has also known in a remarkable way 'the glory that opens midnight windows on eternity'. Every morning she prays with the children before the elder two go to school.

One morning little Gavin said to his mother, 'Mum, will those men who killed my daddy be in heaven?'

'If they say they are sorry and really turn to Jesus and ask him to forgive them, then they will be with him in heaven,' she replied.

He paused and then said: 'Well, Mummy, if they are going to be there I don't want to be in heaven with them.'

'But if Jesus forgives them and saves them, setting them free from their evil sin, they will be completely different people,' she explained.

Another pause and seven-year-old Gavin answered, 'Mummy, let's pray for those men and ask Jesus to change them.'

In 1988 we arranged a festival in Belfast Cathedral called Christians Together at Pentecost. Hundreds of people, Catholic and Protestant, came together for praise and prayer. No one who was there will ever forget Bernadette's powerful witness as she told of the grace that God had given her through that ordeal. God's love shone through her and touched our hearts. When she had finished speaking many Protestant people came to the front of the cathedral. Gathering round Bernadette we asked forgiveness on behalf of the Protestant community for that murder that had been committed in our name.

I describe in an earlier chapter how as a community we pray for all those who have suffered through the violence and write to the families of those who have been killed. It is so moving to hear over and over again the call from the bereaved that there should be no revenge or retaliation for the murder of their loved ones. Behind the scenes of hatred which receive so much publicity those costly acts of forgiveness receive scant attention from the mass media.

Clergy who give constant pastoral care to bereaved families witness to that spirit of true forgiveness. Such a response was characterised by the letter we received from Mrs Travers, wife of Resident Magistrate Tom Travers. Leaving church with his family after Mass, Travers was shot and seriously wounded by a gunman who followed him from the church. As the magistrate lay helpless on the footpath his young daughter, a teacher, was shot dead beside him. Nothing can erase the memory of that Sunday and no one can fill the void in that family. Yet Mary's mother wrote to us:

> Mary was a young woman full of compassion, forgiveness and love and we know that she forgives, and would want us to forgive, those who planned and carried out her murder and the attempted murder of her dad. We, in the name of the Saviour, would like you to remember Mary and our family in your prayers, and also those who were responsible for her death. We would also like you to pray that all men who have murder in their hearts will be overcome by the love of God so that they, like Mary, will one day be at peace with him.

The courageous battle that many have fought in their personal and family lives in Ireland against years of vicious slaughter is an eloquent testimony not easily given. When a whole community becomes victim to ruthless genocide the challenge is even greater. Such mass killing has occurred with devastating frequency in Belfast, Dublin, Derry, Newry, Lisburn and Warrenpoint, to name but a few. Nor has it been limited to Ireland. The murderous campaign of the IRA in particular has extended to mainland Britain and even to the Continent. Communities in London, Birmingham, Brighton, Manchester, Guildford, and Deal in Kent have known the horror of sudden death through planned bombings. Church buildings have not been immune from the mad designs of evil men, such as the incident that devastated the little community of a Pentecostal church in Darkley in South Armagh. People were gathering for worship when there was a hail of gunfire and three of the elders of the church were killed and many men, women and children seriously wounded. Such wanton massacre leaves a legacy of hurt and pain that is hard to erase.

Enniskillen

In recent years I suppose that among all the atrocities that have stained our land none has touched the world more than the Remembrance Day bombing in Enniskillen on Sunday, 8 November 1987. As people were gathering at the town's cenotaph to remember those who died in two world wars, a massive bomb planted nearby by the IRA exploded on the waiting worshippers. Eleven people including three couples were killed, and more than sixty injured, some seriously.

On the Saturday, 7 November Myrtle and I had returned from South Africa where we had been invited to share the message of the reconciling, healing love of Christ with people of all races in that sad but lovely land. The previous Sunday we had stood alongside a thousand blacks and whites who had gathered for a service of reconciliation and to pray for the cessation of the fighting that had caused the deaths of many people in the area around Pietermaritzburg. We could not have foreseen that a few hours after our return to Ireland the people of my home town of Enniskillen would be plunged into grief by the same demonic force of evil.

There were no words left to describe the horror of what happened in Enniskillen that Sunday as innocent people were blown to eternity without a moment's notice.

Yet as I woke in the grey dawn of Monday and switched on the radio a poignant but powerful witness came from that dark place of tragedy. It was the voice of Gordon Wilson whose young daughter had died in the rubble of a wall that had collapsed when the terrorist bomb exploded. Marie, a twenty-year-old nurse, was buried with her Dad six feet below the rubble. She was able to grasp her father's hand. 'Is that your hand, Dad?' she called out. As he held her hand he asked her repeatedly, 'Are you all right?' She answered, 'Yes'. When he asked a fifth time she answered, 'Daddy, I love you very much.' Those were the last words young Marie spoke. She still held her father's hand as her life ebbed away and she passed into her heavenly Father's presence. In the radio interview Marie's father said, 'I bear no ill will. I bear no grudge. She was a great wee lassie. She loved her profession. She's in heaven now. We will meet again.'

That simple yet powerful message of forgiveness and love was relayed around the world. I am convinced that millions of people heard the Gospel for the first time from that place of suffering. As the day wore on it became clear that the eleven who died, some of whom I had known while I grew up in Enniskillen, were humble, dedicated Christian men and women who had made significant contributions to the whole community in their spheres of work and voluntary service.

In the week of mourning that followed, the clergy of the town who conducted the funerals enlarged on the words of Gordon Wilson. They focused faith, looking towards a new day and called us to build communities of harmony where evil could not flourish. By doing that we would ensure that the deaths which plunged the whole country in grief would not have been in vain.

Listening at the cross

The Revd Bertie Armstrong received the news that his brother Wesley and sister-in-law Bertha had been killed in the bombing. In Ballymena, a hundred miles away, he had just shared in a service of remembrance. At Wesley and Bertha's funeral a few days later his words of forgiveness and hope brought light and Christian comfort into the grief-stricken community in Enniskillen. He explained how during the long hours of Sunday night he received the grace to cope with his sudden and cruel bereavement. He recalled how often as a missionary in Jamaica he had shared in the three-hour service on Good Friday and meditated on the words of Christ from the cross. In the darkness he kept that vigil once more.

'You could listen at the cross,' he said, 'and hear all the loud voices of evil and act in the wrong way and please the terrorist groups. Listen to Jesus and there will come repentance, confession of sin, renewal, a new openness to the power of the Holy Spirit and a witness to the power of the Gospel. As I listened I knew God was in the darkness of the cross, and now beyond the agony and suffering there was the dawn of resurrection. This faith is big enough for life and death.'

Out of the darkness a bright beacon of love spread from Enniskillen calling forth repentance in many hearts not only in Ireland but all over Britain and abroad. In her Christmas message, broadcast all over the world, the Queen spoke about the light that shone from that place of suffering, heralding hope in a broken world. Spontaneous gatherings for prayer and remembrance were called in many cities and towns throughout Ireland, north and south, and messages of sympathy were received from many parts of the world.

The way of healing

As a community of Christians we were joining many others in prayer for the people of Enniskillen. It was they who had to come to terms with the terrible grief and the suffering that was bound to last for many years to come. Added to that was the fear and mistrust between the two communities, already severely strained by the hundreds of other murders perpetrated by the IRA in that area of Northern Ireland. On the same day as the bombing in Enniskillen the security forces had safely defused another bomb, also set to explode at a service of remembrance in a village not far from the town. Who was responsible? Were they people who mingled with the folk in the street and at their daily work? Such suspicion creates understandable fear and fear breeds more alienation.

Into that atmosphere we were invited by some people in the town to help the two communities to come together and express their grief and pray for one another. We were known in the town as a community of Catholic and Protestant Christians who might be able to bridge the divide and help the process of reconciliation. When we prayed about the invitation we knew we should accept. We wrote to the clergy of the four main churches in the town informing them of the invitation that had been extended. We suggested that our contribution should be to lead an evening of prayer for healing and that we would bring with us some who had already gone through the trauma of suffering and grief to share witness. The clergy graciously welcomed us and each of the four churches was represented at an evening of prayer that we shall never forget.

About four hundred people came, many of whom had been involved in the tragedy, some injured and others bereaved. The Centre music team led worship and the well-known singer Dana, Mrs Rosemary Scallon, a good friend of the Centre, brought comfort through the songs she sang. Bertie Armstrong and Harry McCann shared consolation, encouragement and hope out of their own experience of suffering and grief. Sister Carmel, a Sister of Mercy from the local convent, near the place where the bomb exploded, conveyed the genuine feelings of sorrow and repentance felt by many Catholic people. Her words, coming from her heart, allayed the obvious fears of people there, especially when she said: 'Before the bomb I would always have thought in terms of "my people". From now on I can only think in terms of "our people", for we are joined as one.' It was a moving and truly holy moment when we all joined in prayer for one another and for those still suffering from the wounds they had received.

That night as we made the long journey back to Rostrevor it was made even longer by a thick fog which persisted all the way. Progress was slow as we followed the road guided by the traffic reflectors marking the centre of the road. We saw a parable in that too. In the mists of fear that enveloped our land we could only find our way together as we kept our eyes on Jesus the light of the world. Since then from Enniskillen many signs of hope have sprung from the ashes of despair.

In 1989 on the second anniversary of the bombing we were invited back to the town, this time to conduct a Celebration of Hope in Christ arranged by Enniskillen Together, an organisation founded after the atrocity to bring people together in supporting cross-community projects. The celebration, held in the town's Methodist Church, was a most moving occasion. People from all sections of the community gathered to pray, to praise God together and to hear remarkable witness to the power of love over hate.

Stephen Ross, a seventeen-year-old schoolboy had been badly injured in the Remembrance day bomb. His face had been crushed by falling masonry and during weeks of painful surgery he recovered. Through it all his faith grew and many people were inspired by the witness which he gave to television reporters from his hospital bed. In the Celebration of Hope Stephen read with great conviction the words of St Peter:

> Praise be to the God and Father of our Lord Jesus Christ! In his great mercy he has given us new birth into a living hope through the resurrection of Jesus Christ from the dead, and into an inheritance that can never perish, spoil or fade – kept in heaven for you (1 Pet. 1:3–4).

Marilyn, a lovely young graduate, spoke of the tragedy that had struck her family. Her father Ronnie Hill, Headmaster of Enniskillen High School, was so seriously injured that he was still in hospital two years after the explosion. The Hills are a deeply committed family and Marilyn joined her mother in the daily vigil by her father's bed, reading the Bible to him and praying with him even though he could not communicate by speech. Marilyn explained how Christ had sustained them in this time of grief and suffering and how through it all she had found God's call to go to Bible College to prepare for full-time Christian ministry. It was moving to hear her report how she, a Presbyterian, had joined a Roman Catholic seminarian in leading a party of Roman Catholic and Protestant children on a visit to the United States. Sister Carmel read the powerful words of St John the Divine from Revelation 7:14. That glorious vision of heaven reveals the victory of love over hate in the lives of those 'who have come out of the great tribulation; they have washed their robes and made them white in the blood of the lamb.'

A miracle and a gift

Although we as Christians regularly confess as an article of our faith, 'I believe in the forgiveness of sins', few would deny that offering forgiveness is the hardest thing to do. Especially so when we have suffered unjustly or seen others abused, injured or killed. In the wake of the Enniskillen bombing some were asking the question, 'What right had these people to offer forgiveness to those who would do such a desperately sinful deed?' We are left in confusion about this question until we come to the cross of Christ, as Bertie Armstrong did on the night after the tragedy. At the cross God 'demonstrated his own love for us in this: While we were still sinners Christ died for us'. Understandably we say, 'If those who planted the bomb will repent and confess their sin, then and only then can we speak forgiveness.' If that had been the way God treated us we would never have experienced forgiveness. It is significant that when Jesus taught the disciples the Lord's Prayer the only petition to which he attached a condition was that on forgiveness. He explained: 'For if you forgive men when they sin against you, your heavenly Father will also forgive you. But if you do not forgive men their sins, your Father will not forgive your sins' (Matt. 6:14–15). We naturally feel sympathy with Peter, when in the light of Jesus' seemingly impossible advice he asked, 'Lord, how many times shall I forgive my brother when he sins against me? Up to seven times?' How many of us would want to pitch it as high as Peter? But Jesus answered Peter: 'I tell you, not seven times but seventy-seven times' (Matt. 18:21–22). Impossible humanly speaking, yes. But that kind of forgiveness that flows from Calvary is a miracle and a gift.

Commenting on Peter's question to Jesus, William Temple wrote: 'We are to show an absolute readiness to forgive, which is undisturbed by any magnitude of the injury done or any frequency of its repetition.'[2] Expanding on this, Temple goes on wisely to suggest:

> We seem to need two words, forgiving-ness and forgiveness. God is always forgiving, in the sense that he desires to forgive; but we are not always forgiven because we persist in the bad self-will which creates an alienation between us and God. For real forgiveness the action of two wills is needed; it cannot be complete till the wrongdoer changes his attitude or, in other words, repents. But he may be led to do this by the love shown in his victim's readiness to forgive.[3]

Few of us could ever forget the remarkable act of forgiveness on Christmas day 1983 in Rome. Pope John Paul II had gone into Rebibbia prison to meet Mehmet Ali Agla, the Turkish-born terrorist who had attempted to murder him two years before. The television cameras recorded that wordless scene that made an indelible impression even in a world saturated by bigotry, hatred, terrorism and bloodshed. The two men talked, their heads close together, seated in the bare prison room. When the Pope emerged from the meeting he was asked by reporters to tell what had happened. 'What we talked about will have to remain a secret between him and me,' he said. 'I spoke to him as a brother whom I pardoned.'

Two weeks later *Time* magazine devoted seven full pages to consider the question, 'Why forgive?' Senior writer Lance Morrow wrote:

Christ preached forgiveness, the loving of one's enemies. It is at the center of the New Testament. Stated nakedly, superficially, the proposition sounds perverse and even self-destructive, an invitation to disaster . . . Forgiveness is not an impulse that is in much favor. It is a mysterious and sublime idea in many ways. The prevalent style in the world runs more to the high-plains drifter, to the hard, cold eye of the avenger, to a numb remorselessness. Forgiveness does not look much like a tool for survival in a bad world. But that is what it is.[4]

One of the best and most practical books I have read on this subject is *A Forgiving God in an Unforgiving World* by Ron Lee Davis, minister of Community Presbyterian Church in Danville, California. He describes this supernatural power to forgive as flowing from God's unconditional love:

It's foolishness to the world, but it's the foolishness of God that confounds the wisdom of men. Unconditional love doesn't have anything to do with the way we feel. Hosea couldn't have felt too loving towards his unfaithful wife. Rob (a close friend) didn't feel too loving towards the man who had tried to rape and kill his wife. Unconditional love is rooted not in emotions but in the will, in our commitment to Christ, in allowing Christ to empower us so that we can love others as he has loved us: volitionally, unconditionally, with no strings attached. God loves us unconditionally. God forgives us freely.[5]

Power to forgive

God's gift of forgiving grace is not only a tool for survival it is a vital ingredient for recovery in a world consumed by hatred and the urge to revenge. I am convinced that the forgiveness that we have seen demonstrated over and over again in Ireland during the years of terrible suffering will be the single most powerful resource for the recovery of our sanity and the healing of our ancient wounds. The gift of forgiveness is the most precious and most costly jewel that Christ is offering to us. To reject it is to perpetuate the cancer of hatred and violence.

The life and witness of Martin Luther King has inspired millions of people around the world to work for a better world built on righteousness and justice. He suffered many personal hurts and insults and died from an assassin's bullet. In the face of all the hatred directed at him he did not allow hatred to degrade his soul. In 1963, five years before he was assassinated, he wrote these words:

> He who is devoid of the power to forgive is devoid of the power to love. Forgiveness is a catalyst creating the atmosphere necessary for a fresh start and a new beginning. It is the lifting of a burden or the cancelling of a debt. The words, 'I will forgive you, but I'll never forget what you've done,' never explain the real nature of forgiveness. Certainly one can never forget, if that means erasing it totally from his mind. But when we forgive, we forget in the sense that the evil deed is no longer a mental block impeding a new relationship. Likewise, we can never say, 'I will forgive you, but I won't have anything further to do with you.' Forgiveness means reconciliation, a coming together again. Without this, no man can love his enemies. The degree to which we are able to forgive determines the degree to which we are able to love our enemies.[6]

As Christians wherever we live in the world there is an urgent need for us to re-learn to use this most precious gift. It is sheer hypocrisy to pray the Lord's Prayer if we do not act on what we say; for the unbelieving world will judge us not only by our words but more by what we do. One man is a living testimony of how that grace of forgiveness can work to change a hard heart. Arie Ben Israel has shared with us in ministry in Ireland on several occasions over the last few years.

Arie was born of Orthodox Jewish parents in a concentration camp in Soviet Siberia. When his parents were eventually released he went with them to their native Poland. As a young boy in Poland, Arie experienced persecution from people who called themselves Christians. Just because he was a Jewish boy he endured endless insults. Other children spat on him and called him names in the street or on the way to school. As he grew into his teenage years a deep hatred towards Christians consumed him. It remained with him when he and his parents emigrated to Israel, where Arie was a social worker and served in the Israeli armed forces.

Yet through all these sad experiences the God of love and forgiveness was working in Arie's life. During a visit to Germany – the land that held terrible memories for Jews – a very significant event occurred. Arie's hatred of the Germans was compounded. One of his best friends was murdered by the bomb planted to kill and maim the Israeli participants at the 1972 Munich Olympics: but in the providence of God it was in the city of Munich that Arie came face to face with the love of Jesus through a young Christian girl. It was the most unexpected meeting of his life. Walking through the city he heard the sound of singing. It came from a group of young people with guitars and he quickly realised they were Christians. Arie's heart filled up with the hatred that had simmered there for years as he recalled the way he had been treated. As one of the girls in the group approached him he opened his coat to reveal the large star of David on his tee-shirt.

The young girl's first words to Arie were, 'Jesus loves you.' He spat on the ground and the words of hatred burst like a torrent from his mouth. To his amazement she did not argue back. He could see an expression of deep sorrow on the girl's face.

She said, 'I'm sorry for all that has been done to you in the name of Christianity. I take that guilt on myself and I repent of it. You can spit on me; you can hit me; you can even kill me but what I said is really true – JESUS LOVES YOU.'

In that moment Arie *saw* the love of Jesus in that young girl. He was impelled to buy a Bible with a New Testament in it. When he read the first chapter of St Matthew's Gospel he found his heart responding to Christ as his Saviour and Messiah.

That encounter changed Arie's life. It has brought him much suffering and loneliness and lots of rejection from his own people who find it hard to understand, but his life now is filled with joy and purpose. To meet him and hear him speak is a sheer delight and benediction. The love of Christ in his heart is deep and real. The proof is that now his life is devoted to the work of reconciliation in Germany.

10

REPENTANCE

We have forgotten God . . . We have vainly imagined, in the deceitfulness of our hearts, that all these blessings were produced by some superior wisdom and virtue of our own. Intoxicated with unbroken success, we have become too self sufficient to feel the necessity of redeeming and preserving grace, too proud to pray to the God who made us . . . (A Proclamation for a Day of National Humiliation, Fasting and Prayer made by President Abraham Lincoln of the USA, March 30th 1863)

Repent, then, and turn to God, so that your sins may be wiped out, that times of refreshing may come from the Lord. (Acts 3:19)

Alexander Solzhenitsyn, the great Russian writer and Nobel prizewinner, is a prophet of our day. His Christian faith was formed in the crucible of suffering. While serving as an officer in the Russian army in 1945 he was arrested for his opposition to the despotic regime of Stalin. Banished with millions of others to a forced labour camp in Siberia and suffering from inoperable cancer his faith in God grew stronger. Miraculously healed, he has lived not only to speak a powerfully prophetic word to his own beloved nation but also to the western world.

In May 1983 Solzhenitsyn was presented with the Templeton Award for progress in religion. In his reception speech in the London Guildhall before the world's media he said:

189

If I were asked today to formulate as concisely as possible the main cause of the ruinous revolution that swallowed up some sixty million of our people (in Russia), I could not put it more accurately than to repeat: 'Men have forgotten God; that's why all this has happened.' And if I were called upon to identify briefly the principal trait of the entire twentieth century, here too I would be unable to find anything more precise and pithy than to repeat once again: 'Men have forgotten God.' The failings of human consciousness, deprived of its divine dimension, have been a determining factor in all the major crimes of this century.[1]

In his letter to the Third Council of the Russian Church Abroad in 1974 Solzhenitsyn enunciated this call to communal repentance:

Since the shiny bauble of unlimited progress has led all humanity into a depressing cul-de-sac, represented with only slight nuances of difference in the east as in the west, I can only discover one healthy course for everyone now living, for nations, societies, human organizations, and above all else for churches. We must confess our sins and errors (our own, not those of others), repent, and use self-restraint in our future development. This solution should be applied universally.[2]

In company with the great prophets of the Bible Solzhenitsyn was calling us back to the heart of the problem. To repent is to have a change of mind; a complete change of heart. It is more than remorse. Repentance is a conscious decision to turn from evil, selfishness and sin to obedience to God's way of truth and righteousness. Repentance, which is both God's gift and man's responsibility, is the first step towards renewal and recovery in our personal lives and extends to national and international relationships.

In the direct line of the great prophets of Israel John the Baptist prepared the way for the Messiah. 'Repent for the kingdom of heaven is near,' he proclaimed (Matt.

3:2). 'Unless you repent you shall all likewise perish,' was the Messiah's warning when he came. The call of Jesus ushered in the most radical revolution the world has known, a kingdom of men and women with the watchword of love, and the foundation of righteousness, truth and justice. Jesus explained that introduction to that kingdom was not by human ingenuity, effort or enterprise but by a new birth. 'I tell you the truth,' he said, 'no one can see the kingdom of God unless he is born again' (John 3:3). That kingdom would endure for all eternity and would challenge all man-made kingdoms and ideologies.

Judgment

By the absolute standard of God's kingdom of righteousness (right relationships with God and with each other), truth, justice and love, our profession of faith in all its varied expressions surely stands judged in Ireland. Before a watching world we stand condemned. More serious is where we stand before God. Have we loved him with all our hearts, our souls, our minds and strength? Have we loved our neighbours as ourselves? Have God's laws governed our behaviour? Before the bar of God we stand judged as a nation that has historically confessed faith in God but so obviously failed. For this he calls us to true repentance. And without that repentance there can be no healing of our nation. Could it be that the cruel violence of these past years might be a judgment on our disobedience, our idolatry, blind prejudice and self-righteousness? On many occasions in the history of God's people in the Old Testament the prophets identified even cruel and ruthless nations as instruments of judgment. The sensitive and perceptive Ezekiel challenged the hypocrisy and apostasy of his day with this searing prophecy:

The end has come upon the four corners of the land . . .
I will judge you according to your conduct and repay you

for all your detestable practices . . . The day is here! It has come! Doom has burst forth, the rod has budded, arrogance has blossomed! Violence has grown into a rod to punish wickedness' (Ezek. 7:2–3,10–11).

With relentless frequency such words come from all the prophets of the Old Testament. Proclaiming the word did not make them popular. Some, like Jonah, did their best to escape it and avoid speaking out the word of God that burned in their hearts. All of them suffered misunderstanding and persecution. Yet they did not stand in self-righteous isolation apart from their people. They identified with them as they exposed the roots of the destructive cancer that was destroying their nation. We can easily understand the anguish that caused 'the weeping prophet' Jeremiah to cry out:

Oh, that my head were a spring of water and my eyes a fountain of tears! I would weep day and night for the slain of my people. Oh, that I had in the desert a lodging place for travellers, so that I might leave my people and go away from them; for they are all adulterers, a crowd of unfaithful people. 'They make ready their tongue like a bow, to shoot lies; it is not by truth that they triumph in the land. They go from one sin to another; they do not acknowledge me,' declares the Lord. (Jer. 9:1–3).

Looking out on all the missed opportunities of a people who had been so richly blessed by God he called to them in warning:

The harvest is past, the summer has ended, and we are not saved. Since my people are crushed, I am crushed; I mourn, and horror grips me. Is there no balm in Gilead? Is there no physician there? Why then is there no healing for the wound of my people? (Jer. 8:20–22)

These men fearlessly turned the searchlight of God's word on all that was wrong at the heart of their nation. That searchlight exposed the cruelty and injustice practised by those in authority in the affairs of state, from the king down to the junior civil servant. It was trained on the shady dealings in the stock markets of the day and on the corruption and exploitation in business enterprises. Discrimination and oppression of the poor and disadvantaged were exposed. Lying and false witnessing was identified and brought to light. Above all, those in religious leadership were held responsible for the ways in which they had deliberately misled the people – false prophets speaking lies, 'peace, peace where there is no peace'. Sexual immorality practised also by religious leaders was ruthlessly brought to light. Amos, the eighth-century prophet, regularly landed himself in trouble as he courageously denounced hypocrisy at the leading religious shrines of the land.

> I hate, I despise your religious feasts; I cannot stand your assemblies. Even though you bring me burnt offerings and grain offerings, I will not accept them. Though you bring choice fellowship offerings, I will have no regard for them. Away with the noise of your songs! I will not listen to the music of your harps. But let justice roll on like a river, righteousness like a never-failing stream! (Amos 5:21–24).

The indignation voiced by prophets like Amos expressed God's anger but they also carried in their hearts his compassion. God longed to restore his people to a right relationship with himself and with each other. In judgment he remembered mercy. Jonah the reluctant prophet knew this well. When the people of Nineveh, the heathen city, had repented and destruction was averted, Jonah petulantly declared: 'I knew that you are a gracious and compassionate God, slow to anger and abounding in love, a God who relents from sending calamity' (Jonah 4:2).

Jesus, the greatest prophet, reserved his clearest condemnation for those religious leaders of his day who misused their privileged positions, compromising God's commandments or reducing them to petty traditions. 'You nullify the word of God for the sake of your tradition,' he charged. 'You hypocrites! Isaiah was right when he prophesied about you: "These people honour me with their lips, but their hearts are far from me. They worship me in vain; their teachings are but rules taught by men"' (Matt. 15:6–9).

If my people

Over the past years in Ireland there is one Scripture that seems to come to us with increasing urgency. It is the word spoken to King Solomon three thousand years ago but it speaks directly into our situation today. After the excitement of the dedication of the great Temple in Jerusalem, as Solomon lay awake in the night God spoke to him. I believe those words enshrine some abiding principles:

> When I shut up the heavens so that there is no rain, or command locusts to devour the land or send a plague among my people, if my people, who are called by my name, will humble themselves and pray and seek my face and turn from their wicked ways, then will I hear from heaven and will forgive their sin and will heal their land. (2 Chron. 7:13–14)

The onus is on the people of God, 'my people, who are called by my name'. We are those who hold so much responsibility when disaster strikes.

There are four conditions which God's people are invited to fulfil:

1   to humble ourselves
2   to pray
3   to seek God's face
4   to turn from their wicked ways.

When we meet these four conditions God makes three promises.

a to hear from heaven
b to forgive
c to heal their land.

It is important to note that these conditions are binding not on the violent, evil and godless people but on the people of God.

In many gatherings throughout Ireland and in the Christian Renewal Centre we have taken this word and tried to act upon it. In times of prayer God has often spoken to us in words of prophecy, warning and encouragement. One such occasion was shared in 1978:

> The state of this land causes me tremendous grief. The attitude of my people is such that it enables the evil spirits to laugh and sneer. The pride of my people frustrates me. Can you say that you love me when you will not bow down to prepare the Royal Robe for the Bride? I shall take away many prematurely, so you will no longer have a chance to work. My dear one, do not think it is beyond a merciful God so to deal with his people. My word is strong and severe in your hearing. I want to awaken my people. And you, my daughter, my son, have never yet been willing to be made free. Because you bicker, quarrel and fight, the demons leap and dance with joy. Let there be repentance before me, so that with your will and my power we shall do great and mighty things. Cause my angels to leap and dance with joy. Only those who love me and bend the knee, and hear my voice, will know my power to tear down strongholds. I appeal to you. Who then will those be who hear and respond, working together with the Holy One?

Another, given in 1985, spoke of the kind of repentance and humbling we need and what would happen as a consequence.

> I come among you with mercy and compassion, with forgiveness and love. I know all your agony and your suffering for they are mine too. I want to give to you my Spirit of healing and comfort and strength. But I desire

first your repentance, for without repentance there can be no reconciliation and without reconciliation there can be no rejoicing. I desire not the formulation nor the form of repentance, for you say with your lips that you have sinned but believe not in your hearts and show it not forth in your lives. I desire a deep realisation of the rift and chasm between you and me and between you and yours. As the mountains of Mourne sweep down to the sea, so the mountains of true mourning will sweep down into the sea of my compassion, forgiveness and love. There shall be such an outpouring of my Spirit that the rivers of repentance will be full once again and waters of forgiveness and the springs of my love will bring forth rich fruit of reconciliation and rejoicing and the land will be healed.

A truly repentant spirit

The last months of 1980 were particularly dark days in Northern Ireland when tension was acute and fears of an escalation of violence mounted. The leaders of the four main churches were meeting together regularly for prayer and discussion: Dr John Armstrong, Church of Ireland Archbishop of Armagh; Cardinal Tomas O'Fiaich, Roman Catholic Archbishop of Armagh; Dr Ronald Craig, Moderator of the Presbyterian Church; and the Revd Sydney Callaghan, President of the Methodist Church, issued a call to an octave of Prayer for Ireland from 28 December 1980 until 4 January 1981. Thousands of people were alerted to pray. I believe that intercession at that time helped to avert greater conflict and possible civil war in the province.

Introducing the week of prayer the Church leaders issued a clear call to repentance:

We need a truly repentant spirit and a sorrowful penitence for our failures. We must become aware of the many ways in which we have come short of the Christianity we have professed. In this way only will our hearts and minds be turned from the sins and errors which are destroying us. We need, too, a practical faith, not in ourselves and in what we are able to do but in the saving love of God that is found in Jesus Christ. This brings us to forgiveness and teaches us also to forgive, that we may find new life and strength in partnership with Christ, our Lord. It is this that gives us hope and it is for this that we must pray fervently to God.

In a divided community like Ireland it is not easy to face that challenge and find meaningful ways to offer and receive forgiveness. Towards the end of 1980 six of us who were leaders in renewal came together to pray about the situation. Two were from the Republic of Ireland, Sister Briege Murphy from Dundalk and Father Martin Tierney from Dublin. Four came for the north, Larry Kelly from Belfast, Peter Yarr and Dr John Kelly from Bangor and myself. As we prayed it was clearly discerned that we should call Christians to come together from all over Ireland on Pentecost Sunday 1981 to pray and intercede for our land in a spirit of repentance. Days of renewal in preparation were held in all four provinces of the country and many observed the Friday before Pentecost Sunday as a day of fasting. The event was truly historic. Ten thousand people assembled from all corners of Ireland in Downpatrick near the site where Patrick began his missionary work in AD 432, and where he is believed to have been buried on 17 March 461.

It is reckoned that never before in Ireland had such a representative gathering of Christians met. We praised God, shared his word and stood together in the open air to pray for our land. As we prayed gentle rain began to fall. I felt God was giving a parable of what he wanted to do in greater measure all over our country. He had called us from our places of separation and division to stand shoulder to shoulder, bowing our heads in prayer, acknowledging him as our one Lord near the place where Patrick had baptised his first Irish convert, Dichu the local chieftain. Was God not calling us back to the simplicity and fervour of those early days? Was he not calling us again to humble ourselves, setting aside the pride and prejudice of centuries of division? Could the gentle Irish rain that fell upon us that Pentecost Sunday be a token of a fresh outpouring of his Holy Spirit in the dry desert of our fading faith?

It recalled a vision given to an English visitor several months before. He saw a map of Ireland. It looked beautiful, green and covered with a network of sparkling blue rivers and streams, moving and flashing with light. The Lord spoke through the vision and said:

> My love will flow throughout Ireland like those rivers. In the past these rivers have been blocked by prejudice and long-held grudges, with unforgiveness and resentment and the waters have been made bitter and become stagnant and no life could flourish . . . but I am moving by my Spirit and there is a new flow of my love throughout the hearts of my people in Ireland, and she will again become beautiful – beautiful and full of my life. The circulation throughout my body in Ireland will be marvellously restored as my people yield to my spirit and relinquish Pride . . . already I am liberating my people into my love and this love will flow from heart to heart as they are willing to move in reconciling love.

Following Pentecost 1981 leaders gathered from all over Ireland in Bangor, County Down for a weekend of prayer, listening to God and intercession. During that time together through prophecy God spoke again a word of encouragement to us.

> This island has a long history of revealing the nature of the Lord Jesus and the Person of the Lord Jesus, but as the age moves to its close God will use this island if you, believers of the people of God, will lay aside every burden and everything that hinders, and let yourselves be poured out even as the Lord Jesus was poured out, to be willing to take up his strength when the burden seems heavy, to be willing to go away from the crowds to pray and seek the mind of the Lord, and the strength of the Lord, and then to come back and minister. In the days when Jesus walked the earth

he fed five thousand with a few loaves and fishes. He was one Man, filled with the Holy Spirit. You are many men and women, filled with the Holy Spirit. If you are willing truly to make Jesus Lord you shall feed not the five thousand but the fifty thousand. Be encouraged and be strengthened and be ready to do the spectacular, because God is looking for a people who are not afraid to do the mighty miracles, the wondrous miracles, to show forth who he is in the earth, that his kingdom might truly come in power and in might and in glory.

Aware of the barrenness of so much inherited religious bigotry and rivalry, and the scandal it presents to the world, a group of evangelical Christians in Ireland came together in 1988 'to look afresh at the Bible in order to identify some principles which we hope will help us become part of the cure'. I was invited to assist in that exploration and the result is a document which has been endorsed by several hundred Christian leaders from a wide spectrum of evangelical commitment in Ireland. *For God and His Glory Alone* examines from a thoroughly biblical base some of the issues that are central to our common witness as Christians in a divided community. Dealing with important topics such as reconciliation, forgiveness, justice and righteousness, peace and citizenship, the document suggests practical ways in which we can move forward in obedience to Christ. To begin with we admit that 'far too often our values, attitudes and actions have been an imitation of society and not of the character of Christ'. The section on repentance declares:

The only way we can become a community of hope is if we come to God (and to one another) in humility, penitence and repentance. Many in Northern Ireland are caught in a face-saving exercise, but there can be no face-saving at the cross. The essential nature of repentance is losing face. We need to say we have been wrong – not merely that we have been the victims of history. We all need to ask for forgiveness from God and our neighbours, repenting and seeking the way of non-violence and the way of the cross as

the effective means of change in our land. However difficult
it may be, we as Christians are committed to Christian
means as well as Christian ends.[3]

It is impossible to re-write history but we can acknowledge
in penitence before God and our fellowmen those aspects
of our history which have been so obviously an offence
to God, rejecting and disowning the attitudes that allow
them to persist today. We are not responsible for what
our forebears did; yet in Ireland we are very aware that
'the sins of the fathers are visited on the children even to
the third and fourth generation'. Thank God, that vicious
circle can be broken by the heart-felt prayer and genuine
repentance of his people.

Changing history

The Bible affords many examples of individuals and small
groups of people who changed the course of history through
repentance and prayer. Ezra and Nehemiah at critical times
in the history of Israel pleaded for God's mercy on a nation
that had turned from God's commands (Ezra 9; Neh. 9).
One of the best examples in the Old Testament is the
remarkable prayer recorded in Daniel 9. Although he held
a high position in a foreign country and had no need to
be involved in the complexities of his nation's problems,
Daniel 'turned to the Lord God and pleaded with him in
prayer and petition, in fasting, and in sackcloth and ashes'
(v. 3). Daniel fully identified with the failure of his people
to keep God's covenant of love:

> We have sinned and done wrong. We have been wicked and
> have rebelled; we have turned away from your commands
> and laws. We have not listened to your servants the
> prophets, who spoke in your name to our kings, our
> princes and our fathers, and to all the people of the
> land . . . We do not make requests of you because we
> are righteous, but because of your great mercy. O Lord,

listen! O Lord, forgive! O Lord, hear and act! For your
sake, O my God, do not delay, because your city and your
people bear your Name. (5–6, 18–19)

As sin is corporate as well as individual, so repentance
needs to have a corporate expression. Historically for
good and ill three strong forces have interacted in this
small island to create the apparently intractable problems
which persist today. English imperialism, Irish nationalism
and Unionist loyalism have proved an explosive mixture.
Out of the whirlpool of our history there is so much
of which each side has to repent and seek forgiveness.
Without that repentance and mutual forgiveness there can
be no lasting peace. I sometimes feel that as a nation we are
somewhat like the poor demon-possessed man Jesus met
on the hills above Galilee. Overpowered and possessed by
a legion of demons he could not find rest or healing. Jesus
commanded the evil spirits to come out of the man and to
the amazement of the onlookers the man who was the terror
of the countryside was 'sitting at Jesus' feet, dressed and in
his right mind' (Luke 8:35).

Only God can deliver us from the guilt of the past as
individuals and as a nation. Only the power of Christ can
exorcise the demons that have dominated us, driving us at
times in our history to desperate deeds of destruction.

We have seen that release take place in small ways which
hopefully will lead the way to more deliverance. In 1985 four
Christian leaders in Derry took a courageous initiative in
this exercise of repentance and mutual forgiveness. Derry,
or Londonderry as it was renamed in the seventeenth century, is a living symbol of that 'triangle of history'. There
for centuries the three forces of English imperialism, Irish
nationalism and Unionist loyalism have clashed with some
disastrous consequences. On Good Friday 1985 Father Neal
Carlin, the Revd Liz Hewitt, the Revd Alan Harper and the
Revd David Gray led a silent procession through Derry to
Guildhall Square. They were from four denominations in
the city, Roman Catholic, Methodist, Church of Ireland

and Presbyterian. Having met and prayed together they were convinced that 'unless we confess our tribal religious sins and be forgiven by one another, no healing will come to these lands'. Standing under a cross in Guildhall Square representatives of the three 'tribes' confessed specific sins of the past which still corrode relationships, asking God's forgiveness and forgiveness from one another. It is significant that for several months after that event Derry saw the longest period without bloodshed for some eighteen years.

This is not an easy peace

In a similar gathering in the centre of Belfast we witnessed the release that flowed from such repentance when approximately a thousand Roman Catholics and Protestants came together from north and south. Men who had been enemies, serving in opposing para-military groups, asked forgiveness of each other. A group of concerned Christians had travelled from mainland Britain to share in the meeting. Among them was Lord Hylton who takes a keen and practical interest in the affairs of Northern Ireland and has often spoken on repentance and reconciliation in the House of Lords. At a meeting in 1981 he said:

> I am conscious of having many friends in Ireland. My father was Anglican, my mother is Roman Catholic. I went to Protestant schools in England but nevertheless remain a Catholic. Perhaps this gives me a certain sympathy for both sides, North and South, Unionist and Republican, Protestant and Catholic. The quarrels of these divided parties are so ancient that we are all involved. None of us is guiltless, none of us can cast the first stone, for like sheep we have all gone astray. I believe that we, here in England, need to repent. We need to repent for the atrocities of the Cromwellians in Ireland, for the harshness of the penal laws, for British inhumanity at the time of the Irish potato famine and for the excesses of the Black and Tans after the First World War. Having repented we should ask

forgiveness for the injustices done to Ireland. We must open
our hearts too in forgiveness of the harm done by Ireland
to Britain. In human terms forgiveness must be mutually
accepted if it is to be complete. As Charles Williams once
wrote: 'Many reconciliations have broken down because
both parties came prepared to forgive and unprepared to
be forgiven.'

In the Belfast gathering God spoke a simple but powerful
word of prophecy:

This is not an easy peace that I would give you, my children.
It cost me the cross to reconcile you to the Father. You must
humble yourselves before each other, listen to each other's
pain, share your brother's burden, seek his forgiveness, if
you would really be reconciled in my love and my way.

The Lord's challenge in that prophecy is expressed in a
prayer which we often use:

Lord Jesus Christ,
You are the way of peace.
Come into the brokenness of this land
With your healing love.
Help us to be willing to bow before you
In true repentance,
And to bow to one another
In real forgiveness.

By the fire of your Holy Spirit
Melt our hard hearts and consume
The pride and prejudice
Which separate us from each other.
Fill us, O Lord, with your perfect love
Which casts out fear
And bind us together in that unity
Which you share with the Father
And the Holy Spirit for ever. Amen.

11

HEALING

Praise the Lord, O my soul,
And forget not all his benefits –
Who forgives all your sins
And heals all your diseases.
                    Psalm 103:2–3

I am the Lord, who heals you. (Exod. 15:26)

The Lord heals today. He heals the bodies, the minds and
the spirits of people now as he did when he was here on
earth. He heals through the skills of doctors, surgeons and
nurses and brings healing as a result of painstaking medical
research. And he heals people by the prayer of faith through
the ministry of love in his body, the Church.

There is a story told that when Jesus returned to heaven
an inquisitive angel came to him one day with the question,
'Lord, what plans have you made for carrying on your
mission on planet earth?'

Jesus replied, 'I have left eleven men to carry on my
work.'

'And what happens if they fail you?' said the angel.

'I have no other plans,' Jesus answered.

God took the amazing risk of entrusting his mission to
ordinary men and women like you and me. We are to
be his hands, his feet, his voice in the world. Jesus
said:

Anyone who has faith in me will do what I have been doing. He will do even greater things than these, because I am going to the Father. And I will do whatever you ask in my name, so that the Son may bring glory to the Father. You may ask me for anything in my name, and I will do it. (John 14:12–14).

It is Jesus who commissions and empowers his church to 'preach the good news to all creation' and to 'place their hands on sick people, and they will get well' (Mark 16:15,18). Gifts of healing are part of God's endowment of the Church in its ministry. As the Lord renews his Church all over the world those gifts are being wonderfully restored as a sign of the presence of God's Kingdom here and now. When we came to Rostrevor we knew that God had called us to a ministry of prayer, renewal and reconciliation. We were not to be specifically a 'Centre of Healing'. Yet we knew that healing of body, mind and spirit is an integral part of the work we were called to do.

All of us need God's healing touch. And it has been our joy to see God perform many miracles of healing in answer to the faith-filled prayer of his people. In the process we have been learning more about these wonderful and mysterious gifts of healing which have never been taken away from the Church but for so long have been sadly neglected. We have come to realise how humble we must be as well as confident in the presence of God's miraculous power to heal. He is sovereign in his working and yet calls us to work with him in faith through love. God is the giver, all his gifts are powerful in their effect and flow from his compassion. As we minister these gifts of God's healing to hurting people we must always insulate them with love.

We are learning to expect God to do the 'unexpected'. In love he is consistently reaching out to hurting, wounded people. We are not the possessors of his gifts of healing but the messengers, who by faith carry them to those who need to be healed. In all kinds of circumstances and at unprepared moments we may be called to deliver his love gift to another in need. It may be on the telephone when someone phones in deep distress; or when the door-bell of the Centre rings and someone in pain or grief or despair is standing there. It may be in a meeting or a day of renewal when a need is realised and Jesus is present to heal and calls us to reach out with his healing gift.

Aware of such great needs in the area of healing, for many years now we have set aside special times of prayer for healing. People with all kinds of needs, physical, spiritual and emotional come. Members of community who have prayed and prepared together beforehand lead these prayer times. Through praise and prayer and in the silence we come with the sufferers into the healing presence of Jesus. Faith is encouraged by reading from God's word about his love for us, and his willingness to make us whole. We explain that we are not the healers, Jesus is. We are simply coming to stand alongside in faith and prayer, bringing those in sickness and need to him. We invite those who come to turn their eyes on Jesus who 'was pierced for our transgressions, crushed for our iniquities; the punishment that brought us peace was upon him, and by his wounds we are healed' (Isa. 53:5). Then, as Jesus has commissioned us, we pray with the laying on of hands for the person to be healed, asking the Lord to do what we cannot do. We pray quietly or sometimes in tongues. In the quietness we invite the Lord by his Holy Spirit to come into every area of the person's life with his healing love and power. Sometimes there will be immediate evidence of physical healing. At other times the healing will be a process. Suzanne explains what God did for her in one of those times of prayer:

For many years I have had Raynaud's Disease, which is a circulatory disease and affects the extremities – in my case my hands and feet; they were never warm, I suffered from chilblains and my hands had deep cracks both at the tips of the fingers and across the length of the fingers. Approximately sixteen years ago I had major surgery and this was most successful – for eleven months – then things were back to square one. I had been warned that this could happen but, as surgery was for once only, there was nothing to do but try again to find an oral medication which might help. Only one sort proved to have any effect but the side-effects were such I had to stop taking it. We had also moved to a smaller house on the advice of my surgeon: we were able to keep it warm and there was less housework to do and thus saved my hands.

In January 1987 my big toe on my right foot was black and my right hand was very painful – I couldn't type and I had great difficulty in opening a car door. My doctor said he was terribly sorry but there was nothing further he could suggest except to keep my hands and feet covered and as warm as possible.

Shortly after this a friend asked me if I would consider going to the Christian Renewal Centre at Rostrevor. My husband and I discussed this suggestion and we decided that I should go and an appointment was made. When we arrived we were welcomed by a member of the community – I think we must have been there for two hours and during this time we talked, read from the Bible, and prayed. I was anointed with oil – my right thumb was anointed – it hadn't healed for at least six months – and then I was anointed for healing for my whole body. During this time I was very aware of our Lord's presence within me – an infilling of the Holy Spirit – a lovely tingly feeling! On our way home, I knew I was being healed – a sharp, searing pain shot up my right thumb – again and again. I felt a tremendous surge of the healing power of the Holy Spirit throughout my body, from the top of my head to the tips of my toes – I continued praying and praising and thanking God for his great love and faithfulness to me. During the evening I telephoned the Centre and told them our wonderful news. That night, in my bath, I looked at my big toe in astonishment – it was pink for the first time in six months – really pink – and it has been ever since. Within two weeks my hands had healed and I went to my doctor. He confirmed that they were definitely better and that my circulation was normal and asked me what I had done. I told him and he rejoiced with me.

I never cease to thank God for his love and forgiveness.

Every morning when I wake up I put out my hand and ask him to hold it in his and grant me strength and grace for the day ahead.

A faith environment

You will notice in Suzanne's testimony how much stress she puts on faith. We learn from the Bible how important that is. Unbelief even hindered Jesus, preventing him in some places from doing healing miracles. Our faith may be trembling and weak. It may be as small as a grain of mustard seed. But if it is offered in simple childlike trust to God great power is released. A clear illustration is given in the Gospel of Mark. A poor woman who had suffered from a most unpleasant illness for twelve years came in great distress but with simple trust to Jesus. She was jostled in the large crowd surrounding Jesus as he hurried in response to an urgent call to the bedside of a dying child:

And a woman was there who had been subject to bleeding for twelve years. She had suffered a great deal under the care of many doctors and had spent all she had, yet instead of getting better she grew worse. When she heard about Jesus, she came up behind him in the crowd and touched his cloak, because she thought, 'If I just touch his clothes, I will be healed.' Immediately her bleeding stopped and she felt in her body that she was freed from her suffering. At once Jesus realised that power had gone out from him. He turned around in the crowd and asked, 'Who touched my clothes?' 'You see the people crowding against you,' his disciples answered, 'and yet you can ask, "Who touched me?"' But Jesus kept looking around to see who had done it. Then the woman, knowing what had happened to her, came and fell at his feet and, trembling with fear, told him the whole truth. He said to her, 'Daughter, your faith has healed you. Go in peace and be freed from your suffering'. (Mark 5:25–34)

We have discovered how important it is to create an environment of faith where those too weak or fearful to exercise much faith for themselves are surrounded by a community of faith. This is well illustrated by an incident Niall Griffin recalls:

There are few things which deepen our faith more than to see our prayers being answered, especially if a healing is involved. One Wednesday in November 1984 this happened when a helper, Sister Helen, who was staying with us, fell and broke a bone in her right wrist. She was taken to a local hospital and two X-rays were taken: one of the front and one of the back of her wrist. The doctor said that the bone was shattered and that it would be in plaster for six weeks. The plaster was put on and, as Helen was in considerable pain, she received pain-killing tablets. An appointment was made for a check-up on the following Wednesday. On the Friday morning after the accident a member of community laid hands on Helen and prayed for her healing. That night she did not need any pain-killers. The next day, Saturday, was one of the monthly days of renewal. The subject was 'The gifts of the Holy Spirit'. During a time for ministering to one another, Helen remembers laying her left hand on her right wrist and saying, 'Lord, if I have faith now you can heal this.' Immediately after this a member of the community was given a picture of two people whose right hands God wanted to heal. Helen indicated that she was one of the people concerned, and those beside her prayed for her healing. The following Wednesday she went for her check-up and had two further X-rays. Then she was ushered into a room with three doctors, one of whom was comparing the first two X-rays with the two just taken. He excused himself and he and the two other doctors went away to consult. When he returned he asked Helen to move her fingers, hand and wrist in various different ways.

'As far as I can gather this is all healed up,' he said in a puzzled tone. 'Keep doing the exercises, but if you have any pain take the tablets – but don't come back!'

When we talked about and gave thanks for the way God had healed her, something she said stuck in my mind: 'It's one thing to believe that God loves you.

It's quite another to experience a broken wrist being healed within a week. When that happens you know he loves you.'

Faith and persevering prayer are closely linked in Scripture. Jesus, introducing the parable of the 'persistent widow', encouraged his disciples 'that they should always pray and not give up' (Luke 18:1). The community of faith extends to all who pray and intercede for the sick, surely one of the most selfless ministries in the whole Church. Persistent prayer was rewarded for John Armstrong when he was Bishop of Cashel in the south of Ireland.

'I have always since student days believed in healing,' he said. 'Then I was struck down by a form of neuritis. I could not walk and was totally dependent on others. The doctor told me I would never walk again, and I had to use a walking-frame. This was hard for a man who used to drive 25,000 miles a year and had been extremely active. I did not believe my doctor because I am a stubborn person, but I did believe in God.'

Many people were praying for the bishop and particularly those involved in the Churches' Ministry of Healing. At his request someone visited the bishop while in hospital and ministered to him with the laying on of hands.

'Nothing outwardly seemed to happen,' Bishop Armstrong recalled, 'but we went on praying.'

During his illness Canon John Gunstone and I were invited to speak at a meeting in Waterford and we called to visit Bishop and Mrs Armstrong in their home in the city. By that time he had been released from hospital but was unable to walk. The bishop explained that he believed in God's power to raise him to health again in spite of the medical prognosis. Before we left his home we laid hands on him, praying that God would honour his faith and answer the prayers of all those who longed to see him fully restored to his important ministry of leadership. The bishop made his way slowly to the door on his walking-frame to bid us goodbye. Writing later in his diocesan newsletter he explained what happened that night:

> Doris, my wife, helped me to bed that night, placing the
> walking-frame near my bed in case I needed to go to
> the bathroom. At 3 a.m. I got out of bed and walked
> to the bathroom and back. When I got back into bed I
> realised that I hadn't used the frame. Doris woke up,
> so I told her.
>
> 'Do you know what's happened? I've just walked to
> the bathroom.'
>
> 'You never did!' was her reply.
>
> That was the start of my healing and I've walked ever
> since. I still get pain, but subsequently I have been made
> archbishop and am able to do my work, which would have
> been impossible before. My healing is not a fairy story, it
> is a fact of experience.[1]

Faith is both a fruit and a gift of the Holy Spirit. The
charismatic gift of faith is a powerful companion to the
gift of healing, especially when we are confronted with
what seem 'impossible' situations, like a 'terminal' illness
or an 'incurable' disease. In practising the ministry of
healing we are not called to diagnose illness but to stand
alongside the sufferer in faith believing in God's power to
do what appears humanly impossible. This is the kind of
faith which Jesus said 'can remove mountains'. We have
seen that happen on many occasions and give glory to God
for his evident working. I remember being called one night
by a local minister to the home of a young mother who had
undergone an operation for a malignant brain tumour. The
doctors had done everything they could for Olive and she
was not expected to live more than another day. A good
friend of ours, Mrs Rita Burke – whom God has used in
the healing ministry for many years after she was herself
miraculously healed – accompanied me. Members of the
community and many of Olive's friends were supporting
in prayer. We prayed in simple faith and laid our hands
on Olive, committing her to the Lord, the Healer. Three
months later we had the joy of greeting her when she drove

her car to the Centre to offer thanks to God for the healing she had received. That was more than seven years ago and she is still alive and well.

In 1985, with a team from the Centre, I was leading a meeting in Cookstown in mid-Ulster. The theme of the meeting was 'Jesus is the answer for our world today'. I had asked people there to express thanks for blessings that God had brought to them in their lives. There was an encouraging response. People thanked God for a wide variety of good things that God had done. Some of them were blessings we often take for granted – friends and loved ones, food and provisions, health and strength and life itself. Then there were thanksgivings for real healings people had experienced. Two women thanked God for healing from cancer. Another woman was rejoicing in healing from epilepsy. Several men had known God's deliverance from addiction to alcohol. With all these people we rejoiced at God's amazing grace and love. For me, however, the greatest joy was to hear the testimony of a young woman I had met three years before. She is a walking miracle.

Emma and a neighbour had climbed into a slurry tank, attempting to save Emma's husband who had accidentally fallen into it while working on his farm. All three were overcome by the fumes in the tank and when eventually rescued were unconscious, and there seemed little hope of survival. They were rushed to hospital and through the skill of the doctors and nurses the two men began to recover. Emma, however, remained unconscious for five weeks and there seemed little that could be done. In Emma's church a group of women joined their minister in regular prayer. They alerted others to pray. Then one day the minister asked me to come with him to pray for Emma in hospital.

We went into the ward with Emma's husband and prayed together. Humanly the situation seemed hopeless and the medical prognosis was bleak. We laid hands on Emma, anointed her with oil as the Scriptures encouraged us to do. In faith we believed that God was working in her body to do what we were helpless to do. Her friends went on praying and at the Christian Renewal Centre we joined in prayer for Emma's healing. Within a few days the news was encouraging. Emma had regained consciousness. Within weeks she was beginning to walk again and able to leave the hospital for some hours to visit her husband and child. Then came the news that she was home and well.

I scarcely recognised Emma when I saw her. She was obviously so happy that she could walk and work again. Her simple witness moved us and we gave thanks and praise to God. And that was not all. Emma shared the joyful news that since the healing she and her husband are rejoicing in God's gift of another lovely child.

The gifts of the Spirit

As a community committed to serving the renewal of the Church we rejoice at the increase in the ministry of healing in local churches. The community of Christian believers that forms the local church is meant by God to be the place of paramount healing; a congregation of love and mutual forgiveness where each cares for the other and ministers God's healing love, spiritually, physically and emotionally. We have to confess how far short we come. Too often people leave the church-gathering as sick as when they entered.

In the area of emotional healing from life's hurts, often inflicted by others, the prayer of faith is accompanied by much counselling. The charismatic gifts of the word of knowledge and the word of wisdom are powerful tools to help in this area of ministry. On occasions as we pray with someone who needs inner healing the Holy Spirit may reveal through a picture or a vision a particular area of need or a hurt that lies concealed. It may be an area of resentment or unforgiveness that needs to be confessed. With the wisdom which the Holy Spirit gives we are then able to pray confidently that the Lord will come into that area of hurt.

Mary was someone who first visited the Centre in 1977.

> I was a very bruised and wounded person, only able to absorb very little at a time, having had several mental breakdowns for many years. I was really afraid of men, having been sexually assaulted as a child, and I now realise that fear remained through life without my being aware of it. I kept coming back to the Centre every year for the Bible weeks and after a few years of the Lord's gentle healing I was able to read the Bible. The Lord has healed me in many ways through his word, and one particular healing was through Colossians 2:9–10: 'For in Christ all the fulness of the Deity lives in bodily form, and you have been given fulness in Christ, who is the Head over every power and authority.' I was very depressed and went to the Centre for ministry and these two verses of Scripture ministered to me and the darkness lifted completely and the sun shone brightly. On another occasion Myrtle and a team ministered to me and the Lord healed my broken heart; this was a very special healing. The day before this healing Niall ministered to me and the Lord enabled me to open up and share my life with him and I received the grace of a deep repentance and for the first time experienced the sweetness of Jesus. I also had great healing through the music ministry at the Centre and can now sing joyfully in my own church knowing that I'm singing to the Lord and giving him the glory.

St Paul wrote to the Christian Church in Corinth: 'You are the body of Christ, and each one of you is a part of it' (1 Cor. 12:27). 'If one part suffers, every part suffers with it; if one part is honoured, every part rejoices with it' (1 Cor. 12:26). In his prayers for the churches which he planted St Paul constantly prayed for a demonstration of God's love in committed relationships and of God's power in healing and transformation. The analogy of 'the body' in New Testament teaching is an important one. For many of us it remains a vague theological concept. In practice it is meant to express the very life of Christ flowing through us, binding us together in mutual love, energised to convey his vitality and healing in the world.

As members one of another we are mutually interdependent. We need each other and we are called to be agents of healing for one another. All of us are 'wounded healers'. Having ourselves received the healing love of Jesus we are able to point others to the source of true healing in him. The world honours those who appear to be strong. The paradox of the Kingdom of God is that 'when I am weak, then I am strong' (2 Cor. 12:10). God's power is made perfect in weakness. Someone who works and cares for prisoners puts it this way:

> Christ is building his Kingdom with earth's broken things. Men want only the strong, the successful, the victorious, the unbroken, in building their kingdoms; but God is the God of the unsuccessful, of those who have failed. Heaven is filling with earth's broken lives and there is no bruised reed that Christ cannot take and restore to glorious blessedness and beauty. He can take life crushed by pain or sorrow and make it into a harp whose music shall be all praise. He can lift earth's saddest failure up to heaven's glory.

What about those who are not healed?

Inevitably when we talk about healing we must address the question which everyone of us has to face. What about those who are not healed? Why? Why? Why? scream the broken hearts of people who have followed the seemingly endless funerals of victims of violence. It calls through the tears after the death of a loved one for whom we have fervently prayed for recovery. Faith was exercised, believing, persevering prayer was offered and the one we loved died. We stand before a great mystery with a question that cannot be fully answered this side of heaven. All the people Jesus healed during his earthly ministry died eventually. Even Lazarus whom Jesus raised from the dead. Death is the one certainty in life. It is the appointment no one can refuse. Healing, when it comes, is merely a postponement of that appointment and a sign of the fullness of the kingdom to come where 'there will be no more death or mourning or crying or pain' (Rev. 21:4). We live in the overlap of those two kingdoms, 'now' and the 'yet to be'. That is why the New Testament reminds us that here we have no lasting dwelling-place. We are pilgrims passing through this world with the opportunity to prepare for the greater life that God provides for those who love him.

In our understandable disappointment in apparently un-answered prayer we must not turn away from prayer for healing nor abandon the wonderful ministry that God has entrusted to his Church. We are right to be angry at disease and death, which have entered into the world through the sin and disobedience of mankind. We are right to feel angry at the needless loss of life through hate-filled violence, yet in the midst of all that suffering we are learning important lessons that God wants to teach us. My introduction to the healing ministry in the Church came when my mother became seriously ill with cancer. After surgery she had a short remission and then died. The shock and pain for me and all our family was very hard to take. She was a relatively young woman and had enjoyed good health all her life. Through the Church's Ministry of Healing, then led in Belfast by Canon Fred Baillie, I received great personal strength and encouragement. My mother too was greatly blessed through the ministry of prayer with the laying on of hands. Many were praying for her and even through her pain her personal faith grew deeper. I have no doubt that prayer was answered in the evident strength she received to face the final battle. When her last moments came it was not defeat for her but victory as she quietly passed over the valley of the shadow of death into the nearer presence of the Lord she loved and trusted. It is in moments like these we discover the meaning of the strong and assuring promises of God's word such as Psalm 23:4–6:

> Even though I walk
>   through the valley of the shadow of death,
> I will fear no evil,
>   for you are with me;
> your rod and your staff,
>   they comfort me.

It is then we discover that for the Christian death is not the end. It is the beginning of a glorious new chapter of life. It is crossing the threshold into a fuller life beyond the grave. For those who remain here, even though our hearts are breaking, the great strong words of St Paul ring with clearer meaning than we had ever heard them.

> Who shall separate us from the love of Christ? Shall trouble or hardship or persecution or famine or nakedness or danger or sword . . . No, in all these things we are more than conquerors through him who loved us. For I am convinced that neither death nor life, neither angels nor demons, neither the present nor the future, nor any powers, neither height nor depth, nor anything else in all creation, will be able to separate us from the love of God that is in Christ Jesus our Lord. (Rom. 8:35,37–39)

The pain of God

Ultimately it is only at the cross of Calvary that we see the source of healing and the key to the understanding of pain. There we see Christ's triumph. The victory of good over evil, of love over hate, healing over disease, not in ignoring these but in his absorbing all their poisonous power and transforming it into the glorious medicine of salvation, peace and wholeness. There is no better way to understand that wordless victory of the cross than to reflect on what God by his Holy Spirit revealed to the prophet Isaiah 700 years earlier. Peering into the future Isaiah saw God's suffering servant, the Messiah:

> Surely he took up our infirmities and carried our sorrows, yet we considered him stricken by God, smitten by him, and afflicted. But he was pierced for our transgressions, he was crushed for our iniquities; the punishment that brought us peace was upon him, and by his wounds we are healed. We all, like sheep, have gone astray, each of us has turned to his own way; and the Lord has laid on him the iniquity of us all. He was oppressed and afflicted, yet he did not open his mouth; he was led like a lamb to the slaughter, and as a sheep before her shearers is silent, so he did not open his mouth. By oppression and judgment he was taken away. And who can speak of his descendants? For he was cut off from the land of the living; for the transgression of my people he was stricken. He was assigned a grave with the wicked, and with the rich in his death, though he had done no violence, nor was any deceit in his mouth. (Isa. 53:4–9)

There is a man in heaven who has been through it all:

> In every pang that rends the heart
> The man of sorrows had a part.

In their profoundly moving book, *In His Image*, Philip Yancey and the world-renowned surgeon and leprologist Paul Brand speak of 'the pain of God', so fully expressed on Calvary. Paul Brand writes:

> I have spent my life cutting into hands, delicately, with scalpel blades that slice through one layer of tissue at a time, to expose the marvellous complex of nerves and blood vessels and tiny bones and tendons and muscles inside . . . I know what crucifixion must do to a human hand.
> Executioners of that day drove their spikes through the wrist, right through the carpal tunnel that houses finger-controlling tendons and the median nerve. It is impossible to force a spike there without crippling the hand into a claw

shape. Jesus had no anaesthetic. He allowed those hands to be marred and crippled and destroyed.

Later, His weight hung from them, tearing more tissue, releasing more blood. There could be no more helpless image than that of a God hanging paralysed from a tree. 'Heal yourself!' the crowd jeered. He had saved others – why not Himself? The disciples, who had hoped He was the Messiah, cowered in the darkness or drifted away. Surely they had been mistaken – this figure could not be God.

Finally, in one last paroxysm of humanness, Jesus said simply, 'Father, into your hands I commit my spirit.' The humiliation of the Incarnation ended. The sentence was served.

But that is not the last glimpse we have of Jesus' hands in the biblical record. He appears again, in a closed room, where Thomas is still doubting the unlikely story he thinks his friends have concocted . . . At that moment, Jesus holds up those unmistakable hands His disciples had seen perform miracles. The scars give proof that they belong to Him, the One who had died on the cross. The body has changed – it can pass through walls and locked doors to join them. But the scars remain. Jesus invites Thomas to come and trace them with his own fingers.

Thomas responds simply, 'My Lord and my God!' It is the first recorded time that one of Jesus' disciples calls Him God directly. Significantly, the assertion comes in response to Jesus' wounds.

Why did Christ keep His scars? He could have had a perfect body, or no body, when He returned in splendour to heaven. Instead He carried with Him remembrances of His visit to earth. For a reminder of His time here, He chose scars. That is why I say God hears and understands pain, and even absorbs it into Himself – because He kept those scars as a lasting image of wounded humanity. He has been here; He has borne the sentence. The pain of man has become the pain of God.[2]

Bill and Sarah were friends of ours, a devoted Christian couple who were using their retirement to work for the Kingdom of God. In a serious car accident Bill was killed and Sarah injured. In a note acknowledging our letter of sympathy Sarah wrote the words of Grant Tullar that had special meaning for her and her family in their deep sorrow:

> Not till the loom is silent
> And the shuttles cease to fly
> Will God unroll the pattern
> And explain the reason why
> The dark threads are as needful
> In the weaver's skilful hand
> As the threads of gold and silver
> In the pattern He has planned.

12

PARTNERS IN MISSION

Those who are far away will come and help to build the temple of the Lord. (Zech. 6:15)

> *In Christ there is no east or west,*
> *In Him no south or north,*
> *But one great fellowship of love*
> *Throughout the whole wide earth.*
>   *John Oxenham*

God has a wonderful family here on earth. Out of every nation, tribe and language he has called a people who belong to one another because they belong to him. At the Christian Renewal Centre we are always conscious of the great international family to which we belong as we are linked with our partners in a fellowship of prayer which encircles the world. People from many nations find their way to Rostrevor. I had a look at the visitors book when I returned after several weeks away writing this book. We had missed friends who came to greet us from as far away as Russia, Yugoslavia, Germany, Italy, France, Switzerland and the United States. I was sorry to miss our first ever visitor from Albania who called while we were away. Even though language may be a barrier and we come from such varied backgrounds, when we meet those who love the Lord we experience a sense of family. When we travel to earth's remotest parts we are immediately at home when we meet God's people.

We have always valued links with friends in England, Scotland and Wales. Our history has been closely bound with these countries which share with us the western seaboard of Europe. For the past twenty years thousands of young men and women from Britain have served in the security forces in Northern Ireland. Many have been killed in a conflict which they found hard to understand. We have always had brothers and sisters from Great Britain as members of the community at the Centre. Their courage in coming and their commitment to sharing in the work of reconciliation in Ireland is a source of encouragement to us. Many from mainland Britain support the Centre with their gifts and prayers and a growing number of people realise that they have an important part to play in the healing of our land. Speakers from a wide variety of backgrounds in Great Britain have enriched our life over the years.

The Netherlands

Tuesday, 1 July 1690 is a date deeply etched in the memory of the people of Ireland. Two weeks previously William Prince of Orange had landed with his army in Carrickfergus, north of Belfast. Marching south he met the army of his father-in-law King James and at the River Boyne the decisive battle of modern Ireland was fought. James, the Catholic king, was defeated, soon to leave for France, and the Protestant ascendancy in Ireland was re-established, leading to centuries of suffering and conflict and building the walls of suspicion and fear which have persisted until this day. In view of those historic events it is wholly appropriate that we are closely linked with many of our brothers and sisters in Christ in Holland. Up to five hundred Christians in that country pray regularly for the work of the Christian Renewal Centre. Many of them belong to a prayer community drawn from different Christian traditions. For almost fifty years that community has been praying earnestly for the unity of the body of Christ. Soon after the

Centre was established in 1974 one of their leaders, Pieter van Heijningen, was drawn by a remarkable revelation to Rostrevor and a close link has been maintained ever since. Members of community are welcomed to the homes of our Dutch friends and some of them come to visit Ireland too. We were enriched by having Pieter's daughter Ruth Yvonne as a member of the community for two years.

South Africa

South Africa, whose story is closely bound with Holland, is another country with which we have enjoyed a close relationship. In the early 1970s the Holy Spirit began to move in renewing power over that great land. In 1975 I had the pleasure of meeting Dr Bill Burnett and his wife Sheila when we were invited to London to speak at a Fountain Trust Conference at Central Hall, Westminster. Bill, who had already made a significant contribution as a Christian leader in South Africa, was then Archbishop of Cape Town. In the same year at an international conference in Rome I met the Revd Derek Crumpton, a leader in the rapidly growing movement of renewal in South Africa. In September 1977 I was invited to South Africa to speak at the first Renewal Conference, held in Milner Park, Johannesburg. That was a remarkable and historic conference. For five days a thousand clergy and church leaders came together for a memorable time of praise and prayer and listening to God together. Another thousand lay people joined them for a further three days. Under the joint chairmanship of David du Plessis, Bill Burnett, Nicholas Bhengu and Bishop Alphaeus Zulu, a committee of sixty pastors drawn from fourteen different traditions worked and prayed together. The massive work involved in organising such a gathering was carried out most efficiently and with grace by Derek Crumpton and his wife Jean, with the help of their Christian community from East London. The spectacle of two

thousand delegates, black, coloured and white, including
Afrikaans and Dutch Reformed clergy, living together in
the same hotels, praying and worshipping together, could
not fail to make a profound effect on a country bound by
racial prejudice and deep fears.

The theme of the conference was a prayer, and a dangerous one – 'Come, Holy Spirit'. He came with great
power among his people, sometimes as the gentle breeze
bringing peace and healing to many lives; sometimes as the
mighty rushing wind tearing away the marks of centuries
of prejudice and fear, and united his people in a deeper
way than they had ever known. The Holy Spirit came as
the fire to burn up a lot of dross and hypocrisy, which
was freely confessed. During the week together God's
power to heal was felt in a thousand ways that heaven
alone will reveal.

Few who attended could ever forget watching black
people and white people, Catholics and Protestants seeking and finding forgiveness from one another. There were
great moments of song and dance too as 'the sons of God
came into their own', and what a joy it was to see white
Anglican bishops and black Pentecostals dancing together
before the Lord!

The prevailing political situation in South Africa, however, brought a stark realism into our meeting together.
Two prominent black leaders had died in mysterious circumstances while in detention during the month of the
conference. One felt a chill in one's spine as Michael
Cassidy the well-known white leader of Africa Enterprise,
and the respected black leader Nicholas Bhengu declared
that humanly speaking they saw no hope for their country.
Yet they both spoke with prophetic vigour, urging the
people to turn their eyes on God who could change the
darkness of despair into a door of hope.

As we came away from the mountain-top experience of
Johannesburg the words of the conference hymn written by
Peter and Gloria Mulligan, an Irish couple living in South
Africa, kept ringing in my ears:

Come Holy Spirit unite us in your love
A love that all the world can see
Come Holy Spirit unite us in your love
A love that only comes from Thee.

After the conference I travelled the country speaking to twenty gatherings in ten days. It was a special thrill to share a day of renewal with Fred Marks, the Irish vicar of a large coloured parish in Cape Town, and to preach in the cathedral filled with an integrated congregation. Black, coloured and white people knelt side by side for Holy Communion.

My next visit to that beautiful country was two years later in 1979 when I was invited to address the South African Christian Leadership Assembly. The impact of that gathering is still being felt and I am convinced it opened many of the doors of hope Michael Cassidy and Nicholas Bhengu had spoken about. Held in Pretoria in July, the theme was 'Christian Witness in South Africa Today'. The gathering was unique in the history of the country. Indeed it was nothing short of a miracle that seven thousand Christians from all racial backgrounds could be mixed together for a whole week – eating, praying, discussing, and in many instances living together. As was to be expected, there was outspoken opposition from both left- and right-wing sources. The assembly was superbly organised by Africa Enterprise, led by Michael Cassidy and chaired by Professor David Bosch of the department of Missiology in the University of South Africa, one of a growing number of Dutch Reformed ministers who are taking a courageous and prophetic stand in South Africa today. Africa Enterprise is a powerful force for reconciliation in the whole African Continent.

Voices from South Africa like those of Bosch, Cassidy, Desmond Tutu and Caesar Molebatsi were calling Christians out from the prisons of history to become 'prisoners of hope'. At the final Communion service, conducted by Bishop Michael Nuttall of Pretoria, I looked out on that vast congregation drawn from so many tribes and peoples and nations and could not help feeling that there is something that God can do in South Africa that he cannot quite do in any other part of the world; for in that Communion service we saw God's multi-coloured new creation. I addressed the gathering with this challenge:

> Over the next ten years South Africa is going to be the focus of attention all over the world in an unprecedented way. You are going to be either a scandal to the world or a visual aid to the whole world of what God can do to heal a nation so divided. I am convinced that this conference has a big place in God's heart not only for Southern Africa but for the whole continent and indeed for the whole world. You need to stay very close to Christ and to one another in the obedience of love if the purposes of God for this conference are to be fulfilled. The eyes of the world are on this land today. Men with human wisdom see great darkness ahead of you and speak with despair about the future of your land. Under God, you, as Christ's followers, have the responsibility to lead this land into a new day of God's healing and reconciliation. It will cost you your pride, pride of race, pride of colour, pride of background, but in paying that price you will demonstrate that the Kingdom of God is within you, and from a place where men least expect it a light will shine forth to the nations of the healing love of Jesus.

From Rostrevor I had taken with me a beautiful banner of Irish tweed, made by Mrs Berti McKee. Based on the words of St John, 'He has given us this command: whoever loves God must also love his brother,' it illustrates the love that Jesus gives across the racial barriers. The banner depicts a black man and a white man embracing. It made a profound effect on the people there and remained displayed on the podium until the end of the conference. Interestingly it was there in a later session that day when an Afrikaans government minister, Dr Piet Koornhof, and Chief M. G. Buthelezi, chief minister of Kwa-Zulu, addressed the gathering, sharing the same platform. There was considerable

demand for the banner when the conference was over, with
Bill Johnston, Dean of Zululand, winning over Pretoria. It
now hangs in the chapel of Unity in Eshowe. Berti McKee
very generously made another banner of reconciliation,
which is now in the Anglican Cathedral in Pretoria, linking
Ireland and South Africa as we pray for each other.

In 1985 Michael Cassidy and other leaders took a courageous step to inaugurate the most comprehensive movement
for reconciliation their country had seen. The National
Initiative for Reconciliation was born. Michael Cassidy
explains:

> As we cast our eyes and hearts across South Africa we
> were watching our nation and its polarised groups moving
> like two alienated people in a crumbling marriage towards
> 'irretrievable breakdown'. Some seventy of us from across
> the land took the initiative to call together four hundred
> church leaders from forty-eight denominations at a short
> three weeks notice for what we called the 'National Initia-
> tive for Reconciliation'. We convened in Pietermaritzburg
> in September 1985 with a full house of invitees – bishops,
> archbishops, moderators, black and white, young and old,
> left and right, radical and conservative: from angry AZAPO
> youth to an anxious but precious fifty-six man contingent
> from the Dutch Reformed Church.[1]

Under the umbrella of the NIR, major initiatives have
been taken throughout South Africa in inter-racial church
activities, projects in education, ministries of mercy and
joint prayer, worship and Bible study.

Since 1979 Myrtle and I have been able to return to South
Africa on a number of occasions. It is encouraging to see
more and more of the barriers coming down and the walls
of division being dismantled. Really costly reconciliation is
taking place in meaningful ways. Especially is this so in
the Christian inter-racial communities and fellowships that
are springing up in many parts of South Africa. One such
community was started by a Roman Catholic priest after he
had read a leaflet about the Christian Renewal Centre. He

felt God saying to him, 'If it can happen in Ireland it can happen in South Africa.'

Israel

It is interesting how often in the media Ireland, South Africa and Israel are compared. We share many similarities in the problems we face. Thankfully in all three countries, despite the obvious conflict, there are growing signs of God's healing and renewing love. Israel has a special place in our hearts and prayers. As we pray for the peace of Jerusalem we long to see the peace of Christ reigning in that land among all its people. Over a number of years we rejoice in the links being forged between the people of Israel and Ireland.

In 1986 some of us from the Centre had the inspiring experience of sharing in two important gatherings in Israel which drew nearly 1,500 Christians from many nations around the world. In the first gathering during the week before Easter 153 Christian leaders came together at Carmel, near the place where, almost three thousand years ago Elijah the prophet challenged the heathen prophets of Baal. The vision for such a gathering to wait on God and hear together what the Spirit is saying to the Church today came first to the Revd Clifford Hill of London. I was asked to join an international team of leaders to prepare and co-ordinate the gathering at Mount Carmel and the larger gathering at Jerusalem over the Easter weekend.

From places as far apart as Finland and Indonesia we had gathered to hear God's Word for the world today. In a week together of prayer, meditation and worship we heard God clearly speak to his Church and to his world. In the gathering at the site of God's victory through Elijah so long ago there was a very clear message.

High up on the slopes of Mount Carmel we were looking down over the valley of Jezreel and the valley of

Armageddon, the scene of many battles throughout history. It was a cold and blustery day for March. The sun burst through the clouds, pouring down like a great searchlight, picking out scenes in the valley below. Nazareth, where Jesus grew up, was clearly visible in the distance and Tabor, the mountain of Transfiguration, was shrouded in cloud. The large flat area beneath the summit, where Elijah rebuilt the altar of God, could easily have accommodated the thousands who gathered to see the fire of God fall from heaven to vindicate God's judgment on a nation that had turned away from him.

All around us there were parables. In the fertile valley of Armageddon one could see a large Israeli army base with rows of tanks lined up in readiness for war. A man-made mountain and forest in the distance concealed more weapons and ammunition and three aircraft runways indicated that the valley of Armageddon was prepared for conflict.

All around us on the Elijah site rocks and stones were lying strewn. The well from which Elijah drew the water to pour over the sacrifice was dry and overgrown. Overhead the storm clouds were gathering in a menacing way. I really felt God was speaking to the Church and the nations through what we were seeing that day. Around the world the storm clouds are gathering; nations are rattling their swords and the guns of war are sounding throughout the earth. Armageddon is being prepared. Yet the Church that should be the instrument of God to shine through the darkness is in so many places scattered and divided. The well that should be supplying life to a dying world has in many places become dry and overgrown.

As we repented together for the sad disarray of the Church today and confessed our sins of pride, of unbelief and complacency we prayed that God's fire would fall again and the showers of revival would come once more. In a remarkable way those prayers were being answered even as we began to leave Mount Carmel. The clouds burst and rain poured over the dry earth, a little sign to us that when God's people begin to turn again to him, 'the author and giver of life', there is hope amidst all the darkness that threatens the world.

We set one day aside on Carmel when all of us could wait in silence on the Lord. He spoke in many ways into our personal lives and ministries, about our churches and fellowships. Many of the words that emerged from the silence spoke of God's sovereign plan being worked out despite the turmoil and confusion in the world. One prophecy was particularly important. Looking back, it is sobering to realise how accurate it has proved to be in several significant ways:

> It will not be long before there will come upon the world a time of unparalleled upheaval. Do not fear, for it is I, the Lord, who am shaking all things. I began this shaking through the First World War and I greatly increased it through the Second World War. Since 1973 I have given it an even greater impetus. In the last stage I plan to complete it with the shaking of the universe itself with signs in sun and moon and stars. But before that point is reached I will judge the nations, and the time is near. It will not only be by war and civil war, by anarchy and terrorism and monetary collapses that I will judge the nations, but also by natural disasters, by earthquakes, by shortages and famines and by old and new plague diseases. I will also judge them by giving them over to their own ways, to lawlessness, to loveless selfishness, to delusion and to believing a lie, to false religion and an apostate church, even to a Christianity without me.
>
> Do not fear when these things begin to happen. For I will disclose these things to you before they commence in order that you might be prepared and that in the day of trouble and of evil you may stand firm and overcome. For I purpose that you may become the means of encouraging and strengthening many who love me but who are weak. I desire that through you many may become strong in me and that multitudes of others may find my salvation through you. And hear this, do not fear the power of the Kremlin nor the power of the Islamic revolution for I plan to break both of them through Israel. I will bring down their pride and their

arrogance and shatter them for they have blasphemed my name. In that day I will avenge the blood of all the martyrs and the innocent ones they have slaughtered. I will surely do this thing for they have thought that there was no one to judge them. But I have seen their ways and I have heard the cries of the oppressed and of the persecuted and I will break their power and make an end of them. Be therefore prepared, for when all this comes to pass, to you will be given the last great opportunity to preach the Gospel freely to all the nations. In the midst of all the turmoil and shaking, and at the heart of everything is my church. In the heavenlies she has joined me in one Spirit and I have destined her for the throne. You are my beloved, who I have redeemed and anointed, you are mine. I will equip and empower you. You will rise up and do great things in my name – even in the midst of darkness and evil. For I will reveal my power and my grace and my glory through you. Do not hold back nor question my ways with you, for in all my dealings with you I have always in mind that you should be part of my bride and reign with me. Do not forget that this requires a special discipline and training. So yield to me that I might do a work in you in the time that is left, for I plan even during all this shaking that the bride will make herself ready.

Do not fear these days. For I have purposed that you should stand with me and serve me. Fear not, for I love you and I will protect you and will equip you. I the Lord will anoint you with a new anointing and you will work my works and fulfil my counsel. You shall stand before me, the Lord of the whole earth, and serve me with understanding and with power. And you shall reign with me during these days. Above all I call you to be intercessors, to serve me in the hidden place, to receive the burdens that I will give you and to co-operate with me until I fulfil my purposes.

Reconciliation in Israel

Both in Carmel and Jerusalem we witnessed the great miracle of reconciliation that is taking place as Arab and Jewish believers meet to share God's word and pray together. In the face of much opposition, and considerable persecution and danger, costly bridges of love are being built. I feel strongly that it is such people who hold the key to the peace of Christ reigning in the Middle East and for them we should earnestly pray. Like many who have gone before in the history of the Church they are often caught in the crossfire as they proclaim the truth, that 'there is neither Jew nor Greek, slave nor free, male nor female, for you are all one in Christ Jesus' (Gal. 3:28).

When we go to Israel we need to go not only as pilgrims to be enriched in our own faith. We need to go in deep humility to learn from our brothers and sisters who are bearing the marks of our Master's suffering in his land today. Because Arab and Jew together are allowing his love to be the dominant force in their lives they are a sign of the victory of the One who 'took the two groups who had been opposed to each other and made them parts of himself; thus he fused us together to become one new person, and at last there was peace' (Eph. 2:14–15 Living Bible).

German links

Some months before we moved from Belfast we met two extraordinary women of faith, Sister Eulalia and Sister Naomi, members of a remarkable community of reconciliation, the Evangelical Sisters of Mary in Darmstadt, West Germany. Their walk of faith encouraged us in taking the first steps towards forming the Christian Renewal Centre.

On the night of 11/12 September 1944 the city of Darmstadt was almost totally destroyed by bombing. In less than twenty minutes 12,000 people were killed and 70,000 left homeless. From the seeds of this sorrow Klara Schlink and Erika Madauss – better known as Mother Basilea and Mother Martyria – founded the community of the Evangelical Sisters of Mary. Founded firmly on the gospel of repentance and forgiveness, it has grown into a ministry of love that has touched the lives of millions. Most notable has been the witness to reconciliation between Germans and Jewish people after the Holocaust.

As we began our own work of reconciliation we knew that the sisters of Darmstadt had a lot to teach us. And they were praying for us. I was to learn something about their way of praying. Travelling together between Dublin and Belfast, Sister Eulalia and Sister Naomi were explaining to me the importance of praise in prayer, pointing out that 'we have a rich heavenly Father' who loves to provide for his children as they walk in his way. From time to time they would burst out in songs of praise based on promises from Scripture. As we passed a field of cattle one of them prayed: 'The Lord owns the cattle on a thousand hills, please sell one for Rostrevor.' Some months later I remembered that prayer of faith when a man I had never met asked to see me. He questioned me for some time about the work and the vision behind the Centre; and before he left he took his cheque book and donated £1,000 as a gift to the Centre. When I discovered he was a farmer I suddenly recalled the Sister's prayer. Some cattle had been sold!

Our fellowship with our brothers and sisters in Germany has grown since then, with many coming as visitors and some as helpers and members of community.

I was present at a European Conference in Brussels in 1979, hosted by Cardinal Suenens. A word of prophecy was spoken then which has become a reality in some remarkable ways:

Before, you have been walking. Prepare to run for I am going to work in a greater way than you have yet seen. What you have seen is like the cool air of the morning compared with what I am going to do. There is a sunrise over Europe. The sun is rising and in its light and heat you will come out of your houses and divest yourselves and meet each other in a deeper way. I want you to be bound together.

We have been privileged to witness the unfolding of that word, which in 1979 would have seemed unbelievable.

One such opportunity came in March 1988. Myrtle and I were invited to conduct a retreat for pastors in the German Democratic Republic, our first visit behind the Iron Curtain. More than a year before, in the letter inviting us, we were informed that 111 pastors would attend. I was amazed that they should know the exact number so far in advance. On enquiry I was told that 111 was the maximum that could be accommodated in Julius Schniewind Haus, the retreat centre, and they always had a waiting list! In the event 120 pastors came from all over East Germany, Hungary and Czechoslovakia. One pastor and his wife travelled for three days by train from Estonia to attend. It was the first time they were allowed out of their country for such a gathering.

It was for us a deeply humbling experience to minister to those men and women who have faithfully served Christ and his Kingdom in the face of considerable hardship. Living under Communist rule with the many restrictions that were placed on Christian witness, they displayed great love and patience. They have learned to become true citizens of the Kingdom of God and have discovered that the seeds of Christian love can grow strong however hard the soil may be. It was a special encouragement that we should come with several other Christian friends from western Europe to share with them. In those precious days of fellowship we knew there are no walls that can imprison the Holy Spirit.

Visits to two churches in Schönebeck, the town where the retreat was held, brought us great joy and encouragement. At the first, a week of united mission was ending with an afternoon service in the Roman Catholic Church. Sharing in the mission were the Lutheran, Roman Catholic, Pentecostal and Baptist churches. That Sunday afternoon the church was filled. About fifty young people were leading praise at the front, and a Baptist pastor was preaching. I thought what a challenge to us in 'Christian' Ireland from 'Communist' East Germany.

The second was a former synagogue which had been renovated to a church, where all were welcome. For years it had stood derelict near the town centre, a symbol of the shame of the Nazi regime. On 'Crystal night', 9 November 1938, the Jews of the town had been rounded up there, in their sacred place, and abused and humiliated. Later they were herded on trains to the concentration camps. In 1983 a group of Christians received permission from the Jewish trustees to renovate the building. As they began their work they found the inscription the Jews had placed there in 1933: 'My house will be called a house of prayer for all nations' (Isa. 56:7).

Beautifully restored, that building now stands not only as a symbol of forgiveness but as a powerful symbol of hope in a broken world.

Our last night in Germany was spent with Dr Paul Toasepern and his wife in East Berlin. Within the shadow of the Berlin wall, nearly thirty Christians packed into the living-room to sing God's praise, read his word and share in prayer. We were asked to tell about the work of reconciliation in Ireland. It was deeply moving to hear those brothers and sisters pray for us in a week when our province had experienced some of the worst violence it had known. 'We will remember you all in our prayers,' they promised as we set off for the border as dawn was breaking.

Some of those friendships were renewed later in 1988 when I took part in two important international events in West Berlin. From 29 June to 3 July a conference took place arranged by an international group of Christian leaders and co-ordinated by Gustav Scheller from England. Over a thousand delegates from forty-four nations took part. One of the purposes was to pass a resolution denouncing the failure of the nations and the Christian Church to come to the aid of the Jews in 1938, to ask forgiveness for those tragic events and to seek reconciliation with our Jewish fellow-citizens. At the conclusion of the conference more than a hundred of the delegates, Jews and Christians, visited Evian-les-Bains near Geneva, the scene of the 1938 conference: what happened there in July 1988 was a real act of reconciliation and a remarkable outworking of the

Brussels prophecy of 1979. A delegate who was present in Evian-les-Bains reports:

> Religious services were conducted in the picturesque Reformed Church, remembering the events of fifty years ago, with prayers of contrition and a commitment that will give hope for the future. On the Friday afternoon before Shabbat (8 July) we were invited to the synagogue for a special service which can only be described as unique in the history of Jewish–Christian relations. In attendance were the rabbi, members of the Jewish community, the Catholic priest and the Reformed Minister of Evian, and approximately 120 Christians and Messianic Jews. Biblical songs were sung in Hebrew, a beautiful rendition of a Psalm was given by a young cantor, prayers were offered by the rabbi and also by Peter van Woerden from Holland (nephew of Corrie ten Boom who with her family saved many Jews during World War II), and the resolution was read in French and in English. Then, during a very solemn moment, on behalf of the delegates present, one of the leaders acknowledged the sins of omission and the failure of nations and the Church to come to the assistance of the Jews. Forgiveness and reconciliation were requested in the name of the God of Israel. We also expressed our solidarity with the Jewish people and offered up prayers for the peace of Jerusalem. The rabbi responded in a quiet and moving way and called us 'brothers and sisters'. The service was concluded with the signing of the Hatikvah.

Just over a year after that act of repentance, it is significant that on 9 November 1989, the anniversary of Crystal night, the Berlin wall was breached and freedom was on the way for East Germany. Equally significant must be the fact that the first act of the newly elected Parliament in East Germany was to apologise for the crimes of the Nazi era. The speaker of the Parliament declared:

> The first freely elected Parliament in East Germany accepts in the names of its citizens joint responsibility for the humiliation, expulsion and murder of Jewish women, men and children. We feel sadness and shame and accept the

burden of German history. We ask the Jews of the world
for forgiveness.

In September 1988 I had participated in another European
Charismatic Leaders' Conference in Germany. At Rostrevor we had hosted the Leaders' Conference of 1986,
when we made plans for the next conference to take place
partly in West Berlin and partly in East Berlin. In the West
we met in a Conference Centre a few hundred metres from
the wall. The welcome we received on arrival in East
Berlin was overwhelming, and the hospitality of our East
German brothers and sisters was further experienced as we
travelled after the conference to churches and fellowships
throughout the German Democratic Republic. It was hard
to believe then what we have now witnessed: the seemingly
impenetrable wall is broken down and people have come
out into the sunshine of freedom 'to embrace each other in
a deeper way'.

All over the world

Besides the countries mentioned members of the community have been invited to minister in other parts of the
world. Niall and Geraldine Griffin led a ministry team
to Nigeria in 1988 which included two other community
members, Maureen Slattery and Mary O'Rourke; and in
1989 Eric and Mabel Mayer were guests of the church in
Indonesia. Also in 1989 Niall and Geraldine, with Gladys
Swanton and Maureen Slattery, joined me in ministering
at an inter-church gathering in Switzerland. Happily on a
number of occasions over the years Myrtle has been able
to accompany me in responding to invitations to speak in
Norway, Sweden, the United States of America, Canada,
Kenya, Mauritius, Malawi, Singapore, Hong Kong, the
Philippines, Australia and New Zealand.

Soon after we came to the house in Rostrevor we discovered that a previous owner, who lived there for many

years, had cherished the wish that it might be used as a
place of renewal, especially for those who had ministered
overseas. Miss Collen, a Methodist, had a lifetime's interest in missionary work. When we welcome missionaries
to the Centre we rejoice that Miss Collen's desire, so
long deferred, is now being realised. The beautiful new
extension, opened in 1986, provides a place of peace and
relaxation where those who have borne 'the burden and
heat of the day' in ministry in difficult and lonely places
can be refreshed. Many who come not only relish the peace
of the place but also the opportunity to share in the prayer
of the community. Writing from a busy ministry in India Dr
James and Willi Barton echo what many have expressed:

> The Centre in Rostrevor has meant for us a place of
> refuge, refreshment and renewal; a place of direction
> and commission and a place to bring others, especially
> Christian workers who often become tired and discour-
> aged. Your sharing with us has encouraged us to con-
> tinue as pilgrims with no 'abiding place' for ourselves.
> The Lord is our refuge and strength, a present help
> in trouble, the protector and provider for our family,
> our only true home. We bless the Lord for your clear
> testimony to the fulness of the Gospel of Jesus Christ, Sav-
> iour, Healer, Reconciler and Baptiser in the Holy Spirit.

Others come as broken, wounded soldiers from the front
line of the battle at home or overseas. In the Lord's house
they are able to meet again with the One who heals the
broken-hearted and gives strength to the weary.

13

LET THE TIDE COME IN

I will sprinkle clean water on you, and you will be clean; I will cleanse you from all your impurities and from all your idols. I will give you a new heart and put a new spirit in you; I will remove from you your heart of stone and give you a heart of flesh. (Ezek. 36:25–26)

> *Shine Jesus shine*
> *Fill this land with the Father's glory*
> *Blaze Spirit blaze*
> *Set our hearts on fire*
> *Flow rivers flow*
> *Flood the nations with grace and mercy*
> *Send forth your Word Lord*
> *And let there be light.[1]*

I watched the dawn creep over Carlingford Lough on a dull December morning. Dark clouds formed a heavy canopy, uniting the Mournes with the hills beyond the Lough in County Louth. Then a shaft of light appeared, piercing the darkness; it folded back a beautiful blanket of blue sky. As I looked a dark cloud in the shape of a sword spread across from the west. It was densely dark and appeared to pierce right into the blanket of blue sky.

Meditating on that quickly-changing panorama, I thought, 'How like the situation over the land.' Many people feel enveloped in the dull darkness of despair, hardly daring to hope for a dawn.

The dark cloud in the shape of a sword stands for the bitterness and hatred that seeks to destroy this land. We have the choice. We can allow that sword to devour us in mutual hatred and dark division or we can ask Christ, the Light of this world, to lead us on a better way of truth and brotherhood. All through the Bible that choice is presented – life or death, war or peace, unity or division.

There is no doubt in my mind that we are facing in Ireland today the greatest spiritual crisis this country has known in its long history. The battle is joined for the very soul of Ireland but I have no doubt that God's purpose is 'for good and not for evil, to give to us a future and a hope'. If we are willing to allow him, God will lead us out of the dark to a new day of opportunity. I firmly believe that if we come humbly before God from our places of division, confessing the sins and failures of the past, receiving his grace and love, then Ireland can help God's healing power. I believe that through the gracious outpouring of God's Holy Spirit, which we have been experiencing over the past twenty-five years, he is providing us with resources beyond human endeavour. It is a day of grace and favour. But it will not last for ever. The day of God's visitation can pass and the Church, by neglect or disobedience, can fail to appropriate what God offers.

Some of the saddest words recorded in the Gospels are what Jesus said as he stood on the Mount of Olives on Palm Sunday. Looking down on Jerusalem, the city of a thousand lost opportunities, Jesus wept: 'O Jerusalem, Jerusalem, you who kill the prophets and stone those sent to you, how often I have longed to gather your children together, as a hen gathers her chicks under her wings, but you were not willing!' (Luke 13:34). Jerusalem, the city of peace had rejected the Prince of Peace:

> If you, even you, had only known on this day what would bring you peace – but now it is hidden from your eyes. The days will come upon you when your enemies will build an embankment against you and encircle you and hem you in

on every side. They will dash you to the ground, you and
the children within your walls. They will not leave one stone
on another, because you did not recognise the time of God's
coming to you. (Luke 19:42–44).

Our religious pride can blind us to God's vision for the
future. Our inherited prejudices can prevent us hearing his
voice. Unwillingness to risk the wind of God's Holy Spirit
can leave the Church becalmed, going nowhere.

'The story of Acts is the story of the stupendous missionary achievement of a community inspired to make a
continual series of creative experiments by the pentecostal
spirit,' wrote Dr Joe Fison, late Bishop of Salisbury:

> Against a static church, unwilling to obey the guidance of
> the Spirit no gates of any sort are needed to oppose its
> movements, for it does not move. But against a church that
> is on the move, inspired by the pentecostal spirit, neither
> the 'gates of hell' nor any other gates will prevail.[2]

The challenge to the Church of Jesus Christ in this country
and the world is to move with God in his eternal purpose,
which is nothing less than 'to bring all things in heaven
and on earth together under one head, even Christ' (Eph.
1:10). Evidence of our failure to do so is the division of
Christendom, so clearly illustrated in Ireland. Our obvious
rivalry, petty squabbles and blatant competition are sad
examples. No wonder observers have frequently asked,
'Are the churches more a part of the problem than a part of
the solution to it?' How can we appeal to divided politicians
to work together, when we who profess to be Christians
are manifestly unwilling to work together? It is a salutary
warning to reflect on the judgment made by Solzhenitsyn
when he spoke about the failure of the Church in Russia at
the beginning of this century:

> The truth requires me to state that the condition of the
> Russian Church . . . is one of the principal causes for
> the inevitability of the revolutionary events . . . Had the

Russian Orthodox Church at the beginning of the twentieth
century been spiritually independent, healthy and strong,
it would have been able to stop the Civil War. It would
have risen above the warring factions without becoming an
appendage to any of them.[3]

Over a century ago in Great Britain there was a great
moving of God's Holy Spirit with a restoration of the
charismatic gifts. That work of God laid important stress
on the unity of the body of Christ. Those involved brought
an urgent prophetic message to the western churches, but
it was little heeded. This was the essence of that message
delivered in 1872:

> God, in his infinite mercy, would now bring all his people
> and his ministers out of their disunion, and reconcile them
> to himself and to one another in the truth. If they will not
> yield, tribulation must effect what love and truth could not;
> and the men who would not be drawn into unity by truth,
> will be driven together by persecution.[4]

It is a sobering fact of history that millions of Christians
died under the Communist regime in eastern Europe; and
the twentieth century has witnessed more Christian martyrs
than any previous one. The warning that those 'who would
not be drawn into unity by truth will be driven together by
persecution' has been illustrated in this century, when from
the shared suffering and prayer together true fellowship
has been realised. In his book, *Open Church*, the German
theologian Jürgen Moltmann recalls his three years of forced
labour as a prisoner of war. Beyond the terrible suffering
and deprivation (he was still a teenager) he remembers the
unexpected fellowship which grew across all the denominational differences.

> Behind barbed wire fences traditional doctrinal differences
> of the divided churches no longer had any special rele-
> vance. Christians got together wherever they were, read
> the Bible, prayed together, and were strengthened in faith.

In situations of need, inter-communion and co-celebration were not so problematic as to prevent Christians from sharing in the breaking of bread. They asked only about the One who is truly important, and they experienced the presence of Christ amid sufferings. This gave them inner strength and firm confidence. Whether one was a priest or a lay person, a student of theology or a labourer, here there was no special precedence or privilege. Here the only things that really counted were the genuineness of faith, the commitment of the person, and the fellowship of confessing Christians. Each one was challenged and had to stand without the support of his or her tradition or the protection of the particular customs of his or her confession. In such a manner each one was tested in the fire of tribulation.[5]

Similar witness came from prisoners of war on the other side of the conflict. My friend Ray Davey, who served in the YMCA and was taken prisoner by the Germans, told us that some of his richest experiences of worship were in the prisoner of war camp, where Christians of different traditions shared Communion. And all they had with which to celebrate the mysteries were stale bread and water from a tin mug.

Significantly it was in the shadow of the cross that our Lord prayed for his disciples. He asked that they would be protected by the power of his name, obedient to his word, consecrated in his truth and filled with his abiding joy. Then Jesus prayed for those who would believe in him through the message of the Apostles.

I pray also for those who will believe in me through their message, that all of them may be one, Father, just as you are in me and I am in you. May they also be in us so that the world may believe that you have sent me. I have given them the glory that you gave me, that they may be one as we are one: I in them and you in me. May they be brought to complete unity to let the world know that you sent me and have loved them even as you have loved me. Father, I want those you have given me to be with me where I am,

and to see my glory, the glory you have given me because
you loved me before the creation of the world. Righteous
Father, though the world does not know you, I know you,
and they know that you have sent me. I have made you
known to them, and will continue to make you known in
order that the love you have for me may be in them and
that I myself may be in them' (John 17:20–26).

I find it very moving that our Lord was praying there for
you and me and all who are his followers today. We are
to be the 'Amen' to his prayer. He who 'always lives to
intercede for us' desires that we should demonstrate in the
world today the answer to his prayer. Specifically he prays
that we should witness to his unity, reflect his glory and
share his love. As William Temple points out, 'It is not
our unity as such that has converting power; it is our
incorporation into the true vine as branches in which the
divine life is flowing.'[6]

United evangelism

At a time when churches are preparing for special programmes of evangelisation it is important to remember that
the visible unity of God's people is the most potent resource
for sharing the Good News. Father Pat Collins, who often
ministers alongside us in Ireland, observes:

> The churches want the last decade of the twentieth century
> to be one of intense evangelisation. But if we lose sight of
> the Lord's teaching about united witness, we may forfeit
> his special anointing and the manifestations of the Spirit.
> They alone can demonstrate the truth of our proclamation
> because 'the kingdom of God is not a matter of talk but of
> power' (1 Cor. 4:20). To receive such blessings, personal
> and ecclesiastical humility will be required. A few years
> ago the Lord seemed to reveal this to me as I prayed in
> Rostrevor. In my mind's eye I could see a number of tall
> flagpoles with their respective flags flapping in the wind. At

the base of each flagpole were groups of people shouting and gesticulating in an angry way at the people grouped about the other flags. Then in the middle I saw the cross. At first the people didn't even notice it. Then one by one, the angry protesters began to pay attention to the crucified One. As they looked at him, their anger turned to shame. Each group began to lower its flag, some slowly, others more rapidly. Soon the cross was higher than all the flags and people began to drift away from their flagpoles to gather around the foot of the cross. It seemed as if the Lord was saying, 'At the moment the flags of your denominational and nationalistic pride are raised higher than the cross. But when you look to him who was lifted up from the earth to draw all people to himself, you will lower the flags of your pride. Then and only then will you find peace, for in the power of the cross the dividing wall of your divisions will crumble.' In many ways those words encapsulate what I have discovered at Rostrevor. When we learn to pay more attention to Christ than to our denominational and nationalistic concerns, his wounded body both in Ireland and in the world will be healed.

Secondly our Lord prays that his glory, 'absolute love in perfect self-expression', will be reflected in a Church that humbly follows him who 'did not come to be served, but to serve and to give his life a ransom for many'. Finally by his love flowing through us in practical ways the world will recognise and experience something of the God whose very nature is love.

A future and a hope

'In Ireland there is no future, only the past happening over and over,'[7] concluded Leon Uris in his story of Irish history. Many puzzled observers of the present scene are tempted to share his pessimism. In the sixteenth century an English civil servant quoted a proverb which echoes the gloom he felt as he surveyed the Ireland of his day:

It is a proverb of old date, that the pride of France, the treason of England, and the war of Ireland, shall never have end. Which proverb, touching the war of Ireland, is like alway to continue, without God set it in men's breasts to find some new remedy that never was found before.[8]

God has set men's hearts to find a better way; through Christ alone who is the way of peace. Behind the headlines that carry the news of fear, hatred and despair the God of hope is powerfully at work in the hearts and lives of ordinary men and women. Those seeds of hope are being sown by the humble men and women in whose lives the kingdom of God is the supreme loyalty. They are those who, often through personal pain and suffering, have been to the cross. They are the Good Friday people who have also walked by faith towards the dawn of the resurrection morning and have seen 'strange victory spring from the fiery embers of defeat'. In the Upper Room they have met the risen Christ and felt the winnowing wind of the Holy Spirit when their eyes have been opened to a wider vision and a further horizon.

With the Psalmist I believe 'there is a future for the man of peace'. The best days for the Church of Jesus Christ in Ireland are still to come. An even greater work than was done by Patrick and Columba will be seen. Ireland will again be a light to the nations, giving glory to God. Through the power of his Holy Spirit hate will be turned to love.

Some of the happiest memories of my boyhood were the summer holidays we spent on the Donegal coast. It was there I learned to swim. What a joy it was to plunge into the Atlantic breakers and be carried along by those tall waves. When the tide was out there was another kind of pleasure in being able to dive and swim in the rock pools that abound around the shore. Exploring those pools underwater had a particular fascination for us. They teemed with all sorts of little fish and sea animals. Rich carpets of seaweed concealed a world of rare beauty. Shells of a thousand hues decorated their walls. Each pool held its own marvellous treasures. At low tide they all seemed miles apart, walled off from each other by centuries-old rock. And then the tide came in. The large Atlantic waves rolled over and submerged those pools. The rocky walls that seemed impenetrable were submerged. All their separate treasures were caught up in the mighty swell of the great ocean.

I have often reflected on that scene in relation to what God wants to do with his Church in this land. Through centuries we have allowed walls of fear and prejudice to separate us from one another, scarcely believing that any valid form of life existed beyond the rocky walls we have built around ourselves. We became preoccupied with our own particular pools; with traditions we have followed and treasures we have received from the past, many of which were good and have yielded rich blessings. But, just as the ocean is greater than its pools and inlets, so when God pours out his Holy Spirit the tide of his love will carry us in his glorious purpose 'to fill the earth with the knowledge of the glory of God as the waters cover the sea'.

Please, Lord, let the tide come in

> May the God of peace, who through the blood of the eternal covenant brought back from the dead our Lord Jesus, that great Shepherd of the sheep, equip you with everything good for doing his will, and may he work in us what is pleasing to him, through Jesus Christ, to whom be glory for ever and ever. Amen. (Heb. 13:20–21)

Appendix

One of our Trustees, David Baillie, drafted a ten-point plan to help people in their ministry of prayer. We have found these most helpful and recommend them to others

1   Before you start to pray, meditate on one or two faith-building Bible verses. You will find it a help to weave the truths and promises of the Scriptures into your prayers.

2   Begin your prayer with praise. Give thanks to God as sovereign Lord of all, and bless God as Father, Son and Holy Spirit, until your heart begins to glow with faith and love. A verse of a hymn may help you in your praising.

3   Claim your position in Christ Jesus: remember that not only have your sins been washed away by his blood, but that as a believer you have been raised and enthroned with Christ, and that through him you are called to be both king and priest.

4   Open your heart wide to God and surrender your whole personality anew – body, mind and spirit – to be a temple for the Holy Spirit to fill each limb and organ and surrender all your thoughts and feelings to him. Yield every tension in your body to God, and yield up also, one by one, every feeling of bitterness, hate, malice, dislike, spite, vindictiveness, anxiety, fear, self-pity, lust, greed, egotism, vanity. Receive by faith the love and peace, the goodness and gentleness, the patience and joy, the self-control and the power of Christ, as

you are filled with the Holy Spirit. Now you can pray effectively for others.

5 Begin your intercessions by praying for the circle of people immediately around you, your own family, your relatives, and members of your own congregation. Be specific here. Write down the names of those you feel led to uphold before God for his blessing.

6 Now move out further, and pray for neighbouring congregations of all denominations, their clergy and some of their members. Be specific here also, as by faith you already 'see' these congregations and their members, alive and aglow with the vitality of God's spirit.

7 Pray specifically for politicians and leaders in the community that the Spirit of Christ may come upon them and fill them. Again be specific. You may find it helpful to make up a list of these people for whom you specially pray.

8 Pray for the binding up and healing of the many wounds in our community. Remember the injured, those maimed for life, people under intimidation, driven from their homes, the bereaved, grief-stricken, lonely, needy, those in prison, those in the grip of resentment, suspicion, fear, hate, despair.

9 Pray, as far as possible specifically, for the men and women of violence, and for those who embrace ideologies that have rejected God. Pray, forgiving, and pray positively with faith and hope, remembering that whatever people say, the Holy Spirit bears witness in each heart. And remember that you have authority in Christ to restrain evil and withstand Satan.

10 Have a vision of Ireland, a land of justice, mercy, love and peace, and with a Church restored to New Testament vitality in all its parts.

Notes

1 The Power of the Cross

1 Bob Gillman, 'Bind us together'. Copyright © Thankyou Music, Eastbourne. Used by permission.

2 The Wind of the Spirit

1 J. B. Phillips, *The Young Church in Action: a translation of the Acts and the Epistles* (Bles, 1955), Preface, p. vii.

3 A Vision is Born

1 Graham Kendrick, 'Rejoice!' Copyright © 1983 Make Way Music. Administered by Thankyou Music, Eastbourne. Used by permission.
2 David Watson, *You are My God*. Hodder, 1986.

4 Living in Community

1 Dietrich Bonhoeffer, *Life Together* (SCM, 1954), p. 18.
2 ibid. p. 10.
3 ibid. p. 15.
4 Brother Lawrence, *Practice of the Presence of God* (Burns & Oates, 1977), p. 41.

5 Prayer

1 Joseph Duffy, *St Patrick Writes* (Irish Messenger Pubns, Dublin), p. 12.
2 ibid. pp. 15-16.
3 Frank C. Laubach, *Prayer, the Mightiest Force in the World*. Fleming H. Revell, NJ.
4 Ruth Wieting, Fisherfolk, unpublished.

6 Spiritual Warfare

1 C. S. Lewis, *Screwtape Letters*. Fount, 1982.
2 Frank C. Laubach, *Prayer, the Mightiest Force in the World*, op.cit. p. 32.
3 J. B. Phillips, *Letters to Young Churches*. Bles, 1965.
4 H. Berkhoff, *Christ and the Powers* (Herald Press, Scottdale, Pa), p. 32.
5 Ronnie Wilson, 'I hear the sound of rustling'. Copyright © 1979 Thankyou Music, Eastbourne. Used by permission.
6 *Irish Times*, 23 May 1983.

7 Renewal

1 Richard Trench, *Synonyms of the New Testament* (Macmillan, 1880), pp. 64-5.
2 Lesslie Newbigin, *The Household of God* (SCM, 1964), pp. 91-2.
3 ibid. p. 95.
4 ibid. p. 92.
5 Official Report of the Fourth Assembly of the World Council of Churches, Uppsala, 4–20 July 1968, p. 298.

8 Reconciliation

1 Leckey's *History of Ireland*. n.d.
2 W. Williams, *Personal Reminiscences of Charles Haddon Spurgeon* (Religious Tract Soc., 1895), p. 54.
3 'Ulster will fight and Ulster will be right' in R. F. G. Holmes, *Studies in Church History*, vol. 20, *The Protestant Churches and Ulster's Resistance to Home Rule 1912–1914* (Blackwell, n.d.), p. 321.
4 quoted in ibid. p. 333.
5 ibid. p. 329.
6 Francis Shaw, 'The canon of Irish history: a challenge', *Studies* (Summer 1972), p. 117.
7 ibid. pp. 122-3.
8 G. B. Caird, *Gospel of St Luke*. Pelican Gospel Comm. (Penguin, 1971), p. 104.
9 ibid.
10 David Watson, *You are my God*, op.cit.

9 Forgiveness

1 Michael Hare Duke, *The Break of Glory* (SPCK, 1970), p. 28.
2 William Temple, *Christus Veritas* (Macmillan, 1925), p. 266.
3 ibid, p. 268.
4 *Time* magazine, 9 January 1984.
5 Ron Lee Davis, *A Forgiving God in an Unforgiving World* (Harvest House, 1984), p. 108.
6 Martin Luther King, *Strength to Love* (Fontana, 1969), pp. 48-9.

10 Repentance

1 A. Solzhenitsyn, *The Address at the Eleventh Presentation of the Templeton Foundation Prize for Progress in Religion*, tr. A. Klimoff. Lismore Press, Grand Cayman, BWI, 1983.
2 N. C. Nielsen, *Solzhenitsyn's Religion* (Mowbray, 1975), p. 154.
3 C. Kerr et al., *For God and His Glory Alone*, ECONI, Holywood, 1988.

11 Healing

1 from Christian Healing (Ireland).
2 Philip Yancey and Paul Brand, *In His Image* (Hodder, 1984), pp. 285-6.

12 Partners in Mission

1 Michael Cassidy, *The Passing Summer: a South African pilgrimage in the politics of love* (Hodder, 1989), pp. 279-80.

13 Let the Tide Come In

1 Graham Kendrick, 'Lord the light of your love'. Copyright © 1987 Make Way Music. Administered by Thankyou Music, Eastbourne. Used by permission.
2 J. E. Fison, *Fire upon the Earth* (Edinburgh House Press, 1958), p. 79.
3 N. C. Nielsen, *Solzhenitsyn's Religion*, op.cit. p. 152.
4 Anon., *The Purpose of God* (Thomas Laurie, 1872), p. 355.
5 Jürgen Moltmann, *Open Church* (SCM, 1981), pp. 88-9.

6 William Temple, *Readings in St John's Gospel* (Macmillan, 1961), p. 312.
7 Leon Uris, *Trinity* (Corgi Books, 1976), p. 900.
8 J. C. Beckett, *The Making of Modern Ireland* (Faber, 1966), p. 13.